UFOs
A Great New Dawn for Humanity

Enrique Castillo Rincón jumping for joy following his second encounter with the Pleiadeans

(Realistic reenactment photo by D. Villiamizar)

"The case of Enrique Castillo Rincón began physically on November 3, 1973, and, taken as one of several other contacts, I personally classify it as a concrete reality, with certainty, by UFO behavior standards, which I have followed and investigated for twenty-five years."

—Fabio Zerpa, director ONIFE,
founder, *Cuarta Dimension*

"As far as I am concerned, I have not the slightest doubt that the events described by Enrique actually took place. This does not mean that I have to believe that what the extraterrestrials told him is true, for a very simple reason: as an investigator, I have information from people in other countries who have been given similar information through contacts with supposed extraterrestrials."

—Carlos Vilchez, N., author,
founding member ICICE

"[Enrique] has a clear mind and an impressive memory. Being a 'contactee,' he is the only one who has become a tireless investigator, widely recognized in Europe and America as one of the most dependable and knowledgeable."

—Ricardo Vilchez, N., author,
founding member ICICE

"Today, even more than before, I believe that what Enrique says about the 'sky people' is more valid than ever, because now more attention is paid to the contactees, due to the more frequent occurrence of abductions and cattle mutilations, etc., that have been taking place lately. It is no longer possible to ignore these events, odd as they are, especially when the very survival of the planet may be involved."

—Andreas Faber Kaiser,
founder, *Mundo Desconocido*

UFOs

A GREAT NEW DAWN FOR HUMANITY

The True Story of a Contactee

and his encounter with intelligent beings who have visited planet Earth for thousands of years from their central sun, Shi-el-ho, in the Pleiades

Enrique Castillo Rincón

Translated from the Spanish by
Hugo A. Castro

Blue Dolphin Publishing
1997

Published by Blue Dolphin Publishing, Inc.
P.O. Box 8, Nevada City, CA 95959
Orders: 1 (800) 643-0765

ISBN: 1-57733-000-5

Library of Congress Cataloging-in-Publication Data

Castillo Rincón, Enrique, 1930–
[OVNI. English]
UFOs : a great new dawn for humanity : the true story of a contactee and his encounter with intelligent beings who have visited planet earth for thousands of years from their central sun, Shi-el-ho, in the Pleiades / Enrique Castillo Rincón ; [English translation by Hugo A. Castro].
p. cm.
ISBN 1-57733-000-5
1. Castillo Rincón, Enrique, 1930– . 2. Human-alien encounters. I. Title.
BF2050.C3713 1997
001.942—dc21 97-11568
CIP

Spanish original: *OVNI: Gran Alborada Humana*
Primera Edición: Abril 1995
Enrique Castillo Rincón
Apartado Postal 836-1002, San José, Costa Rica, A.C.

English translation by: Hugo A. Castro, A.A. 4854, Cali, Colombia
First edition: November 1997

Cover painting by Franco Rosso, Venezuelan-Italian painter, inspired by the encounters of Enrique Castillo Rincón.
Interpretation: A naked man half-kneels on Planet Earth, with the Book of Knowledge and Law. A dove with a leaf in its beak, links terrestrial man with his cosmic origin. Pleiades stars appear shyly within the frame of the Universe, while the Pleiadean ship carries the seed of life to Earth.

Printed in Canada by Best Manufacturing

10 9 8 7 6 5 4 3 2 1

Dedication

TO ALL THOSE WHO PARTICIPATED WITH ME as group companions in the reception of the messages and sharing of experiences, without whose backing this information would not be the document that it is.

To my friends from Colombia, Venezuela, Costa Rica, Guatemala, Mexico, Spain, Germany, and every country that I visited, where I found the strength of friendship and understanding.

To my wife, Ana Gertrudis, force and sustenance in my life, who with her love and patience has been able to surmount the greatest difficulties of the last seventeen years.

To my Greater Brothers, the Men from the Stars, who trusted me and gave me their teachings, which I now give to Men on Earth, in this Great Human Dawn.

To all Humanity, for which this Knowledge exists.

To all who have been victims of scorn, attack, and vituperation, or have been derided and treated as insane, and for those who have suffered pain in their own lives for making the truth known about this event, which can change history and throw down all the plots that have been mounted and conceived to control and manipulate the inhabitants of the Earth.

Enrique Castillo Rincón
Caracas, January 5, 1997

Contents

Foreword

IF THIS BOOK HAD BEEN PUBLISHED shortly after the events took place, it surely would have been considered an invention of the author. Its publication several years later may have decreased its impact or novelty because the abductions that Enrique describes have now proliferated everywhere, and this only increases the credibility of the encounters. Two decades ago, when the "contactees" first began describing their unbelievable experiences, it was natural that people would refuse to listen to them, or else take them for crackpots. Now, public opinion and specifically Ufology are much better prepared to receive these facts, because they have learned much since Kenneth Arnold's sighting.

Even so, we must accept that some of the so-called Ufologists have not taken full advantage of the substantial information provided by contactees, and insist on studying the phenomenon at an elementary level, verbalizing and dogmatizing about places of origin, cataloguing different shapes of space ships, or collecting rather irrelevant data. This is all right, but it belongs to the elementary stages of Ufology.

I don't mean that catalogued data are not necessary; they are fundamental, because important conclusions can be deduced from them. But it is a great mistake to stay there without moving forward, centering the investigation on said data, without finding, or at least glimpsing, the astounding reality that lies beyond.

Those of us who investigate the UFO phenomenon are always in danger of taking at face value what the contactees say, and even more so what we see with our own eyes. It is a completely logical reaction, as we are used to interpreting at face value the data received through our senses. With the UFOs, we must remain aware that we are bordering on another reality, metaphysical and paraphysical, where the governing patterns that command our mind are not the same, and if we interpret them as usual, we will arrive at wrong conclusions.

It is to be expected that contactees make this sort of mistake, because they may have been overexposed to the vortex of the events, and their minds may have been manipulated to make them see what is not really there. It is about time for many investigators to realize that this phenomenon is sort of a symbol, or shadow, of a larger and more mysterious reality that lies beyond it.

Some contactees (not so Enrique Castillo) get angry when told this, because they are sure about the absolute reality of what happened to them. However, the actual reality may be different from what it seems to be. For instance, on a radar screen, what seems to be a small, moving, luminous dot, is not a dot and probably is not luminous. No one denies that a dot was really moving on the screen; what we deny is that the screen image is exactly equal to the reality that caused it.

In the face of books as fascinating as this one, it is wise to take the above into account. I do believe that all that Enrique Castillo relates, actually happened to him. But what interests me most is to take the experience as a whole, to penetrate into the astonishing panorama located behind the UFO phenomenon. The mysterious and camouflaged setup behind the specifics of an abduction is more important than its specific details, although in this case the details that the author gives are extremely interesting.

Another aspect deserving of emphasis is that, more and more, this phenomenon loses its "frivolous," hobby-like flavor, in favor of becoming a keystone that unravels the mysteries of human existence, the Universe, and God. This is the transcendental aspect of the UFO phenomenon, which some are not willing to accept, entertained as they are in its secondary, picturesque facets.

It is in this transcendental direction that I aim all my efforts, and although such an objective implies navigating frequently through abstract metaphysical sciences and forgetting minute details valued by many ufologists, books such as this are the raw material for the construction of spiritual theories. Without experiences such as those of Enrique Castillo, we could never have arrived at the conclusions that we have already reached.

As odd as it may sound, the stream of human history, the cultural and religious currents, the divisions between races, and to a great extent the deep crisis in which the planet finds itself, not only have to do indirectly with the UFO phenomenon, but also are their direct consequence and to some degree their manifestation.

I understand perfectly well that this may seem to many a delirious self-delusion. But do not be afraid, dear reader; I am not going to use this foreword—where the kindness of the author has permitted me to enter as a visitor—to defend or promulgate my personal theories. I simply leave them here for the reader to reflect about at leisure, such as when he or she finds that the facts in this field do not match any of the "official theories."

Back in 1974, when I met Enrique Castillo at a restaurant in Caracas, Venezuela and listened directly from his own lips to the vivid narration of his incredible saga, I wondered how I was going to temper his natural and unbounded enthusiasm about such fascinating facts and his dedication to the grandiose mission that he outlined.

When I exposed my viewpoints, I found that regardless of the intensity with which he had lived his experiences, his remarkable intelligence, his impressive memory, and his professional training as an engineer, those experiences had made him suspect that beyond the witnessed events there might be something deeply mysterious and disquieting. I believe that conversation served us both: to him, to make the point that his experience was much more complex than previously thought, and to me, to confirm existing suspicions and compare his data with that of other contactees.

After all, in spite of boycott and debunking on the part of several national and international authorities and organizations, such as news agencies, the number of the contactees like Enrique Castillo increases every day, all over the world. And this, even though many may disagree, is something that should fill us with great concern.

Salvador Freixedo Tabares[1]
San Juan, Puerto Rico, 1980

---

[1]Spanish writer, author of many enlightening books about UFOs, religion, the unknown beyond, etc. Former member of the Society of Jesus for thirty years, author of the following books: *My Church Sleeps; Israel; Contactée People; Let Us Defend Us Against the Gods; When the UFOs Land . . . Dogmas Fly Away; The Diabolic Unconscious; They, the Invisible Owners of the World;* and *The Extraterrestrial Menace,* among others. A brave soul.

Preface

MY FULL NAME IS ENRIQUE DE JESÚS CASTILLO RINCÓN.[1] I was born in San José, Costa Rica, Central America, on August 24, 1930.

The Spanish original manuscript of the present book was completed in Bogotá, capital of the Republic of Colombia, in September, 1976, and, after long and difficult delays, was finally published in Spanish in 1995. The present translation into American English was carried out in Cali, Colombia.

All the events described in the book took place between June, 1973 and February, 1976 and are narrated as accurately as possible. They are not the product of hallucination, astral travel, or any other type of paranormal phenomena. They physically happened over that period of time, of about two-and-a-half years. Many trustworthy and reliable people participated in the events: professionals, businessmen and women, housewives, college students, employees, and even two illiterate individuals. All the details, names, dates, and places can be verified by any investigator willing to undertake this task.

I am not a mystic nor a religious fanatic. I do not belong to any of the traditional organized religions, and I am not an atheist. Neither have I considered myself a "chosen one" to save humanity, and I detest those "contactees" who pretend to have been appointed by some divinity to carry some message to the suffering and almost disgraced human race. The teachings and messages contained in this book should be taken only as a warning about future events, which are predicted to take place between now and the year 2011.

It is relevant to add that under the influence of various contactees, pseudo-religions have sprung up, with fanatic followers, some of them called the "leaders of the extraterrestrial parliament." Because of them, many investigators refuse to listen to what they should, and rightly so. I have struggled against this situation for over twenty years. I have not permitted that under my name or sponsorship any groups be created that could be manipulated by any "leader" of the moment, who might be promoting "purification" campaigns aimed at creating a new race that will people the earth, all under inspiration of the "Space Brothers."

These "leaders" argue that a privileged group will be rescued and taken to other planets, to guarantee a continued human presence on Earth in the future. These types of announcements have failed several times, such as when the "Ashtar Command" announced, with exact dates, a false evacuation.

I became a modest and humble investigator of the UFO phenomenon in order to find a logical explanation, not only for my own experience, but also for everything related to our beliefs and history, which through the centuries has puzzled man without adequate answers.

I have traveled almost all over the world, have attended at least twelve Congresses on UFO and Paranormal subjects, have met and exchanged views with the greatest world investigators, and have read most of the books on the subject. Sometimes I have felt thoroughly misled and confused, at other times close to finding the answer to all the mysteries, and I have sometimes believed to have had in my hands the "universal panacea," as well as the reason as to "why me?"

Over twenty years have passed, and I still don't know why I was contacted. Was it plain chance? Was I selected by chance to transmit a message or knowledge from the stars? Why was an individual belonging to the "sandwich-class" (middle-class), such as myself, assigned such an "ungrateful" task as this one, which has meant jeers, calumnies, epithets, and nicknames against my person and my dignity?

I have been called humbug, charlatan, swindler, liar, and accused of inventing a story, in order to make a living off of believers or fanatics. On the other hand, I have been extolled to unusual heights, and in public, called one of God's "chosen ones," because he sent his angels to contact me.

Thus, terrible things have been said about me, and also the opposite. To be suddenly and unexpectedly involved in such an affair made me an outcast in the eyes of many of my friends. Some of those who met me shortly after the encounters assure me that I am a smart-aleck with a well-conceived story. Others tell me of their belief in what I say, admire and respect me, or simply become astonished, do not comprehend, and shut up.

Today, I am conscious that this book can unleash frictions among the UFO fans, because herein I disclose many truths about phony "contactee groups" and their so-called "spiritual" messages. I do not pretend to be the bearer of eternal Truth, nor the "Spiritual Master" of anybody.

I only wish to be allowed to be what I am—a man with a unique experience that few people have suffered, for good or for evil. Besides, I shall continue my search for the real values of the spirit and the acquisition of knowledge that will give me the answer or answers about this interrelationship of elevated beings and spirits, throughout history, who without any doubt have intervened in the eternal struggle between good and evil.

Sometimes directly, and other times very subtly, they act upon all human beings, allowing us to know The Law and delivering us the knowledge and wisdom that will give us, in the end, victory of peace over violence and of love over hate and vengeance. This acquired Knowledge will be the fundamental basis for a new mental state, which will give us the Universal Laws, for strength and enjoyment of the Spirit.

Enrique Castillo Rincón
January 5, 1997
Caracas, Venezuela

---

[1]According to custom, after my last name (Castillo), I use my mother's maiden last name (Rincón).

Seven Eternal Minutes

"The number of worlds in the galaxy capable of developing some type of oxygen-based life is 100 million, one for each two suns or stars in our solar system. . . . Can anybody dare to say that terrestrial man is the King of Creation?"
—HAROLD UREY, Nobel Laureate, Chemistry

MUSING OVER THE BEGINNINGS, memories drifted into my mind about that lovely Central American country, Costa Rica, for which I harbor indelible feelings of gratitude. In 1963, I was employed with the maintenance department of ICE (Costa Rican Institute of Electricity) and working on the installation and improvement of the communications network that was to connect the country with the whole world during the visit of the U.S. president, John F. Kennedy. The North American president, in a goodwill mission, participated that year in a summit meeting of the heads of Central American countries, regarding their regional economic and political future.

Until then, my life had elapsed normally, combining the exercise of my profession as an electrical and communications engineer with that of a practicing Mormon, the religion I had joined some years before.[1] I had been looking for that "lost identity" that we all may sense at one time or another but find difficult to explain. Happy and contented about having found a measure of peace and harmony through the exercises imposed by church obligations, I learned to navigate satisfactorily among the contradictory tendencies of life, in relative peace and harmony.

The preparatory tasks for the summit meeting advanced quickly. Headquarters "boiled" with the heat of multiple activities. The security agents assigned to the protection of the U.S. president watched all participants carefully during the preparations. I learned through them that the majority of the U.S. presidents had employed Mormons for their security services, which made me feel very proud.

Exactly as planned, the tasks were completed on the eve of Kennedy's arrival, and for three days Costa Rica became the center of international attention. Even though few people knew the true objectives of the meeting, people in general overflowed with enthusiasm and curiosity, eagerly taking in all the details. Among many other things that happened that day, a slight ground tremor occurred a few hours after the arrival of the presidents, which went unnoticed by the majority ofthe carefree people of the capital. In light of later events, it must have been a warning from nature,calling attention to what was about to happen in the near and sudden future. For, some weeks after the end of the conference, Costa Rica shook violently, generating chaos and confusion. This was not just another earthquake: in the distance, about sixty kilometers away, one of the largest volcanoes in the country, Irazú, expelled a great column of ash, which darkened the sky and threw the country into desperation.

The regional economy, based mostly on coffee and banana crops, suffered the most, due to the hot, sulfurous gases that saturated the countryside, along with a thick layer ofvolcanic ash. As a result, commerce was affected adversely, and a shortage of the main staples occurred.

The government, seriously worried, took actions intended to stop the damage caused by the eruptions, designating special commissions in charge of keeping track of the lava flows. Recognized vulcanologists and technicians, after a quick look into the crater of the volcano, diagnosed an "early pregnancy" because, according to their estimates, the crater surface had risen about one meter.

The advice from the experts was to evacuate the slopes of the volcano. They knew that if it expelled its igneous mass, even San José could be in danger. Among the numerous remedies popularly proposed to relieve the internal pressure was the suggestion to use TNT inside the crater! Another inspiration, very daring indeed, was to install a huge tarpaulin over it, to keep the ashes from blowing out, since the ashes reached San José in about two hours, carried by the winds, carpeting the streets, andblinding the people, who took to protecting themselves with plastic bags in order to prevent feared diseases.

Like any disaster, the eruption had its consequences: schools closed, and commercial activity was ostensibly affected.

The Civil Guard organized an emergency plan: an observation post would be established near the crater, manned by police officers, in order to report continuously about the lava movements, in case it overflowed the crater. The observation post was to be equipped with a telecommunications network connected to a central station, which would coordinate an evacuation, if necessary. There would be a two- to three-hour safety margin.

Once the plan was approved, our department at the ICE was ordered to install the network. We got ready to carry out the orders, and accordingly planned an itinerary, choosing a Sunday for making preliminary calculations and necessary measurements. That day, together with two other engineers to whom I reported, in two jeeps, through an excellent road, we traveled to the previously designated place. We had to climb to an altitude of 3,342 meters above sea level to reach the volcano's summit.

On the way up we saw many people: some of them were impressed tourists, and many were simplyidle people looking for excitement. The crowds mocked the police instructions to stay away from the volcano and recklessly endangered their lives by approaching too close. Days before, a man had been hit and killed by a stone flying from the crater. It was difficult to make people obey.

We parked our jeeps on the esplanade next to the crater, at around 5:15 p.m., and waited until the crowd and the police finally dispersed, in order to get started with our work. It was 5:30 p.m. when we started working. A cold draft chilled our faces. It was a clear and cloudless day. The sun was still high enough to bother our eyes. At that altitude, weariness soon took control of our bodies, and with a great effort, we took the measurements and photographs very carefully. Next, after a few seconds of reflection, we selected a location for an observation post.

Walking on the volcano's surface was not easy. In spite of the protection of our lightweight, asbestos suits, at each step we felt hot steam as it ejected from the ground. We were in front of one of the largest craters in the world, but at the time we didn't really feel very proud of this fact.

Rather, we yearned to return to San José as soon as possible. To gain one last look, our boss decided to walk some distance away from us, about thirty-five meters to our left. The volcano continued to crackle. My fellow engineer glanced at his watch: it was 5:45 p.m. I took off my gloves and started to remove the asbestos suit. I had barely begun when the engineer next to me yelled loudly, "Look, Castillito,[2] that orange plane!"

I looked carefully at the object, which, followed closely by another very similar to it, silently approached the volcano. Our first guess was that these could be some type of aircraft from President Kennedy's escort forces; however, we could not identify them.

1963 eruption of the volcano Irazú and the site where Enrique Castillo R. saw two UFOs.

Besides, we were very surprised at the way they flew, "skimming" the jagged peaks, in maneuvers that were unheard of for contemporary military or commercial planes.

At 5:47 p.m. the two craft hovered together, stationary, at an altitude of some 300 meters above the crater.

The object closest to us suddenly dropped a few meters in a straight line, stopped abruptly, and then started falling slowly, gently swaying from side to side, like a dead leaf falling from a tree. It finally "parked" three meters above the surface of the volcano's crater, about sixty meters from us.

This "vehicle" was lenticular in shape, about forty-five meters in diameter and twelve meters high. A series of windows emitting blue light was visible around its diameter. It had a well-proportioned, greenish dome, seamlessly joined to the main body, which was smooth and the color of lead. When the two machines approached, they looked orange or reddish in color, but when stopped, they lost that hue.

The second object had moved towards the far side of the crater, and once it crossed the column of ashes, it executed similar maneuvers, until it disappeared behind the volcano, right in front of the lead engineer, who was some distance from us. Both craft induced a whirlwind, as we recalled later, as if produced by a propeller rotating at high speed.

At that moment, far from feeling fear, with our willpower numbed, we felt at first as though we were pinned to the ground, and then as if we were standing on top of an ant hill, because we felt a strong itch all over our bodies, which blocked our otherwise sensible intentions to flee for cover.

We had been watching this imposing spectacle for only a few seconds, when a piercing, high-pitched, whistle-like noise assaulted our ears and made them ache almost unbearably. A door opened over the dome, and something like a periscope emerged through it. Above this, another object, shaped like a hammer, rotated rapidly while emitting a violet light, a different hue from the blue that filtered through the peripheral windows. The periscope rose about a meter and stopped. We thought we might be being photographed, but this was just a hunch.

The hammer continued to rotate, and, in spite of our ear ache, we could perceive a low-frequency, quite rhythmic, musical tone.

Totally conscious of everything around us, with our senses more alert than ever, but at the same time perplexed and immobilized, we feared for the worst. An answer to our fears didn't take long in arriving: a second and different noise reached us, announcing the end of the show. The periscope retracted, the door closed, and after a fraction of a second, the craft lifted up a few meters, as if it were falling upwards; then it tilted slightly and shot off into infinity at a fantastic speed. The second ship followed silently, leaving behind a multicolored trail, first white, then orange, then reddish, changing to strong blue, and finally fading into violet. The stupendous speed made the craft look oval rather than round. As suddenly as they had appeared a few minutes earlier, they were gone, and we saw them no more.

The wind, true and silent witness of our sighting, blew with renewed vigor, forcing our minds to react. Instinctively I shook off my unhealthy stupor as I felt a sharp pain in my left shoulder. I crouched and turned my head to see my companion nearby, who, like me, was also holding his hand to his shoulder. He then let go and silently left me alone for a few minutes.

Our chief engineer approached us, walking rapidly. Confusion and anger showed on his face, such as I had never seen him display.

"I'll be darned if those were not flying saucers!" he said, throwing away his gloves and uttering an unpublishable curse.

I was not in a position to assert or negate this conclusion, preferring to wait a few moments until our spirits simmered down a little. Then we attempted to rationalize the details of the sighting. In our work, we were acquainted with electrical fields, and these could explain the uncomfortable itch and our loss of freedom of movement, presumably induced by the machine.

But we could not classify these flying objects, because they were different from any man-made thing known to us. With a simple calculation, we figured the duration of the sighting: seven minutes, time enough to imprint it indelibly upon our memories.

The next vexing question was whether or not we should tell about our experience. We fully realized the impact that such a strange event could cause on traditional minds. We agreed together to keep it to ourselves. It was far more difficult to explain than to keep secret, we felt, and we decided accordingly. Pledging silence, we pretended to forget about the entire incident. Unfortunately, circumstances would soon make us change our minds.

It was already dark when we picked up our gear and headed for San José. A few minutes later, we experienced a strange discomfort, marked by dizziness and vomiting. We had to stop and remain quiet until the ill feelings passed.

Fearing that we might have received a strong dose of radiation from the objects, we drove our jeeps quickly to the nearest health center, located in the city of Cartago, some forty-five minutes from Irazú. Along the way, we were forced to stop several times, distressed by stomach cramps and the need to evacuate our bowels, always with negative results. These false alarms scared us, because our bodily functions seemed altered, and in our panic we feared that we might even die.

At the Cartago health center, we persuaded the doctor to examine us, on the grounds of a possible poisoning by the noxious volcano emanations. He gave us no medication, but with suspicious curiosity about our high degree of excitement, he sent us to the San Juan de Dios hospital in San José, for a more thorough check up.

Once we arrived at the capital's hospital, thanks to the timely action of the doctors on duty, we received adequate attention. Our eyes and tongues were examined, and we were given a white powder in a glass of water. They sent us home with the assurance that nothing was wrong with our health, which was calming medicine after such a hectic and traumatic day.

Since the jeeps belonged to ICE, we returned them to a place called Colima, near San José, and even nearer to San Juan de Tibás, where I lived. We then parted, each one submerged in his own thoughts, lost in the intricate network of questions without answers.

I was up late that night at home. I was not tired, just wanting to think. I told the full story to Beatriz,[3] my wife at the time, who did not believe a word of it. That night I meditated as never before, powerless under the avalanche of questions posed by my curiosity about the event, related to life, religious beliefs, and the scarce scientific knowledge that I had.

I promised myself that I would find a logical answer to properly explain those strange machines that had appeared in front of my eyes and then left, leaving no trace other than our physical discomforts.

I believe this is what happened to me at Irazú during those . . . seven eternal minutes!

CHAPTER NOTES

[1] Church of Jesus Christ of the Latter Day Saints.

[2] An endearing term for Castillo, the author's last name.

3 Beatriz was my first wife, born in Ecuador. We were married in 1952 and were separated in 1974.

2

The Siege Begins

"Through trial and error, selecting all possible demonstrated falsehoods, the true order of the great significant events of the past can be established. . . ."
—ROBERT CHARROUX, *The Masters of the World*

THE NEXT DAY, with all due haste, I ran to the bookstore, Libreria Universal, in San José, with the intention of purchasing a volume that might shed some light on our sighting at Irazú. The salesman, a bit confused, was unable to advise me, and he picked up from an old shelf a dusty book whose title seemed to fulfill the requirements of my emerging interest.

That book, *The Case for the UFO,* by Morris K. Jessup, was my first informative exposure to the world of the "flying saucers."

From this book and many others, I learned that my experience was far from unique, but it also served to show me the divided opinion of the scientific world regarding the authenticity of such phenomena. For some, UFO events represented nothing but normal confusion about well-known natural phenomena, or perhaps devices and gadgets derived from the new space race between the world powers. For others, UFO phenomena became the victory of magic over the wrongful positions of an imperfect and hesitant science.

To be honest, neither explanation satisfied my curiosity completely, but I had to accept them because nothing else was available in our limited Costa Rican milieu. My investigations were always informal, because I lacked the means to tackle them more seriously. This research activity included making albums, consisting of newspaper clippings and pictures taken from journals and magazines, some of them courtesy of the bookstore attendant.

On the other hand, because of my new and fortuitous relationship with the "flying saucers," I couldn'thelp being dragged along by the already uncontrollable desire to talk about my experience. Having pledged silence to my companions of adventure, they considerately agreed to let me talk, as long as their names were omitted.

In hindsight, I realize that this was a naive and reckless action, born from my good intentions. Without knowing in depth the consequences of my action, I dared to share with others the details of the sighting. What a great mistake it was to step in the way of religion and science, without any other shield than my innocence. . . !

The frightful mechanisms brought to bear against me, aiming to defend the principles that are entrenched in the depths of the listener's minds, were unleashed almost automatically, in a hurling of energies against something that, to me, was only an unexpected incident. I narrated the Irazú sighting only with the intention to inform about it, never to explain it. However, to my misfortune, the public never stopped to consider my intentions, and, like a heretic, I was shouted down and effectively prevented from speaking out further. A wave of malicious comments and ridicule hurt my feelings badly.

That was the price of my daring. Although no one within the public dared to speak openly, I couldperceive some discrete, relatively favorable comments. Well, after all, I was not completely alone, but the experience served to make me more cautious in the world of the unknown.

The stubborn attitude of my fellow workers, entrenched in showing how silly my stories were, was eroding my already weakened investigative will, and all would have died off, were it not for something that took place two months after the Irazú sighting.

One night I arrived at my home at San Juan de Tibás, about two hundred meters away from the school "Miguel Obregón," where I had completed my primary studies. Exhausted, I soon fell asleep. At 1:00 AM, a violent sound reverberated in my head. I woke up startled and indescribably frightened, trying to identify the origin of the noise. It was like a swarm of bees fighting fiercely inside my brain. Covering my ears did not help at all.

Composing my thoughts, I recalled suddenly that only once before had I heard such a noise: at Irazú, in front of the UFO. . . !

I swept the room with my gaze. My wife, asleep, was not aware of anything. Quickly, I stood up and, grasping an old broom handle (I was afraid of some disgrace), inspected the entire house. My children[1] rested peacefully in their rooms, unaware of what was going on. Visibly affected by terrible feelings of foreboding and not knowing what to do, I came back to my room, where, while I was trying to open the window, the noise ended abruptly. A cold sweat covered me, and I was shaking all over. Finally, the incident was over.

In the morning, over coffee, I questioned my wife discreetly about the night before. I dared not do so directly. However, she instantly deduced where I was leading and cut off the conversation rather sharply: "The UFO has made you psychotic," she said.

What could I say? I had no answer either. How I wished at that moment that she could understand the inexplicable sequence of events promoted by the unknown something, the meaning of which was impenetrable to my limited intelligence. Whatever it was, it was now continuing to manifest itself openly, providing calculated doses of enigmatic riddles, with the perhaps intentional effect of confusing me further.

The next night, before dawn, when we had already forgotten in part our fears, a strong tremor woke both of us up. Beatriz, visibly disturbed, tried to call my attention to a strange noise that was mercilessly jostling the house. Her panic helped to form a terrible knot in my throat. The surprise left me cold with fright!

Once again, I grabbed an old broom; grasping it, ready to wield in defense, I tried to find out what was shaking the house. The children slept placidly, and only three of us were conscious at that moment: my wife, nearing an uncontrollable nervous breakdown and following me closely; the cat, purring and leaning against my legs, looking at my eyes as if searching for an explanation; and myself, powerless and also nearing hysteria.

I walked to the bathroom, where everything shook. The window panes seemed ready to fall to the floor. The walls "danced" to the same tune. We were possessed by chaos! Our ears ached desperately. Deathly afraid, I ran for the door, and when I opened it, all noises ceased, replaced by a sudden, eerie, quiet. A minute had passed, two at the most.

It was possible to compare the two latest frightening events: I discerned that the awful noise this time had been louder and more piercing than the first time.

I stepped out into the yard and surveyed the beautiful, starry sky. There was nothing in sight. A soft breeze was blowing. Terribly ashamed, I looked down at myself, at the broom clutched ridiculously in my hands. How far things had gone! Here I was, dressed only in my underwear, fear having forced me to pursue the cause of the noises and vibrations, seeking protection against them. Of course, my actions were unconscious, born of automatic self-defense.

I reentered the house, in order to try to calm Beatriz. She looked shocked, dazed, and was shaking nervously. I could not go back to sleep, and I remember that when she woke up, she had exclaimed, "Enrique, they are here!"

Then, as if nothing had happened, life continued, day after day. I never had an explanation for these events; nobody had one, but I never was able to forget those two, terror-drenched dawns in Costa Rica.

One day I visited a friend, an old school buddy, probably the most intelligent man I had ever known; his name was Julio Acosta. I told him my story. He listened attentively, weighed all the facts for a few seconds, and said, "They are following you; there is no question about it!"

Julio[2] is today manager of the Costa Rican National Mail Post Office Department, and he was the first to suggest a heretofore unsuspected but possible relationship between the "flying saucers" and myself. Of course, this idea surprised me, because I never expected such a statement, but it acted as an excellent sedative. Julio would become my closest advisor and confidante, and together we would discover many things that exist in this world, which have never been scrutinized, for lack of proper criteria to unravel them. For example, many people have experienced unusual events, but the lack of coordination and lackadaisical attitude of the press towards these events frustrate any attempt to clarify or publicize them.

One afternoon, Julio and I took a cab. We casually began talking about UFOs and, immersed in our conversation, failed to notice the curious gaze of the driver through the rearview mirror. He was paying attention and finally decided to interrupt us, saying that he himself was building a flying saucer! Apparently, he was lacking only a motorcycle engine to drive it. We could not help smiling to ourselves at his endeavor. For a long time we had not heard of anything so outlandish. Nevertheless, he gave us a card with his address, along with a cordial invitation to his home. We never went; I can't recall why. Most probably, his invention never flew!

Sporadic conversations such as this confirmed the visible interest of the general public about the unusual experiences that many people undergo, without meriting adequate investigation or explanation. For this and other reasons, we decided to organize a study group, charged with the task of gathering and processing all the available information on UFOs. The group consisted of several of my friends, among them Julio Acosta, at that time a salesman for Universal; Felipe Segura, maintenance operator for the Tropical Commission Company, old acquaintance of mine; and others whose names have faded from my memory, but who were all united by the same interest.

We began gathering all data within our reach, which was not very abundant, for lack of adequate sources of information. We compensated for this drawback by writing to prestigious existing organizations in the UFO field. Two of them answered us, Aerial Phenomena Research Organization

(APRO), of Tucson, Arizona, and National Investigation Center of Aerial Phenomena (NICAP), in Washington, D.C., assuring us that they had in their files over 20,000 investigated cases of people who had been involved in some type of sighting. This was something to think about seriously.

We fully realized the complexities involved in these investigations, and the difficulties in correctly outlining the questions in order to obtain adequate answers. We had to resort to related sciences in our attempt to clarify the existing theories about life in the universe, and its not less enigmatic consequence—humankind. And the task was not as simple as we first thought it would be.

We used to meet in an old garret, away from outside noise, for pleasant talks that often lasted until the late hours of the night. Of course, we made no transcendental discoveries, but we did have satisfactions that eased to a degree our voracious longing for the weird. Among the many conclusions arrived at, one was significant: most of the mysteries remain so, due to lack of information on the part of the public, and are compounded by ignorance and fertile imaginations, which balloon them out of proportion.

Of course, this phenomenon helps to generate some of the senseless news that appears in newspapers around the world. Then, another thing makes matters worse—thousands of reports from people of varying social and cultural levels regarding apparitions of unknown flying objects maneuvering in various fashions, have never received adequate attention on the part of the experts. This remains a persistent problem.

To our chagrin, various difficulties frustrated our good intentions about continuing our meetings: the accumulation of unanswered questions, the lack of new data, routine (the early enemy of non-scientific minds), and each one's own occupations, which took up most of our available time. Eventually, we

Enrique Castillo R. at the headquarters of the Costa Rican Institute of Scientific and Ecobiologic Investigations (ICICE) in San José, Costa Rica.

Photo: Ricardo Vilchez, Costa Rica

were forced to dissolve the group, thus finishing an honest endeavor, devoid of extraordinary discoveries or conclusions, but satisfactory for ourselves.

Of course, I never quite forgot my pastime, but gave it only a normal amount of attention, under the circumstances. When my daughter Asuramaya was born,[3] I had to pay more attention to my family, who felt a little abandoned during my long absences at the nightly meetings, and also to my church, which I loved very much.

Once I made a comment about the Irazú incident to one of our Mormon ministers, hoping for some type of explanation from him. Not only was there none, but I received a severe warning from my superiors to keep silent. Abiding under this new passive attitude, my curiosity subsequently became aroused when one of the "elders" volunteered this confidence: "One of my brothers, who is an Air Force pilot, saw a 'flying saucer,' but his superiors 'amiably' suggested he forget about it."

I was always alert to listen to any story that was being circulated. I heard one upon receiving an assignment to inspect the telephone system of the U.S. Embassy. There I met an ex-midshipman, a veteran of the Korean war, who accompanied me to inspect the main switchboard of the diplomatic headquarters. I was handling a selector, when he mentioned its similarity with some flying objects he had seen in the past, and I took the opportunity to ask him his opinion about UFOs.

He answered that while serving as a sergeant in the U.S. Army, he was ordered to investigate a guerrilla pocket near some large rice fields in Korea. Eight soldiers accompanied him. They heard a noise and silently decided to split into two groups, to surprise the enemy from both sides. They did just that, and while crawling further, the noise increased. When they gazed upward, to everyone's surprise, they found themselves in front of a machine about four meters in diameter. Around it were six small beings, each accomplishing assorted tasks. Some were fetching water, and one was leaning against the machine, seemingly cleaning his nails. They walked with a peculiar gait, like penguins. They had big eyes and were about sixty cm (two feet) tall at the most. Their skin was purplish, and they wore no helmets.

The sergeant lifted his weapon, aimed through the telescopic sight, and examined the black uniforms of the diminutive astronauts. Something kept him from firing at them. The one "cleaning his nails" alerted his companions that the soldiers of the U.S. patrol were about to fire from behind him! The six occupants, yelling in an unknown tongue, climbed into their machine and disappeared from sight instantly.

The sergeant reported the sighting to his superiors as a matter of routine. Soon thereafter, he was discharged from active duty, ordered to shut up, and relocated as a security officer in the diplomatic service. That was why he was in Costa Rica.

Another story came my way shortly after the gigantic Riomacho hydroelectric dam was built; wevisited it in order to inspect its telephone system. The watchmen posted there made comments about the sighting of mysterious objects flying at low velocity; they made no official report because nobody was interested.

My investigations were thus limited to data collection, a mere pastime such as collecting stamps or butterflies. Since Costa Rica was not very rich in this type of information, the days passed without my receiving any new significant data.

About this time, I found myself with a new talent—that of writing poetry, with an irresistible drive whose root I was unable to comprehend. Some of the poems were published in newspapers as prominent as *La Nacion* and *El Diario de Costa Rica*. The by-then director of the SIP (Inter-American Press Service), Ricardo Castro Beeche, referring to my work , called it "poetry of the future." This was all somewhat paradoxical. From one moment to the next I found myself gifted with talents unknown before, and I searched in vain for an explanation for them, but found nothing special. My childhood was a happy one; in fact, not many children have such wonderful parents as mine.

My mother, a Colombian from the highlands of Boyacá, gentle, kind, and intelligent, filled our lives with her personal example. While we lived in Costa Rica, she practiced writing, under the pseudonym of"Esmeralda Colombiana" (Colombian Emerald). Highly esteemed in the intellectual circles of Costa Rica, she held important public positions in that country. Young people loved her; teenagers and children were her friends. Her concept of life, notably advanced for the epoch, probably would make many winceeven nowadays. My father was likewise a great man, who, in spite of all its difficulties, was able to face all life wisely.[4]

They were a beautiful married couple, with never a complaint, an offense, or an argument between them. They loved each other with all the strength of their immense hearts. In 1948, during my adolescence, my father died, a few days before the cowardly assassination of a great man he admired: Jorge Eliécer Gaitán.[5] I would no longer be able to listen to their vibrant voices: that of Gaitán the popular leader, and that of my father!

By mid-1964, new professional opportunities appeared for me. One of them was in Cali, Colombia, and it offered an excellent position. The decision was made to go to Cali, and I relocated there. As my mother often said, "You have a mobile spirit, Enrique!"

CHAPTER NOTES

[1] My children were Enrique Jr., Mauricio, and Alexandra—10, 8, and 6 years old, respectively, at that time.

[2] Julio Acosta was the postal manager until 1979.

[3] In San Jose, on May 13, 1964 (our fourth child).

[4] My family had retuned to Colombia, their country of origin, together with my brother Roberto, my sister Leda, and myself, in 1944, during the second world war. My brother Leonardo stayed in Costa Rica, where my parents had lived for twenty-five years. Julián, my older brother, has lived in Bogotá since the beginning of 1944. Four years later, my father died in Bogotá, Colombia.

[5] Jorge Eliécer Gaitán was a very popular liberal candidate for the presidency of Colombia. He paid for his socialistic ideas with his life, on April 9, 1948, when he was shot by an unknown assassin who was in turn lynched by the crowds.

3

Are Those "Things" Following Me?

"The simultaneity of many of these observations implies that there really was not one, but several of those aerial ships of similar characteristics. This very intriguing wave of sightings has been unearthed by several modern investigators, through delving into the press of that time. These investigators were the North Americans John Keel, Jerome Clark, and Donald B. Hanlon."
—ANTONIO RIBERA, *De veras los OVNIS nos vigilan? (Are the UFOs really watching us?)*

QUITE THRILLED ABOUT THE NEW JOB, I oriented all my aspirations towards Colombia, cradle of my ancestors, and about which I harbored pleasant remembrances, thanks to my parent's decided effort to preserve their nostalgic ancestral customs. Perhaps this was why I accepted going back to Colombia so quickly. Besides, I had heard interesting comments from friends and acquaintances, which also helped me make a quick decision.

Cali was by then a prosperous city, outstanding in its industrial progress. Its streets, graced by beautiful women, had an air of happiness and celebration, where sadness held no place. My stay there, very pleasant indeed, was rather uneventful. Even though we led a quiet life, I could not break away completely from my experiences in Costa Rica, which were subtly impressed forever in my mind, and any confusing situation, inexplicable event, or sensationalist announcement was enough to associate those facts with the mysterious objects I had seen. This was an interior, automatic process, almost impossible to control. At the same time, I noticed my judgment and conclusions becoming more acute. However, I avoided acknowledging any reason for these changes. Also, I refused to accept any gratuitous explanations: I wanted to know the truth, not empty or irrational answers that would in any way slight the subject.

In that brooding state, I often turned my gaze to the stars, my thoughts lost in contemplation of things I could not define. That is how I weighed certain strange events that went unnoticed by other people—unimportant events, perhaps, but still interesting to me.

I witnessed two such events: the first one together with my wife, during a clear night. We were looking at a new housing project, when I saw a meteorite moving slowly, tracing a perfect zigzag in the sky. Very excited, I yelled to some construction workers, who, without wasting time, ran and watched the show with me, which lasted for about thirty seconds. Very strange, indeed.

The second event caused more commotion among the people of Cali. During a summer afternoon in 1964, one of my sons pointed to an orange-colored aerolite crossing the sky at great speed, horizontally, moving south. After fading in the distance, about four minutes later, a loud explosion boomed and was heard all over the city, terrifying both people and animals. That night the TV news report presented a detailed account, according to which the object had fallen near Jamundí, burning the vegetation at the site of the impact.

Also, the newspaper from Cali, *Occidente*, published some notes about the subject that were somewhat contradictory. One of them mentioned an expert from the Universidad del Valle, stating that natural causes produced the event. Another mentioned a group of farmers armed with machetes and sticks, who supposedly had visited the site of the impact and found a thatch and some grass burned—and also had seen the "aerolite" just taking off! No crater was found, and there were insistent rumors about strange beings moving in the area. Nothing could be confirmed. People, as expected, did not help, and we decided to forget about the incident.

Steeped in a disagreeable monotony, time elapsed in Cali with an incredible slowness. In order to overcome it, I distributed my time between work and going to the movies, reading, or attending church services. A Mormon since 1961, I was very fond of my church. Seduced by its teachings, I became submerged deeper and deeper into the tenets of its faith. Although not a mystic in the strict sense of the word, I acknowledged the need to find tangible links with a Superior Truth, independent from obscure human feelings.

Convinced of the teachings of the Mormon prophets, I strove to find my true self in them. I knew that it was a safe harbor, and thus I surrendered easily. As might be expected, I found myself involved in a priestly career full of satisfactory experiences, about which I have never felt remorse. When I came to Cali, I did so as a presbyter, and as such received approval for operating a "branch" of my church at my home.

Without wasting time and with the help of two "elders" or veteran priests, the Mormon Church was finally established in Cali. The first ceremonies took place at my home, until we could obtain a more suitable location.

With certain envy, the laboriousness of Mormon priests has been criticized. The truth is that in a short while, we enticed a goodly number of people, some of them working companions, others, neighbors of the house, to convert to Mormonism. Our church community grew rapidly, and with it, my personal satisfaction, although I had to put up with the hot afternoons of Cali.

Because of reasons already known, I never tried to mix the religious subject with that of UFOs, and I even refused to discuss this matter. Nevertheless, pressed by chance circumstances, I found myself involved in an unexpected argument on the subject, wherein my bosses, subordinates, and a friend, José Miller, took part. So, the cat was let out of the bag, and my experiences became known. Jose Miller later dubbed me *El Marciano*, "The Martian." Because of this discussion, I was forced to do something that I never dreamed I would do.

My working in Cali involved installing rural telephone networks for the sugar mills. At the urging of a resident engineer at the sugar mill, I agreed to give a talk on the UFO subject at one of them, Ingenio Pichichí, in 1965, for the first time in my life. Far from suspecting the extraordinary interest that the subject would provoke, at first I was reluctant, arguing my lack of experience, and so forth, to no avail. To my surprise, I was faced with a very receptive audience, who applauded me long after I finished, while I recovered from my emotion.

The same José Miller, my old friend from Costa Rica, along with Felipe Segura, who happened to be attending a telephony course in Cali, sponsored by his company, had attended the conference. They were very moved and were the first to approach and congratulate me about the talk.

There is no doubt that the success of my talk contributed to exposing my hidden craving for the UFO subject, which had until then been kept jealously hidden during my stay in Cali. Afterwards, many people approached me, shyly at first, and later openly, to tell me their own stories, some of them many years old, others recent.

Among the many secrets that surfaced, I remember two watchmen from the Central Castilla sugar mill who had watched an object overflying the worker's living quarters at 4:00 a.m.; they aimed their flashlights at the UFO, and it had answered, flooding the whole neighborhood with a powerful light.

Experiences such as this were numerous. Unfortunately, I could not give people any adequate explanations, and I adopted a rather passive, receptive

May 8, 1977.
The author during his address at the First UFO World Congress in Acapulco, Mexico.

May 9, 1977. Enrique Castillo R. and Jim Orenzen, U.S.A, Director of the A.P.R.O., attending the First UFO World Congress in Acapulco, Mexico.

May 7, 1977. Dr. Walter H. Andrus, Jr., Director of MUFON, and Enrique Castillo R. during the First UFO World Congress in Acapulco, Mexico.

May 7, 1977. Left to right: Hilda Menzel (Investigator), Major Colman von Reviczky (Director of ICUFON, U.S.A.), Antonio Ribera (Writer-Investigator, Spain), and Enrique Castillo R. during recess at the First UFO World Congress, Acapulco, Mexico.

attitude that would not conflict with my priestly condition. The seed had been planted in the minds of many; it was only necessary to cultivate it.

My tenure in Cali ended, thanks to a new contract in Bucaramanga, capital city of the northern Colombian province of Santander del Sur, this time with General Telephone International. I became chief engineer in charge of indoor installations for the Public Central phone system.

Following the pattern already established in Cali, in Bucaramanga I did exactly the same: founded a new branch of the Mormon church. This time my ecclesiastical efforts had to be increased twofold, to the point that the UFO subject might have died out within me for my own good, had my stay there only been long enough.

Truly, my plans and goals were not clear, even to myself. I traveled from one city to another, searching for something impossible to describe, and I never wasted an opportunity to visit new places. That is how I came to accept an offer from Brazil. Somewhat dazzled by the possibility of acquainting myself with new lands, and also by a satisfactory economic compensation in the capital of the largest country in Latin America, I decided to follow my new destiny. I left for Brasilia in 1968, on my birthday.

Designed from scratch to house the government agencies and the diplomatic delegations of the whole world, Brasilia presented an imposing physical profile. The great number of recently constructed buildings required many technicians, which were not very plentiful in that tropical territory.

Separated by many hundreds of kilometers from the main coastal cities and surrounded by dense jungle, Brasilia left one with a gloomy impression and lacked all types of recreational facilities. A weekend at Brasilia was unbearable. I had no access to social clubs, where the jet set socialized. I had no friends, because of the language barrier. That's why I used to drive my sporty car to São Paulo, to spend most of the weekend there, while getting a tan at the ocean beaches.

The early dawn of a Monday during the month of October 1968 caught me driving at high speed towards Brasilia, on the Trans-Amazonic highway. It was 4:00 a.m., and for a long stretch the road was completely empty. At 100 kph, my car was performing beautifully. It was a clear, cloudless night, with no wind. Suddenly, an unknown force shook the steering wheel with a strong vibration.

Through the windshield, I saw a ball of fire that crossed the sky and lit up the tops of the jungle trees. I stopped at once, parking at the side of the road. At first, I thought it might be a plane in trouble, but it looked more like a luminous sphere. It pulsed, as if it were breathing!

Pulsing, its lights sparkled intermittently. I got into the car, exceedingly scared, and accelerated, intending to put distance between the object and myself. To my chagrin, the object followed me for many kilometers, ahead or above the car, moving to the left or to the right. When close, the steering wheel shook and the radio lost the station to which it was tuned, and garbled unintelligibly. This circumstance was repeated several times, increasing my panic towards the object.

It moved parallel to the car, keeping pace, whether I increased or decreased the velocity. Several times, when it dove over the car, I thought it would crash, but in the end nothing happened. In the distance, a light became visible over the road. The object, sensing it, quickly got lost over the jungle. There was no witness for its appearance or disappearance.

The light was at a toll gate. An officer and a soldier welcomed me. Babbling a few words in my rudimentary Portuguese, I asked them for a glass of water to regain my serenity, and then, after a few seconds, I told them about my odyssey. It didn't surprise the officer at all, who said very seriously, "Those apparitions of 'spirits' are frequent around here."

A man changing a tire was attracted by our conversation, and he roundly confirmed the officer's appreciation.

Fear of another encounter detained me at the toll gate until another car showed up, and together, after goodbyes and thanks to the military, we reached Brasilia.

That Monday afternoon, I mentioned the incident to a group of engineers, but only one of them, who worked for ITT, showed any interest, and he called me to one side of the meeting room and confided his childhood experiences.

I was already used to the momentary interest of people and the early oblivion of the facts of such events. My story, besides entertaining some, was soon forgotten.

My six-month contract elapsed very fast. While still in Brasilia I met a Japanese engineer, a representative of OKI, manufacturers of telephone equipment. He offered me a job possibility in Venezuela, where he had a representative. I accepted at once and traveled to Caracas.

On my way to Caracas, I stopped in Bucaramanga, rested for two days, visited my family, and again full of illusions left for Venezuela. I stayed at the Lincoln Hotel, in the Venezuelan capital, in quiet surroundings, between Miracielos and Hospital streets. Unfortunately, right from the beginning, things did not go as planned.

After two weeks, the Japanese still had not shown up. Penniless, and with the hotel owner asking for her money, I went to the only place where I could find refuge: the church. With the help of a Baptist minister, I located the Mormon congregation. Happily, all the brethren welcomed me, especially brother Robert, who was kind enough to offer me a room in his beautiful

Caracas home. There I stayed for four months, until I could save a few bolivars and move to a nice apartment in San Bernardino, Plaza de la Estrella, on the fourth floor.

What great luck! I could not complain. Finally I was able to achieve some stability and bring my family to live with me in Venezuela.

4

A Swissman Who Was Not Swiss

"One of the hottest scientific issues contemplates the possibility that the Universe may contain, in far away planets, intelligent beings who, although very different from us, may have reached the high degree of intellectual development inherent to scientific investigation and technical control over nature. A lot of attention is currently given to this issue, in all research fields."
—Professor PASCUAL JORDAN, co-author of *The Theory of Static Transformation*

LIFE IS STRANGE AND DISCONCERTING. Around it, people, important events, and interesting ideas orbit and remain as indelible memories.

My experience with Mormonism was fundamental in the structuring of my basic living principles. It taught me profound respect for people in general. I learned to follow the principles of reciprocal good behavior, avoiding in this way the common and normal frictions in social relationships.

I tried to harmonize with people and with everything. Whatsoever I encountered that did not agree with these principles, provoked in me feelings of rejection and repulsion. I avoided getting involved in pointless arguments and stayed away from commotion and fights. Rather, I persistently looked for and enjoyed solitude.

A few days had elapsed after I moved into my comfortable apartment in San Bernardino. It was located on a fourth floor, overlooking Avila, a beautiful mountain on the north side of Caracas, somewhat isolated from the heavy traffic of the metropolitan network of highways, with its multiple interwoven bridges.

I used to work hard, and I was living alone, far from my family. My intention was to save some money to be able to bring them with me to Caracas. According to the Evangelical teachings, I complied with my religious duties and then yielded to what I accept is for me one of the most pleasant "bad habits" or pastimes: the movies. Watching a movie would break the routine of the daily work, allowing me to escape to the deep recesses of the movie plots.

Then, a monumental chain of events began at a movie house, one Sunday in 1969. As usual, after the religious services, I went to the "Canaima" cinema, alone, although I did not dislike company. There was a big crowd. That day, in order to buy the tickets without trouble, I arrived early. While standing in line, I happened to look up to one side.

A young fellow stood there, looking back at me curiously. He smiled and walked towards me.

"Hello, elder!" I saluted him, thinking that he could be a Mormon priest.

Half ashamed and half cordial, he answered, "Sorry, but that is not my name."

I excused myself, explaining that his looks were similar to that of the priests of my religion.

He understood immediately, and taking advantage of my privileged place in the line, he asked me to please buy him a ticket. He handed me a ten bolivar bill.

"Sir, are you escorting somebody?" he asked shyly. I said no.

"Then, do you mind if I stay here with you?"

"No, not at all," I answered quickly.

We walked together into the theater. I bought some candies and offered some to him. He accepted very courteously. We introduced ourselves.

"My name is Cyril—Cyril Weiss—of Swiss nationality, representative of a wholesale distribution house from my country," he said, and added, "I am here in Caracas with the purpose of opening the market for Latin America."

When the show ended, I invited Cyril to my apartment. He did not accept, for reasons he didn't disclose, but I made him promise that he would visit the next day.

Driving my small Simca 1000, I drove him to his hotel. He asked me to drop him at a corner, from where he walked off with great strides.

My impression about this young Swiss fellow was good. He was pleasant and very well-behaved, although cautious.

The next day, as agreed, we met after work and I took him to visit my apartment. We were very hungry, and I offered him a carton of milk and some delicious "cambures," as bananas are called in Venezuela.

Cyril made himself comfortable in a rocking chair in my small living room. He noticed some tape recordings on a table.

"Enrique, I'd like to listen to this recording." He handed me the "Trout Quintet."

Pleased, he relaxed, breathing deeply, giving the impression of being lost in his thoughts at the harmonies of this beautiful musical composition. Once in a while he came back to reality and asked details about my collection of classical music. Our friendship had established itself quite firmly. We exchanged ideas and opinions. I told him about my life. He appeared startled when I told him that my religion prohibited coffee, liquor, and tobacco.

Later in the evening, I offered him some cheese and sausage sandwiches.

"I cannot eat that, Enrique; I am a vegetarian."

I felt like laughing, and I did it with such élan that Cyril was speechless.

"It's all right, Cyril, it is just that I also decided to become vegetarian some time ago."

"You are doing the right thing, Enrique." And he enumerated a series of advantages for those who do not eat meat.

"Enrique, there is something else that bothers me a lot."

"May I know what it is?"

"How is it possible that someone who likes classical music likes also tangos by Carlos Gardel?"[1]

"Well, Cyril, it is just that I am one of those weird combinations that nature concocts once in a while!" I laughed.

The evening was interesting, but time elapsed slowly.

"Cyril, have you ever heard about UFOs?" I tried to motivate him with this question. His answer was more of a courtesy, rather than true interest. His expression turned more serious.

"Enrique, the latest investigations of the U.S. government, related to UFOs, have shown that they do not exist. As of today, the phenomenon has been sufficiently explained. I do not wish to discourage you, but I agree that they are pure hallucinations. Furthermore, I dare to say that they are a safety valve, a product of the cold war among the world powers."

I kept silent and did not insist on the subject, because I was afraid of offending him with my opinions.

The meeting lasted into the wee hours of the morning, because we continued deepening this "coincidental" friendship, since we shared so many viewpoints. I had found a good new friend and intended to integrate him into my framework of activities. I decided to invite him to church. He accepted the invitation twice.

At that time, I was carrying out a decided evangelical effort among my group of friends. One of them, Manuel Bonell, barber by profession, his wife, and their young son attended, along with Cyril and myself, a baptismal ceremony, by immersion, of adult new members of the congregation. Manuel and his wife refused to be baptized, because some of the Mormon principles did not agree with their beliefs. Cyril did not want to be baptized either. Later I found why he refused; nevertheless, he always was very respectful of other people's beliefs.

My friend Cyril had the characteristic physical traits of the Nordic race. His looks enticed women. His blond, well-kept hair shone under the sun. He protected his fair, white skin from the sun's rays, staying in the shade as much as possible. He was about 1.78-1.80 meters tall (or almost six feet), and looked twenty-seven years old at the most. His countenance was proud, but he dressed informally and neatly. His face projected serenity, and his speech denoted peace of mind.

He was always calm and never completely lost control of his emotions. I was able to verify this in a series of events isolated from each other, but ample to reconfirm my impressions. One of them was related to the theft of some electrical cables from the company where I worked. Suspicious about a young employee, I decided to talk to him, because I was aware of the difficult economic situation he faced. On a Saturday, I decided to clarify this matter. On the way out of the office, I saw Cyril and asked him to please accompany me. We drove to the barrio where the employee lived, with its steep, narrow alleys, where it was difficult to drive a car.

Returning, on the north side of the city towards Avila mountain near the Vargas Hospital, a car ahead of us seemed not to notice a boy and his dog, who were crossing the double-laned road. The boy had reached the sidewalk, but not the dog. The driver, with a certain savagery, aimed the car towards the dog and knocked it soundly against the hard concrete surface. In a cowardly action, the driver then sped up, screeching his tires, and was lost from sight.

Fearing a collision, I had slowed down while the reckless driver crushed the little dog. I got out of the car and approached the boy, who, numbed by the surprise, could not yet react. He looked at his small pet with somber eyes, full of sadness. The little animal convulsed in the throes of death. A man, amidst the shouts and utterings of the people who gathered about, covered the body of the dying animal with a newspaper.

"Where does the boy live? Who knows him?" I asked the curious crowd. A lady recognized him and promised to take him home. The boy started crying.

With my hands full, attempting to console the boy, I felt behind me a cold stare, alien, insensible to pain. It was Cyril, who had walked slowly to the place of the events. His coldness impressed me strongly. A strong horn blast reminded me that I was obstructing the traffic. We ran to the car, started it, and drove away as fast as possible.

I was very angry and cursed humanity, spouting to Cyril about the brutality of people. With his usual aloofness, he interrupted me forcefully, saying, "Enrique, don't worry so much about the boy; after a few hours, his sadness in the face of the inevitable will end. We all possess a brain mechanism that overcomes everything; even children have it. Thanks to that mechanism, we finally accept the events that hurt us, no matter how cruel and unjust they might be. There is such a mechanism, I assure you, Enrique, and what happened was inevitable, Enrique."

Astonished, I was open-mouthed. I had expected him to back me up in my position, and instead he reproached my attitude indirectly. Cyril was not moved at all. Undaunted and seemingly inhuman, as if his feelings were about inferior beings, he hardly looked back at me. Restraining myself with all my fortitude, I changed the subject. He hadn't even shown pity. In this way, Cyril was baffling. He seemed indifferent to everything.

In spite of his handsome looks and being a center of attraction for girls, he showed no interest in the opposite sex. This provoked satirical comments among my fellow workers, who described him as "queer," with all the implications carried by this word. However, I never noticed anything unusual about him in this respect.

Cyril avoided parties and the like. At one of these meetings, the girls of my church group went overboard to provoke him, and for the first and only time I saw him mad, although a few moments later he was back in his usual nonchalant mood.

I often encouraged him to enjoy social events, trying to keep him away from what I considered abnormal solitude. I do not recall that he had any friends. He always behaved correctly, and I insisted frequently that he join me in promenades and the like, and during one outing I came to appreciate how nice he could be when he tried.

That weekend we went to the beach. Cyril did not swim, because, according to him, salt water, wind, and sun would affect his skin. He rested under a beach umbrella and spent the time reading a book on the famous UFOs.

"Don't worry, Enrique, take your time; swim as long as you wish." He laughed all the while, very easygoing. I invited him to refresh himself in the water.

"Enrique, if I swim, my skin will be ruined completely, keeping me from getting dressed for the rest of my life!" he yelled, half-kidding and half-serious.

After a while, I left the water to accompany him. I saw him enjoying the book. When I got close, he asked me, watching to see my reaction, "Have you ever heard about the 'BLUE BOOK'?"

"Yes, of course! I believe it is the smoke screen of the U.S. Air Force to discredit the belief in the existence of the UFOs and to ridicule the witnesses," I answered.

Immediately he replied (recall that very recently he had expressed that extraterrestrials did not exist, and that everything along those lines could be very naturally explained), "Personally, reconsidering the matter, I believe that there must be some type of intelligent life somewhere in the Universe, but I don't think they have arrived at this planet yet.

"Perhaps those 'entities' have advanced more than ourselves, and their evolution is such that for now it is difficult for them to contact Earthlings; don't you think so, Enrique?"

"Well, myself, I do believe in the existence of intelligent beings in the Universe," I said, "and I also believe that some of them have arrived on our planet in remote times. There are traces and hints of evidence, Cyril, only our science is reluctant to accept them. There must be several reasons for this, and I feel that two of them are pride and arrogance."

Cyril didn't answer. He was silent for a few seconds, deep in thought about my belief in worlds superior to our modest airborne dwelling.

It was difficult for me to find a pastime or activity wholly satisfactory for Cyril. I tried everything, including sports. Though knowing that he disliked terribly those that generate violence, I decided to invite him to a soccer game.

At the time, there was a contest for the "Libertadores de America Cup," a well-known championship, between Deportivo Italia from Venezuela, and Union Magdalena from Colombia. About halfway through the game, one of the two teams provoked a wrangle, during which the umpire expelled several players. The violence on the field was indescribable. With fists and kicks, the players fought each other, making it necessary to call in the police to control the situation.

Cyril, thoroughly disgusted, stood up to leave. Among the curses of the spectators, I realized his intentions. Then I asked him why he wanted to leave, just as the show was getting more interesting.

"I'll wait for you outside," he mumbled.

The game was suspended, and I went out to find him. I found him enjoying a luscious orange, of the type cultivated at Valencia, Carabobo State. We got in the car, but he still looked grim.

"I don't like violence, Enrique."

I regarded him silently for a second, affirming mentally that Europeans had strange attitudes!

"Well, then, why don't we go and watch a boxing match?"

"No, I do not like that."

I tried to interest him in something, unaware of the fact that all my invitations involved a show of violence.

"What about a bullfight?"

Cyril looked at me calmly and answered serenely, "Haven't you ever thought about the philosophy contained in violence? Haven't you noticed the bloodshot eyes of all the spectators of the type of shows that you have just named? Enrique, violence is contagious, and violent shows, without a doubt, are for individuals who are insufficiently evolved."

I kept silent. Nobody had spoken to me with such authority, about something so evident. Only after the course of some years was I able to grasp those words in their fullness. For the moment, Cyril made me feel guilty. Maybe because of that, I paid great attention to all his actions, because there was something about him that made him interesting and different from anybody else.

For some reason, Cyril seemed eager to convince me of his identity, as if he were concerned about being suspected, and he never wasted a chance to confirm it in my presence. Whenever possible, he showed me his identification papers and the contents of his dark attaché case, which he always carried with him. But he did so indirectly, almost accidentally most of the time.

Not less intriguing was his speech. His Castillian was excellent, for a foreigner, and was devoid of any accent. He had a very academic way of talking, carefully worded, and lacking any regional expressions that could expose his origin. He was sober and expressed his ideas, always profound, with precise words and no verbosity.

I continually presented different subjects in the course of our conversations, in order to discover his ideas. I found that certain subjects didn't interest him. We covered many facets of life in this world. He was persistent against violence, and he often repeated a characteristic expression, "That is something classical among us."

Sometimes he preferred to change the subject. One of his favorite topics was that of religion. He already knew my viewpoints on religion and especially on Mormonism.

"Enrique, I don't profess any religious belief. It is my belief that all religions are the product of a temporary need inherent to people, and I think that you are through that stage at the present moment. By the way, have you studied other religions?"

"No, I haven't."

"You should. That way you will be able to fully respect them." When Cyril avoided certain subjects, he gave the impression of not knowing them, or of bypassing them in order not to answer certain questions.

Most of the time, he became impervious if I asked about his sentimental or personal life. He never mentioned his family, although from scattered comments I could guess that there was a possible separation of his parents.

It is impossible not to mention the great interest that Cyril showed in the letters that my mother sent me weekly. He enjoyed my reading them aloud to him, and once he requested me to please read the letter over again. Cyril enjoyed the contents of the letters, and he stressed the notions of love, and of adherence to the highest standards of respect for all human beings, that were in them.

Often he inquired whether my mother had written. His interest was centered in learning, in detail, about what united my mother and myself with such a tremendous bond of love, besides the mother and son relationship, and on some wholesome advice towards accepting things that cannot be changed by religion or advice, acceptance for things as they are.

Our friendship lasted almost four months. One afternoon he arrived in a hurry to tell me some important news.

"Enrique, headquarters has called me. I must leave as soon as possible. Possibly they will send me to another southern country."

Surprised, I didn't answer. We embraced each other strongly. I was moved. For the first time, his eyes expressed some feeling. Without a second thought, I gave him my mother's address, just in case he was sent to Colombia. There he would find a home, family warmth, and a lot of love.

Cyril thanked me. The day he traveled, I phoned him and offered to drive him to the airport.

"Don't worry, Enrique, my boss is with me, and we will travel together. I will write you."

These were his last words. I was sorry about his absence, because I never heard from him after that. He never wrote. Such is life, here today and gone tomorrow. He left pleasant memories, and he was a good friend.

But things didn't end there. A few years later I would see him again, under very different circumstances.

I had observed Cyril at close range, with his case full of samples of men's toiletries, ostensibly opening a distribution channel for his company—lotions, talc, deodorants, soaps, and shaving creams. How far I was from suspecting that those products were not made in any laboratory anywhere on earth, and that they were only an excuse for staying in the city of Caracas, while "selling" a more sophisticated and transcendental product.

Cyril's "product" was one with which not only myself, but the whole of humankind, along with some beings alien to our world, would be involved—a product that is destined eventually to change, through subtle but radiant teachings, the behavior patterns of humanity and the races that populate Planet Earth.

Chapter Note

[1] Famous Argentine singer who died in Medellin, Colombia, in a plane crash.

5

The Initiation

"There is nothing in the world as fraudulent as the Ideas. The Ideas are pitfalls, great opportunities for deceit. They seduce man, take him away from reality and mislead him. . . ."
—JULIAN CASTILLO, *De mi edad del Sol (About my Solar Age)*

NEAR THE END OF 1969, I returned to Colombia, very concerned about my mother's health and afraid of a fatal outcome. I had quickly canceled my commitments in Venezuela in order to be with her. Seeing her exhausted on her death bed was very painful and sad, as she exhibited only a weak reflection of the greatness that had marked all her endeavors.

Attempting to describe her fascinating personality, enclosed in such a fragile frame, is an impossible task; nevertheless, the memories crowd through my mind like a visible testimony, forcing me to recount some of the interesting facets of this woman, whose influence provided the strength and drive of my existence, even in the bitter days to come.

"La Esmeralda de Colombia," as mother was known, died that year, on October 21. Costa Rica felt her death. It was there that she carried out with utmost dedication her campaigns to benefit children. She was founder of "La Casa de la Madre y el Niño" (The House of the Mother and Child), one of her many projects on behalf of the community.

A wise woman with a sharp wit, she filled our souls and minds with timely advice, always practical and adorned with kindness and cordiality, qualities that were very prevalent in her. One of her "spiritual sons," a Catholic priest who criticized the church and made himself a leader for the poor, Monsignor Eduardo Valencia Cano, called her "mother." Months before his tragic death, the "red bishop," as he was called, nostalgically mentioned the kindness that she had bestowed on him, voicing her sincere and encouraging message, very timely and necessary at his lonely post in Buenaventura, a Colombian harbor on the Pacific coast, where he gave hope to the poor.

It is worth recalling the warm conversations of these two intellectuals, deeply engaged in discussions intended to show the listeners that the correct attitude of man towards the world should be one of respect and understanding.

She never became a burden for anyone. Even when her physical strength was lost, she multiplied her intellectual capacity, leaving us a bequest of love and wisdom. The "elders" knew it and fought cordially for the chance to talk to her.

How much I would like to feel her presence again. From her we learned that death is painful only when visualized as an end, but it is not painful when we view it as a transition to a higher stage of life, becoming a comforting encouragement for all men to accept the present with its struggle and pain, which are but necessary ingredients for betterment and true happiness. That was my mother; her absence meant a lot to me. I suffered terribly, although I had to accept the reality of her loss.

I went back to my new job as manager of an important company in Bogotá, INSTELCO, founded by a former co-worker at the Bogotá Telephone Company, Januario Moyano. Within the next two years, another strong tremor was destined to shake my inner world.

By the year 1971, I still regularly attended religious services. As a priest, the possibilities for meeting many people were truly amazing. The great majority were looking for help and advice, sometimes in order to solve difficult problems. Some came as sincere seekers of spiritual matters and eagerly imbibed the teachings of the Church. One such person was Rafael, a small Negro boy, his skin as dark as coal, but with such a shining soul that it sparkled at the contact of our words and teachings. He was saintly but black, and he became the turning point that opened my eyes to a totally different reality. As presbyter, I prepared him for the evangelical life, and he speedily assimilated all the rules.

At the church, the blond priests had already suspected certain "sin" in his blood. They searched in their holy writings and found that the little boy belonged to a sinners' race, eternally punished by the Mormon god: Cain's race!

Cain committed the first manslaughter, motivated by frustration, noticing that Jehovah underestimated his efforts as a tiller, and instead was pleased with the presents of Abel, the shepherd, who slaughtered his innocent lambs and burned them in His honor in a bloody sacrifice, repulsive to our sensitivity.

According to the Mormons, Jehovah damned the aggressor with a genetic curse, blackening his skin and stigmatizing him, his children, and the children of his children, for ever and ever, until the end of time!

This is the way, according to Joseph Smith, the founder of Mormonism, that the black race originated on our planet.

A wind of rage swept my mind. Since my childhood I had been taught not to discriminate against people by virtue of the color of their skin, religion, or ideas. However, according to the Mormon church, the black were condemned for life to be a damned race because of a disobedience of God's will. According to them, this precept included the little boy who wanted to be a Mormon priest. (However, now colored people are being accepted as Mormon priests.)

Also, in those days, an illness endangered the health of two young brethren. They urgently needed blood donors, and I ran to the church, looking for someone who could spare a few minutes of his time and a little of his blood. They received my plea with sour faces, to my unbelieving surprise. Those men, representatives of an American Christian church, recoiled shyly at first, and then openly refused, as if insulted.

At this, something exploded in my conscience. I was facing disenchantment with the church. This was not a matter of maintaining a rigid stance in life, but rather of acting in accordance with reason and justice. I had to accept reality, aside from sentimental or emotional considerations, which are normal in any thinking individual. Suddenly I could see the blindness that had affected me for many years.

As could be expected, I protested emphatically, thus breaking the humble acceptance rules, important in the scheme of any religion, and criticism grew inside me. I could no longer justify so many regulations, full of incongruent statements, where reason was not as important as pretending to belong to an artificial world, saturated with "happiness."

I realize that those two incidents were not terribly important in themselves, but they served the purpose of making me question other important implications.

My elders attempted to make me believe that my viewpoints were unimportant and even prominently senseless. They entangled themselves in a series of Biblical technicalities, intended to explain my sudden rebellion. Truly, my mother's death had erased all mysticism from my heart. That is why everything was so utterly clear to me.

I sent a letter to the "living prophet" in Salt Lake City, asking for some explanation, but it was never answered.

Thus it was that I canceled my relationship with the Mormons, simply because they could not answer all my questions. I could not accept that people with a different ideal should be excluded from the salvation plans of Mormonism. I have never regretted my decision. I finally comprehended what Cyril, the "Swissman" in Caracas, meant! The moment had arrived.

It is incredible, but these critical moments went by without major mishaps occurring to affect me. Soon, with my full mental capacity applied to professional tasks, I achieved some level of worldly success. With two old friends in the field of telephony, we started a company of our own, Conmutel Ltda, and left Instelco, the partnership we had with Januario Moyano. My associates Pedro Murcia and Isidro Contreras and I struggled arduously to succeed, and excellent sales increased our possibilities. We shared an office in downtown Bogotá on 13th Street and 8th Avenue, with Dr. Alfonso Blanco. At the end of our daily tasks, we discussed that old subject, almost forgotten and exhausted for me, of UFOs. Some excellent publications by Antonio Ribera, Jessup, Aimé Michel, and the like, crowded my small library, withered with the passing of time. My office became the obligatory meeting place for all who felt attracted by this subject, for one reason or another. Of course I enjoyed talking about it, because I had some knowledge of the subject.

One Friday afternoon in 1973, while together with my friends, I received a telephone call. It was a woman, her voice soft and quiet, with a pronounced foreign accent.

"Good evening, Enrique," she greeted me. "My name is Karen, and I have just arrived from Buenos Aires. I have with me the address and telephone number of your office. The purpose of this call is to discuss certain subjects that interest us both."

1978. Left to right: Ricardo Vilchez (Costa Rica); Dr. J. Allen Hynek (U.S.A.); Carlos Vilchez (Costa Rica); and Enrique Castillo R. in Federal District, Mexico, attending the International UFO Congress during an interview between Dr. Hynek and Enrique Castillo R.

She said she was Mexican and was staying with an Argentinean family. Right after that she started talking about UFOs, and a message that some "Martian" masters had supposedly sent to me. Actually, I took this to be a jest from one of my friends, but decided to let her talk further, pointing to one of my associates to lift a receiver and listen silently to the conversation. Thus, she continued: "Enrique, my Masters have sent me to prepare you with certain exercises for telepathic communication with them. I want to meet and talk to you."

This conversation lasted ten minutes. We agreed to meet in a well-known ice cream parlor on the north side of town, by the name of Monte Blanco, at 70th Street and 7th Avenue, on Saturday afternoon, the following day.

The next day, after 3:30 p.m., we drove there in a company jeep, along with my friend Alfonso Blanco. I never suspected, even for a second, the chain of events that this woman would initiate. Her presence affected not only me, but all who had any contact with her.

"Karen the Mexican" was sent by "destiny" to accomplish a strange mission, the full nature of which I am not sure even now. The truth of the matter is that the precise events put into motion by her were always planned to the minutest detail, and calculated to perfection, because everything took place swiftly and astonishingly.

Karen awaited me in the Monte Blanco ice cream parlor, and I did not want to keep her waiting for long. . . .

6

The Preparation

"No matter how diverse the statements may be at first sight, all coincide in announcing an experience of a type that fifty years ago would have been qualified as spiritual, and fifty years hence will be adequately classified, based on the comprehension of the phenomenon."

—ALEYSTER CROWLEY

KAREN ARRIVED AT 4:00 P.M. As if we had known each other forever, she approached and greeted us with a warm embrace. I introduced Alfonso Blanco to her, and together the three of us walked into the ice-cream parlor.

Without wasting time, she addressed her conversation to the "flying saucers." For the sake of courtesy and politeness, I did not interrupt the fantastic story that streamed from her lips. She talked about some "Martian" masters who had given her my address and telephone number, and also about some courses taken from a Mexican lady called Marla, who had left her career as an opera singer in order to spread the teachings of her masters.

I could not understand much of what she was saying, but my acute interest in everything related to UFOs stopped me from severing her conversation for good. Karen had come to Colombia with the sole purpose of teaching her courses and bringing me up-to-date on cosmic matters.

For this purpose she gathered together a group of people and began teaching them some "techniques for communication with extraterrestrials." Thanks to some successful negotiations, we arranged to use the conference room of the National High School, "Camilo Torres."

So, for three days Karen told us about her experiences with the "Martians" and the conditions of life on that planet. Without exception, we were all baffled and stared at her with disbelief. Time passed and tension mounted. The group of listeners, very select professionals in various specialties, abstained from making a final judgment, because they lacked information on which to base it. Karen completely captured the public's attention. Not a whisper was heard while she talked.

Then she announced a course for the following week, charmingly called "Introduction to Cosmic Science."

People whose lives have been framed by the boundaries of rationality, whose habits have been perfectly sketched by society, for whom life may have become a meaningless routine, may feel at heart the need to break with this style of handling things. Perhaps such people clamor inside for liberation but remain solidly bound by their habits, by their past. In such people, Karen found a fascinated audience.

The voice of this woman, convinced about her own ideas, had an insidious effect. It subtly pervaded the minds of the listeners and broke their past convictions into a thousand pieces. Science and religion took for granted for many centuries the solitude of man in the Universe, but now Karen talked about the Martians as if they were some neighbors from Asia or Europe!

I can't deny it; I also fell to her charms. She talked about "universal love" and the need for interplanetary communication for the benefit of humankind.

After the talk, an architect offered a smaller room at his home as a meeting place for the next course, and that was where the first classes in "Cosmic Science" were taught.

The awe for Karen increased. She gathered to her a group of people with certain paranormal capacities, and she taught them techniques for communicating with the masters of the cosmos. There were seers, mediums, telepaths, a whole retinue of beings endowed by nature to see in places where others were blind.

Among this group, one woman was reputed to be able to get in touch with a doctor who had been dead for many years. Her name was Graciela Torres, better known as Chela, who was the bridge to Dr. José Gregorio Hernández, a Venezuelan physician who had died in 1919. Through Chela, Dr. Hernández carried out his miraculous healings.

It was decided to move headquarters to the home of a gentleman who was well versed in esoteric and occult sciences, Richard Deeb, who in the course of time became one of my best friends.[1] I did not participate actively in these meetings. Chela, because of her mediumistic endowments, was in charge of directing the first concentrations and meditations. The first group was made up of many people, all connected to the first talks given by Karen.

During one of the "communications" received by this group, the name of Enrique Castillo was suggested by some supposed extraterrestrial from An-

1992. Left to right: Graciela Torres, who received the first extraterrestrial communications; Enrique Castillo R., and Mrs. Marjorie de Hollman, in whose home many instructions and messages were received, in Bogotá, Colombia.
Photo: Gloria Ortiz

ICIFE (Instituto Colombiano de Investigacion de Fenomenos Extraterrestres—Colombian Institute for the Investigation of Extraterrestrial Phenomena) building, 1978

dromeda. Karen, without wasting time, contacted me to update me about the messages. She almost forced me to attend the meetings. I accepted willingly, but only with curiosity. The meetings usually took place twice a week.

The group was able to communicate through Chela with "beings" from Andromeda. She received the messages, sometimes through automatic writing and other times through spoken mediumship, through what I considered to be a kind of conscious mediumship. Karen zealously made sure that the techniques of relaxation were followed to the letter. She emphasized the need to first contact your "OVERSELF."

We achieved certain routines during our meetings. Twice a week, during the months of August and September of the year 1973, we met at the home of Richard, or the home of Chela. We always placed ourselves in the same positions, Chela at the center, Karen at one side, and myself at the other side. At the beginning of the sessions we turned the main lights off, leaving a small lamp on. With pencil and paper we awaited the messages.

Once, the communication centered on the satisfaction of the visitors from Andromeda about my participation in the exercises. According to them, three ships hovered above the city, expecting a physical contact with three members of our group, previously chosen.

In general, the majority of the messages had to do with messianic warnings, stressing our behavior patterns and encouraging us to improve our attitudes toward life. Interest in the meetings increased so much that nobody missed them. Chela, with the ease characteristic of those born specifically to accomplish certain functions, entered quickly into successful communication. The days elapsed, and the exercises and training went on day after day, until we were told the date when our first physical contact was to take place: October 11, 1973.

We looked at each other, baffled. Finally, the so much desired visit!

The chosen day, at 10:00 p.m., we left together for Chela's home. We were sixteen in number, but only three would have the opportunity to board the ships. The meeting place was "La Calera," a suburb north of Bogotá.

We stopped and got out of the cars at Kilometer 8. It was a cold night,[2] the wind blew, and a drizzle soon drenched our clothes. We were expected to reach a hill, some distance away, by crossing some difficult terrain. Half an hour later, we got there. Meanwhile, a bitter dispute took place about the presence of four strangers who had come along uninvited. These people, determined and even aggressive, were reluctant to go back to Bogotá. They knew somehow that a "contact with extraterrestrials" was to take place that night. I was not willing to get into a fight, and my friend Alfonso Blanco finally accepted their presence.

At the top of the hill, we prepared for the contact. First there was to be a telepathic communication, and then the "beings from Andromeda" were to give the names of the ones to board the ship.

We stood in a circle, holding hands, feeling very nervous and insecure. I was making some fun at Dr. Cosme Mejía, one of our group. Cosme confused any star or cloud with "flying saucers," and I was laughing about this situation. I was very skeptical about the expected results of that night.

Chela received a first message. "We are here, brothers. In ten minutes we will give the names of the 'contactees.'"

We all gazed upwards, searching for some signal that would indicate the presence of the ships. Each one thought about being selected, but nothing happened, and no more communications were received. Somebody yelled, pointing to a light on a cloud, but it was only the reflection of the lights of some distant car. Tension grew, and we were on edge, to the point of breakdown.

The medium broke the silence after twenty minutes of no communications: "We are here, brothers; we have decided that five of you will come on board. Please wait five more minutes."

Not only minutes, but half an hour elapsed, without anything happening. The reflections on the clouds continued, and although I was satisfied with the explanation of distant car lights, something led me to watch them more carefully.

Just before midnight, a voice broke the silence through the medium. Quickly and anxiously, Chela's voice announced, "Brothers, operation Andromeda has been canceled. Please go home. Tomorrow at noon we will get in touch with each of you. Good night." The message ended.

A wave of protest was felt all around. I shared in this feeling, offended and disillusioned, about being fooled by the "extraterrestrials," wasting our time. Here we were, close to becoming ill because of the cold night, and the Andromeda beings had decided to postpone the meeting for another day. This was intolerable! How could it possible be that highly evolved entities had played such tricks on us? Richard and Karen, with soft voices, tried to calm our spirits.

Those are simply tests given by the "Masters," they said. As for me, I was not very convinced about this explanation.

Without paying attention to the advice of the others, in a bad mood and cursing indiscriminately, I climbed down from the hilltop to where the cars were parked. Alfonso Blanco, nicknamed "Poncho," followed, encouraging me to reconsider my stand.

"The heck with extraterrestrials, darn it!" I protested—feeling the object of the best-organized joke in all human history. Walking crestfallen, slightly more settled down, but still mad, I suddenly heard a final order: "Halt! Stop there!"

I lifted my face; a bright light shone in my eyes, half-blinding me. However, I was able to perceive an imposing-looking sub-machine gun, aimed at my body. Poncho also stopped, and so did the rest of the group.

From the brush-like vegetation, some uniformed shadows emerged.

These were not extraterrestrials; they were officers from the Colombian Army and Police!

One of the officers asked what we were doing there. They had been warned by some peasants, who had called the central police station after seeing a strange "helicopter" hovering over the fields. They thought it could be smugglers and decided to warn the authorities.[3]

I immediately associated the strange lights, which we had blamed on cars, with "flying saucers." There was no doubt, the country people had seen the same objects! They were not cars, they were. . . .

Richard Deeb, the oldest in the group, approached the commander of the patrol and identified himself. As a coincidence, Richard carried a calling card from a friend of his, a general of the Republic. When the officer looked at the card, speechless, he saluted him, thinking he was the general himself.

Richard explained to them that our presence at that place and hour was part of certain contemplation and meditation exercises that were to be practiced outdoors. The officer was satisfied and, after looking at the faces of each one in the group, allowed us to go our way.

We breathed freely again. At least, for a short while, we had forgotten the purpose of our visit to La Calera. Several countryfolk around the soldiers stared at us with curiosity. We were a rather unusual sight, at midnight in such a place. We walked down to our cars, without a word, and once inside them agreed to follow exactly the instructions given by the "beings from Andromeda."

Each of us would await a message the next day at our homes at noon sharp, and at 8:00 p.m. we would meet at Richard Deeb's home to compare our information. Then we left for our homes.

I arrived home very late that night. My wife didn't ask anything. She assumed that I had been busy working late, perhaps installing a computer or taking care of some important business. She had no idea where I had been.

The next day was October 12, "Dia de la Raza" (Race Day), a holiday in Colombia, celebrated with special ceremonies about the "Discovery of America." Minutes before noontime, I tried to persuade my wife to leave me alone in the house for a couple of hours. I lived in the barrio "Santa Isabel" in Bogotá, well-known because of the many emerald traffickers who lived there.[4]

My wife protested angrily, and in a moment of rage, confronted me with this statement: "Enrique, if you get involved with those Martians, you are going to become insane!"

She slammed the door and left with my dog Dingo, who, happily wagging his tail, ran away after her.

I was finally alone. I disconnected the doorbell and retired to the bedroom. I readied paper and pencil and sat on the bed, starting my relaxation and concentration exercises. I removed my watch from my left wrist. It was almost 12:00 noon. Time passed quickly, but nothing happened. I decided that I was not one of the chosen ones and that I should end the concentration. I got up and walked towards the window.

I looked at the sky and asked myself: "How can a 'flying saucer' possibly arrive at my home, at 12:00 noon, on a holiday, and with all these people on the street? Nonsense!"

I had barely thought about this folly, when I heard a voice: "Enrique, write!" I turned around and, surprised, ran for the bedroom door. I opened it, but there was nobody in the living room.

"Enrique, write!" the voice repeated.

As fast as I could, I took paper and pencil. I looked around, trying to locate the source of that order. Then I felt the strangest sensation I had ever felt: a steady, buzzing sound, like the sound of bees, affected my ears. Panic got the best of me. The voice persisted.

At the center of my brain, I heard a rhythmic drum beat. My breathing sped up abnormally. I held the paper on my legs and started writing what the voice dictated. This was at 12:25 p.m., October 12, 1973, a Friday. Minutes passed, and I wrote. It was my first communication with extraterrestrials.

Tears, or perhaps perspiration, dripped on the paper. Pages were filled at the speed that my hands permitted. A strong shivering affected my whole body, and a strange force took hold of me. I was so moved that I could no longer think.

The notes had to do with a "Third World War." They ended by telling me that there would be no contact that night, but that other space brothers had already arrived. "Continue with the group," the voice said. "They will get in touch with you. Goodbye!"

The voice also stressed our poor behavior during the preceding night, during which basic rules of conduct had not been respected, such as when we had argued furiously over the incidents just described. According to them, this line of conduct did not help the group. I trembled when I heard this observation.

The communication ended. I stood up and went into the bathroom.

I turned on the faucet and looked at the image in the mirror. My eyes were bloodshot. My arms and legs still shook. It was not perspiration that had fallen on the paper. They were tears, which streamed from my eyes uncontrollably.

Around my nose and my nails, a purple line appeared. My body itched all over. I washed my face and returned to the bedroom, rested for a while, then gathered and ordered the sheets just written, reading them over carefully. I was deeply moved. I then folded them and put them in my pocket. Then I lay on side of the bed and rested again.

Much refreshed, I went back into the bathroom and could see that the purple lines were gone. I washed my face again and felt renewed. I arranged my clothes, reconnected the doorbell, and opened the door of the house. Then I whistled, calling one of my sons, who was playing soccer some fifty meters away.

When my family returned, Beatriz could not control her temper. She asked me why I was so pale and again criticized my activities with the UFOs. I had spoiled the lunch hour. At this moment, my brother Roberto arrived, and offhandedly I showed him the written pages.

"Enrique, where did you get that?" I didn't explain anything to him, and he said, "I know that the Third World War is being held back, but it will come, no matter what," and that was all.

I put the pages back in my pocket and left, seeking the company of a friend of mine, to whom I could relate the recent events. I invited her to the movies, and while there told her about the message. She listened, surprised, and suddenly cut off my monologue with a warning at what she termed as cheap spiritism or imagination. I decided that I would rather not continue with my story.

That night, among nightmares and insane thoughts, I barely slept. Flying saucers landed at my house, doors slammed, footsteps echoed through my dreams. The next day, a Saturday, I was late arriving at the office. It was nine o'clock. Four people from the group were waiting for me. One of them spoke up for the rest, saying, "Enrique, Karen is offended. Why didn't you go to the meeting? Several of the group received messages, ordering them to go to such and such places. We were at Fontibón, El Rosal, La Calera, Choachí. We waited in vain until 3:00 a.m. Nobody showed up."

I listened to them silently. Calmly, I answered that the reason for my absence was due to the message received the day before, in which the beings from Andromeda informed me that there would be no contact that night.

My friends looked at each other. I handed them the handwritten pages, and they read them eagerly. An idea crossed my mind. I warned the four members of the group to maintain their silence about the messages I had received until that night's meeting. I wanted to discover for certain whether anyone else in our group had received a message such as mine. That night, at the moment of reading the messages given to each one, no other messages were announced.

All agreed that I had been selected in some way by the beings from Andromeda to relay a message, and that mine was the true message. With this unexpected result, I read aloud the message. No one discussed the truth of my report; it was self evident. The others didn't want to talk much about the subject, and the meeting proceeded quite like any other. Sitting in our usual places, at 8:15 p.m. on Saturday, October 14, 1973, we started our relaxation.

I was sitting with my back to a window that opened to the street. I was dressed in informal clothing, wearing a blue shirt, scarf, and leather jacket. All were looking at Chela. Ten or fifteen minutes elapsed with no communication. Then I felt that same buzzing sound, same as the day before. A voice, this time very tenuous, said, "Enrique, write!"

The message started this way: *"We are messengers from Pleiades, the same who gave knowledge to the Inca and other races."*

Shuddering, very uncomfortable, almost breathless, I tore open my shirt and tossed the scarf away, which landed on Marjorie Hollman's lap. This time we were connected to beings from the Pleiades, not Andromeda!

I fell into sort of a mediumship spell, with my tongue tied. All my friends noticed it and rubbed their hands and placed them on my head. A new message started, and at that point I lost track of time and place.

I remembered nothing. After half an hour, I opened my eyes. Marjorie and Maria Teresa wiped perspiration from my face. Karen was holding my head, and without thinking, I asked, "Karen, what happened?"

She replied categorically, "My child, you were gone very far away!"

The message read that I was the one selected in Colombia by the extraterrestrials to make direct physical contact on a date that they would give soon. Until then, I was the only person in the country to undergo this experience. Paulina, Richard's wife, brought me a cup of warm milk with brandy. I stood up with the same drowsiness as the day before.

Marjorie and Jorge Eduardo rubbed my arms vigorously. I was put to bed. Luckily, there was a doctor, Rafael Contreras, who, after examining me using his stethoscope, said that other than a slightly elevated heart rate, I appeared to be in good health.

He complained bitterly about not having a movie camera to capture the moment when I drew some strange symbols in the air with my hands. Much of the information given made reference to a golden disk, hidden in a temple in Perú, and to some papyri and manuscripts. Everything had been recorded on tape, and this allowed us to end a small argument over some misinterpreted words. Then we agreed to meet again the following Tuesday.

A throbbing headache tormented me each time that communications were received. It was no longer Chela who received the messages; it was I who had to bear the consequences of the communications. The terrible headache forced me to skip work for two days. Twice I refused to receive more communications from the extraterrestrials. They said that after two or three more sessions, the headache would go away.

At one time I heard that they were taking measurements of my brain. They even gave a figure. According to them, the vibration rate of my brain was 829 "valiums." I thought maybe that was a voltage, the natural frequency of my brain. However, they never clarified this point.

It is extremely difficult to put into words the full depth of the meaning of these experiences, because most of the time, with all the attendant reactions and consequences, the impact was blended and interwoven on many levels with internal events, invisible to the eyes of the other people in the group.

Karen's role was not clear anymore. She had been the initiator, but once her mission was completed,the shine of her "aura" faded. Karen insisted on my need to strengthen my bonds with the "OVERSELF."

I carried out, step-by-step, her recommended techniques for contacting, but I felt frustrated, for I realized that I lacked the paranormal faculties of others. I tended to blame it on the "unconscious." Certainly, I did not know about the forces that dominated us. Anyway, our group was organized, at first with seventeen people. Later it grew to twenty-seven members. Because of the importance of the events that sequentially took place, I will give the names of the initial group:

1. Mr. Richard Deeb
2. Mrs. Paulina Deeb
3. Marjorie Hollman
4. Maria Teresa Paladino
5. Graciela Torres (Chela)
6. Alfonso Blanco (Poncho)
7. Cosme Mejía
8. Heberto Cediel
9. Dr. Rafael Contreras
10. Pedro Avila
11. Gloria Avila 12. Alba Avila (daughters of Pedro Avila)
13. Alcides Camelo
14. Victor Rodríguez
15. Fernando Márquez
16. Jorge Eduardo Silva
17. Adriana Turner (Karen)
18. Enrique Castillo (myself)

Sometimes the group grew as a result of invitations made by some of the members. The opposite also occurred. As time passed, several of the members left, convinced that what was going on was fraudulent, or the manifestation of witchcraft, spiritism, or insane minds. Others left because they expected something more spectacular. We met regularly, Tuesdays and Fridays, at 8:00 p.m.

During another communication, we were told about an old temple in ruins in Perú, where the true history of humankind was hidden. But they said that not only in the Peruvian temple was there such information: It was also hidden in different locations in Central and South America, where there are lost cities, located somewhere in the Andean mountain ranges.

Once the riddle is put together, with the information taken from temples, pyramids, and forgotten cities, humanity will have no other alternative than to accept the facts of this knowledge, which is quite different from what we are presently taught about the history of the planet. All of this was news to us. We were excited about the possibility that we might be the first to receive such information. In a way, we were a privileged group.

Still, sometimes, in spite of having the evidence at our fingertips, we doubted. By the end of October, 1973, the "emissaries" from Pleiades announced the date of a physical contact with them.

The moment had arrived, and we were prepared!

CHAPTER NOTES

[1] He died to physical life in September 1990, at the age of eighty-three.

[2] Even though close to the equator, the altitude at La Calera is approximately 8500 feet above sea level.

[3] At that time, Colombia had not yet been afflicted by drug trafficking.

[4] For as long as the country has existed, and before 1492, Colombian emeralds have been world famous.

7

The Contact

> *"Is mankind the sudden product of the will of some Creator, whose image we see in imperfect form in the human species? Was mankind put on Planet Earth by means of a "fiat," a sudden decision, a personal act of an utterly superior intelligence? If God as superpowerful intelligence, were there, someplace in space, creating mankind, then surely He, in His infinite wisdom, would have wanted that we were sure of this fact. But we aren't; some believe it blindly as part of a religious dogma, whereas others reject this notion as unscientific and illogical."*
>
> —Dr. HANS HOLZER, *The Human Dynamo*

By late October, 1973, during one of the telepathic sessions with the "Emissaries from Pleiades," they announced to me an appointment for November 3, near a nondisclosed lake. Having been chosen as the only person in Colombia to undergo such a relationship, I suffered a series of experiences related to its preparation. The first one was during a dream.

During four successive nights, I repeatedly saw faces pointing to a lake surrounded by forests and low hills. Unable to explain this to my friends of the group, because they probably would attribute it to abnormal influences over the subconscious, I decided to keep it to myself and to follow through on my own with whatever directions I received. It would have been impossible to explain something that by itself seemed illogical, anyway. Besides, many doubted, given the failed attempt at La Calera, which in spite of having been carefully analyzed, still evoked certain suspicions as to its authenticity.

My friends from space, anticipating this, and interested in the success of the mission, intensified their personal communications, detailing the exact coordinates of the place selected for the meeting. Besides this, they gave me a plan to follow, once I arrived at the lake and the forest that surrounded it. I was told to follow the instructions from the dreams, for finding a clearing. There should be a tree, and under its roots, hidden by a medium-sized stone, I should find a sphere, take it in my hand, and walk to the designated place.

They set the time for the meeting at 8:00 p.m. They forbade me to carry any knives, etc.

I got up early on Saturday, November 3, and afraid of some unforeseen event, alerted my wife and associates to expect a possible absence of a few days, without further explanation.

I had lunch as usual and, around one in the afternoon, headed for the bus station. The bus left at 3:30 p.m. and was on its way without any unusual incidents, except for the folkloric activities of the many peasants who boarded or left it along the way.

After two-and-a-half hours, I got off the bus. It sped off, leaving behind an annoying cloud of dust. I watched it until it faded in the distance, while reviewing in my mind the sequence of events that would lead me to the physical encounter with the extraterrestrials.

My apparel was simple: cotton trousers, working shoes, a ruana,[1] and a hat, property of Richard Deeb, which made me look like a country man, so as to avoid arousing any suspicions. After taking a look at the scenery and gathering all my forces, I began walking determinedly. For two hours I walked, stopping only to regain my breadth. The path was difficult, and the effort made my heart pound.

I recalled with some fear my childhood difficulties with asthma. The region was very fertile. Its green color contrasted with the blue sky. Nature's noises didn't predict anything unusual. Once in a while, the acute yell of a woman who was not visible, protested for something that I could not perceive, and disturbed my thoughts.

Approaching sundown, I arrived at the edge of the lake. Stepping on soft ground covered with abundant vegetation, I sank into the mud and got my boots and feet wet, forcing me to climb back to firm ground and take a detour via a seldom used "bridle path." I realized that there were two forests, separated by a finger of the lake, which stretched between them. The water was calm, breaking quite softly against the shore, driven by a very weak but chilling breeze.

I checked my automatic watch, trying to figure out if I was going to be on time, and made a renewed effort to move faster. The groups of trees were in front of me; I recognized the first one and walked fast in its direction. When I entered it, I was impressed by the density of the grove. No wonder the extraterrestrials looked for lonely places such as this. The peaceful swaying of the trees back and forth, driven by the wind, were a far cry from the noise of the city traffic. I could perceive everything very clearly: the sound of my feet crushing the dry leaves, the whisper of the forest, the water at the lake.

I stopped in a clearing, as if in a dream. Among a group of trees, there was one that I could single out easily. I ran in its direction, looking around just in case there was somebody watching. I noticed a medium-sized stone. I moved it easily and, shocked, felt my blood surge up to my head. There it was, the sphere, within my hand's reach!

I picked it up and examined it closely: it looked like stainless steel but was light in weight, ice cold, and its surface was punctured by several small holes, as if it had been drilled by a very thin needle. I kept the sphere in my hand, looking at it constantly as I walked, also paying attention to the sky and the forest, without seeing anything. Then I walked away from the lake shore and into the trees, until it got dark.

The phosphorescent hands on my watch showed a few minutes before 8:00 p.m. The moment was approaching, relentlessly. With surprise, I noticed that the sphere now felt unevenly warm. At first, I thought this was a natural effect of warming up under the ruana. The doubt cleared up when tiny, deep-dark blue rays of light emerged from the orifices of the sphere. The idea of an explosive bomb crossed my mind instantly. The light emission must have been triggered by something, because it was increasing. I listened to it closely, but it was silent. Because of its rising temperature, never hot enough to burn my hands, I held it on and off with one corner of the ruana.

I thought about my "Greater Brothers" and prepared myself to make matters easy.

The watch showed 8:10 p.m. Nobody had showed up yet, and my left hand held the warm, shining sphere, the size of a golf ball. Suddenly, time stood still, my mouth agape at what was beginning to happen. My ears perceived a low rumbling noise, and the whole area was flooded as if by direct sunlight. In the light of this false dawn, I perceived two craft slowly moving above, some 200 meters above the trees. I looked at them, perplexed. Water dripped from their slanting surfaces. They were huge, forty or forty-five meters in diameter, by twelve to fifteen in height.

Over them, I could discern great domes, casting a surprising luminosity. The temperature changed noticeably. When they passed overhead, I felt heat. I was terrified and didn't know what to do. They had been waiting for me at the bottom of the lake; that is why a water noise was heard! All nocturnal noises stopped, and time stood still.

The momentary, day-like illumination gradually extinguished. The ships hovered about 100 meters from where I was. One of them silently moved behind the other. Now there was no more light, just a small halo surrounding the closest one. This one approached as if getting ready to greet me. Moving slowly and swaying slightly from side to side, when it was about 60 meters away, it shot downwards two beams of light, strong orange in color.

Two silhouettes slid down the light beams until they disappeared behind the trees. From where I was, I could see only the great ship. About the orange light beams, I must say that they do not radiate like regular light does. I saw how the beams of light retracted until reaching the bottom of the craft, apparently "absorbed," or reeled-in.

A crackling of broken branches and the stepping-upon of dry leaves announced the arrival of the two beings. Ten meters from me, I noticed a luminosity. They wore dull, lead-gray uniforms, orange or tangerine-colored boots, and helmets with glasses that permitted seeing their eyes, as I noticed later, when they were closer. Their belts supported five odd-looking buttons, three on their right side, and two on the left. Some of them were larger than the others, and two emitted light: one white, the other green. The two astronauts dressed exactly the same and stood about four meters from each other.

They both approached me. I smiled nervously, not knowing what to do, because my mind went blank, and I was able only to watch the scene. When I stopped, a voice was heard in my brain: *"Enrique, don't be afraid; we are incapable of hurting you!"* My reaction was of fear, walking backwards three or four steps, and wishing to run away, until my back hit against a tree. Calming down a bit, I decided to face the situation, and I heard the voice again: *"Enrique, we are your friends; we are not going to hurt you.* We are going to take you on board. Don't be afraid. If you don't want to come in, it is all right, but we *need this meeting; it is vital."*

I approved by nodding, desperately trying to keep control of my emotions. My hands perspiring, I clutched the sphere in my left hand. The astronaut on my right side came closer, and I could see his eyes through the glass in his helmet. A flexible, corrugated piece around his neck connected the helmet to the rest of the uniform. At the height of the ears, some coiled cables protruded and went towards his back. Looking at his eyes, I heard the voice say: *"Come with us."* They turned around, and I could see a backpack where the coiled cables ended. At the tops of their helmets was something like an "electronic eye."

They walked ahead, and I followed closely. The elegant but very masculine shape of their bodies emphasized their height: 1.78 to 1.80 meters tall. One of them placed himself at my side, and the other walked firmly ahead. I smiled constantly, and they looked at me frequently. We arrived at a clearing, free of

vegetation. The one walking ahead turned around and told his companion and myself : *"Wait!"* He gestured, putting his hands snug against his body. *"Stay there; we are going to lift you on board."*

The ship approached, as if having received a signal. The closest one moved closer to me, and, touching slightly my right arm and shoulder, said, *"Enrique, I am your friend, don't be afraid."* When he said this, I finally relaxed, the fear went away, and I felt a great peace of mind.

From the ship above, the orange light-beam was projected, which surrounded me about one meter around. I noticed how small leaves and dirt particles on the ground jumped at the contact with the light. A prickly sensation was felt through my whole body and my brain, like pins being stuck into my skin. I left the ground and slowly ascended. When the tips of the trees were surpassed, I could see the lake.

I went up about 50 meters, feeling a terrible "vacuum" sensation in my stomach. I moved my right hand, nervously, and felt that the light was "solid." Like glass. Bothersome electronic fluids traversed my body. I kept on moving upwards. A gate opened above me, I entered, and the light ray softly dropped me onto the floor of the ship. No one waited for me. I could breathe freely, because the air was wholesome. The hexagonal room was empty. There was light, but its source was not apparent, because no light bulbs or lamps were visible. When I took two or three steps, I noticed that there were no shades, either.

I moved my ruana and hat, and could see that they projected no shade. The light was pleasant to the eyes, the temperature was cool, and I felt comfortable. Then a voice was heard: *"Enrique, please undress!"*

With a certain amount of distrust, I got rid of the ruana and hat, keeping the sphere in my trouser pocket. I heard the order again, and started undressing slowly, very fearful. Finally the voice thundered, imperatively: *"You have to undress; it is necessary!"*

I removed the remaining pieces of clothing and covered my nudity with my hands, because I felt embarrassed. An instant later, a sort of smoke issued from the joint of the floor and the walls. Alarmed, I thought I might be poisoned, like the Jews at the hands of the Nazis in the gas chambers! In fewer than five seconds, the room was saturated with this smoke, which surrounded me but let me breath normally. It was blue-colored, with a delicious scent similar to lemon or lime. In a few more seconds, the smoke drained back through the same openings from where it came. I could find no explanation for this smoke.

Moving inside the room, I thought about how I was going to get out of it. There were no doors, rivets, or seams that might indicate an opening. I was wondering what might happen next, when a voice was heard: *"Get dressed, Enrique!"*

Unlike at the beginning, when I had to be told repeatedly, I now obeyed the order as quickly as I could. Another soft sound, and a door slid upwards, or bi-parted horizontally. *"Enrique, my friend,"* one of the beings saluted. I extended my hand in answer, while he introduced me to his friend, who had just walked into the room.

"This is Krunula,"[2] he said in Spanish.

I extended my hand, but to my surprise, he only touched it slightly and bowed slightly in salutation. I turned to my first acquaintance, and a surprising conversation took place with the exchange of a few words, but at first I did not fully grasp what was going on.

"I am Cyril, Enrique."

I answered, "I am Enrique Castillo."

"Yes, I am Cyril Weiss."

I repeated once more, "I am Enrique Castillo; you are Cyril Weiss."

He added, *"Don't you remember, in Caracas in 1969, at the entrance to a movie house? I am your friend of those times; don't you remember?"*

It finally dawned upon me what he meant. With boundless rejoicing, and with all the memories rejuvenated, I expressed all my repressed sentiments. I asked him, "Cyril, my Swiss friend, what are you doing here?"

"I am a crew member of this ship."

"What?"

"Follow me, I'll explain everything to you." They asked me to give them back the sphere, and so I did.

Walking along a semicircular corridor, we entered a large room, where four people were waiting for us, seated in front of a large table, which was made of clear, transparent material, like the white of a raw egg. Two of them wore uniforms that were reddish-brown in color, and two others wore silver, different from the lead-gray of those who had descended to the ground to meet me.

Drawing prepared by Jesus Alberto Balbi for the magazine Fourth Dimension (Cuarta Dimensión) *of Argentina, Nov. 1975.*

Saturday, November 3, 1973 (exactly 8:25 p.m.)
The Pleiadeans

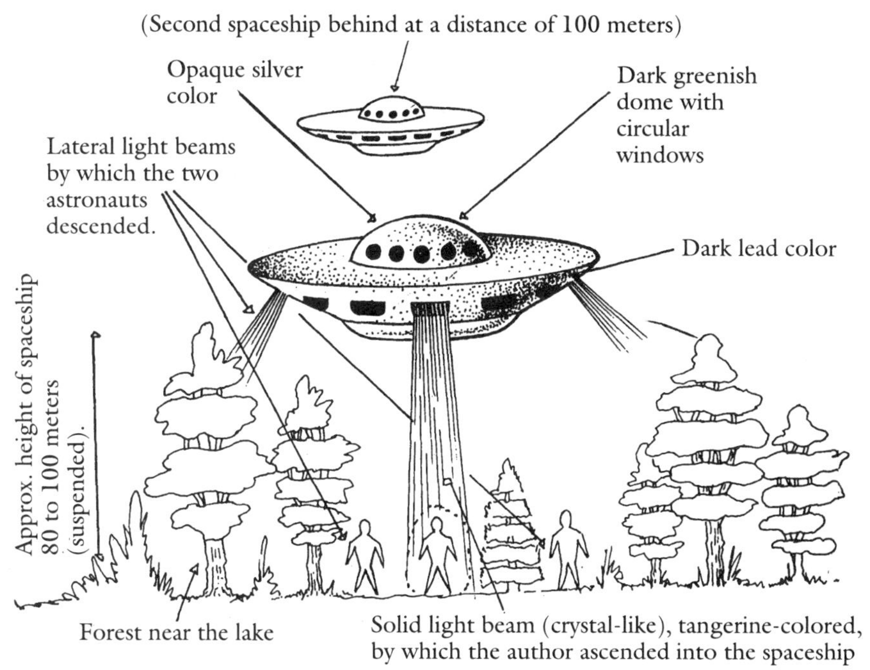

Note: 1) Spaceship's diameter, approximately 45 to 50 meters.
2) Height, 12 meters
3) Interior - three floors

Diagram prepared for the magazine Fourth Dimension *of Argentina, issued November, 1975, in accordance with the design and narrative of engineer, Enrique Castillo Rincon.*

Cyril hurriedly told me, *"My name is Krishnamerck, and I am an extraterrestrial."*

At that moment, I thought that my friendship with him in Caracas must have influenced the selection of me for the contact; however, I had trouble believing that he was an extraterrestrial. His features were slightly changed, with more prominent cheekbones and thinner, almost nonexistent lips; when he smiled, he showed perfect teeth. His nose looked very straight, his eyes a little slanted and deep blue. His long hair reached to his shoulders and was truly yellow.

At 8:25 p.m., the meeting took place that changed permanently my outlook on life because of the deep implications that developed therefrom. I could see the men sitting at the transparent table. They wore no helmets.

Their height and features were almost identical, with yellow hair and perfect skin, like a baby's. Their foreheads were ample and their chins straight. They had no wrinkles, blemishes, or moles. One of them turned his head and I could see the perfection of his ears. Without being athletic, their bodies were perfectly shaped.

Upon greeting me, they repeated the light touch with the palm of their hands and the brief bowing, then pointed to an empty seat in front of the table. They wore no gloves, and their hands were white and silky, the fingers a little longer than normal. The one whom I presumed was the leader sat down last. Cyril introduced him as Commander of the Ship, and Mission Chief. His name was Kramier. He then introduced the others, Krensa, Kramakan, and Kruenenyer, who together with Krishnamerck and Krunula made up part of the crew.

Mutely, we examined at each other in minute detail, again and again. In the middle of the silence, my heart was about to explode, but I waited, and they were the first to break it. Finally, the Commander went ahead, pronouncing first some strange wordings, with many S and Z sounds, and in an almost imperceptible voice, he said, *"Welcome!"*

I answered, "I am very happy to be here with you, brothers. But I would like to know why I am here, and where you come from." Smiling, they answered my questions one at a time.

"We come from the Pleiades."

"Where are the Pleiades?"

"What you know also as 'The seven daughters of Atlas' or the 'Seven Little Sisters.'"

I spoke in Spanish, and the Commander answered telepathically, without moving his lips. I heard his voice in my head, quite clearly.

"As far as why you are here, you know the answer perfectly well, because for the last eight years we have been following you," he said. I was flabbergasted and did not know what to say, because to this day, while writing this book, I have never known the reasons behind my encounter with the extraterrestrials. What qualifications did they discover while following my life step by step? Why did they choose me? I still don't know why, and this bothers me to desperation.

The conversation in the ship continued. I had with me a questionnaire written on a piece of paper by some member of the group, but I forgot about it at that instant. The questions and answers were produced as they came, spontaneously. The attitude of the crew members was more one of giving me confidence than of supplying information, as such. Krishnamerck and Krunula, standing up with their arms folded—almost in military fashion—listened attentively.

The room was large, rounded, about six meters in diameter, with translucent, geometric-shaped partitions in sections. Four projections from the floor above were visible, shaped like beams. There were two columns, which had the appearance of plastic. The chairs where we sat seemed leather lined. While sitting on them, they felt soft and yielding, shaping themselves to one's body, and moving to the correct height for comfort.

Several pictures decorated the walls, some representing strange animals, sort of winged serpents or dragons. Others showed flying birds. And there were space themes—stars, planets, and stellar routes—straight or spiral, funnel-like shapes. Some folders, wrapped in ribbons, seemed furred and contained very thin, plastic-like sheets (navigation charts?).

The style of the room was sober. A decoration contained inside a dome exhaled a sort of fog or vapor, around plants or flowers. The soil inside was wet and had small stones, visible through the transparent dome. It was oval-shaped, about two meters long. It was placed on a table supported by eight legs, about 1.2 meters high. It was like a terrarium and looked like an undersea scene, but without water, just the humidity inside the crystal dome.

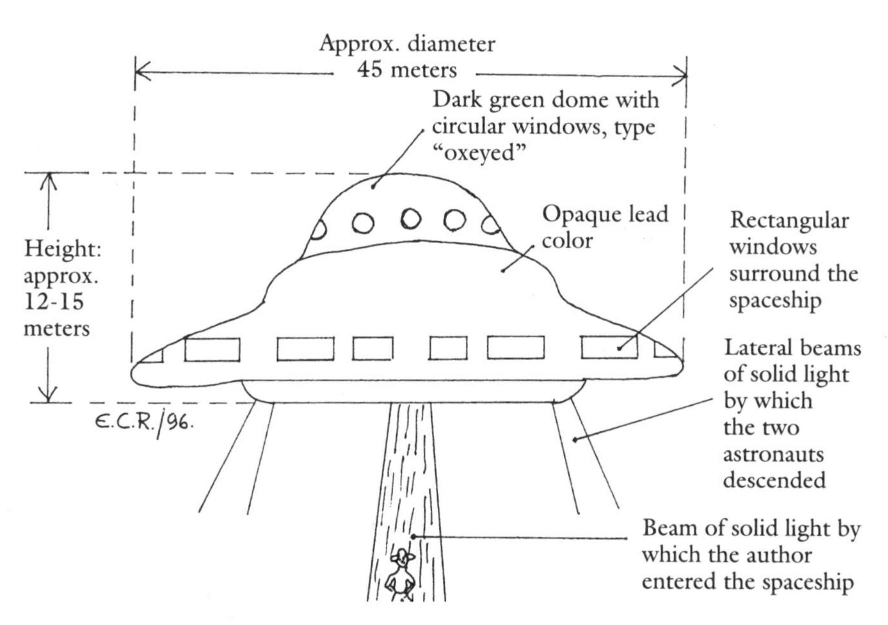

Model of the Pleiadean spaceship (with possibly five floors) used for interstellar voyages with a capacity of twelve to twenty crew-scientists, that contacted Enrique Castillo Rincon on November 3, 1973, at 8:25 p.m. near a lake north of Bogota, Colombia.

I mentally questioned if there were women on board, and the Commander answered: *"Yes, there are, but you are not going to see them at this time."* He had read my mind, making me feel embarrassed. They must have been doing this ever since I entered the ship. I could not keep my mind off the handsomeness of their features.

I happened to think about the gigantic distance between the Pleiades and our planet, and could not refrain from asking them, "When did you leave your planet?"

"We just left it!"

"I don't understand."

"For you, it was millions of years ago, when your planet had not the conditions for intelligent life. For us, we just left." Gesturing with his left arm, he snapped his fingers.

I supposed they reckoned their time on a different basis than ours. They smiled.

"How far away are the Pleiades?"

"You have the figures in your books. We are over 500 light-years away."

Later, I checked and found that the figure is 410 in some books, 328 in others.

I asked if their means of travel have to do with Dr. Einstein's Theories of Relativity and the Unified Field. Commander Kramier answered: *"For the Theory to be correct, it will be necessary to modify it at least three times. Besides, the speed of light is not 300,000 kilometers per second. It is closer to 400,000; it's just that light slows down in the atmosphere, because of the electrostatic, electric, or ionized layers of the planet, the belt that you call "Van Allen," and other fields not yet detected by your scientists, which have the shape of two apple halves."*

I am ashamed of not having delved further into this conversation, but truly, my limited scientific knowledge kept me from asking additional questions about a subject that was unknown to me. My effort for now is to transcribe faithfully the answers given by my interlocutors. Once the formal introduction and initial interchange of ideas was completed, Krishnamerck invited me to visit various sections of the ship.

We exited through another door, into an adjoining relaxation room, which had several cushions on the floor. The wall was illumined by a very comfortable halo of light. This room was also circular in shape. I asked no questions. Again in the corridor, we encountered more rooms, all curiously interconnected to the large room where we were before.

In one of the rooms were bottles, large flasks, slanting slightly and hermetically sealed. I asked what they were.

"It is chlorophyll extract, which we take from forests and jungles, extracting it from the best trees. This is basic for our food. We eat, the same as you do. We are very fond of the fruit cultivated in the southern part of the continent—peaches, grapes. . . ."

"Chile, Argentina?"

"We 'borrow' the fruit from some of the farms, and then, by night, with certain ionizing rays, we speed up the growth of the fruit. A few hours later, the fruits are ripe for picking. You must believe; it is true. We carry out a directed alteration of plant metabolism. Our technology allows it."

Other bottles which held either coffee-colored or clear, very transparent liquid.

"Aboard our ships, we operate laboratories to process all of our foods."

As we continued our tour, when we passed in front of a room I thought was for relaxation, I could see books, with transparent pages and written symbols very similar to Japanese.

They persisted on the subject of their food.

"We need this type of food because we have stopped the process of mitosis. We have a technique for keeping alive the cells, stopping the aging process."

I deduced that he considered aging to be a disease. On the other hand, I thought I understood from his words something about immortality. They did not say so directly, and I didn't dare to confirm my suspicions.

"We are here carrying out a very special mission. We belong to a very developed civilization, sister to others, from which we have received specific orders regarding Planet Earth. From antiquity, we have contacted other men, belonging to various cultures. We have influenced their thinking through what you call 'Masters.' But not only on this planet, also on others; we have contributed to their scientific, cultural, and spiritual development. Besides, some of us have been 'born' here, or incarnated, if you prefer, since ancient times."

Then we approached a metal, spiral staircase that took us to another floor. Three men were going in the opposite direction; they turned their heads and greeted us. One of them went out through a doorway leading to another room; the other two stopped in front of a control panel, where others were busy and did not pay any attention to us. We passed unnoticed by them. Krishnamerck said that twelve men made up the total crew.

I took a long look at the control room, located on the third floor of the ship. Various maps were unfolded. Crossing my arms behind my back, I examined them. *"They are cosmic maps,"* my guides said. They seemed to have come out of the wall, in order to be seen by me. The control panel, with lights that blinked on and off, like neon signs, must have had something to do with

Interpretive drawing by the artists at the Revista Mexicana: *"Extra-terrestrial Contact" in 1977, about Enrique's contact.*

Reenactment, years later (1978), of Enrique's encounter in the woods by the lake. Photo: Samuel Medina

the maps. These appeared to be marked with multicolored lights, representing zones. Some were well-defined lights, and others were without apparent function, picturing galaxies, nebulae, suns, and planets.

"We have technological and cultural exchange with thousands of inhabited planets. We often also exchange raw materials." I asked if I could know the names of those planets.

"It would be useless, because we know them by different names."

Next, the Commander located Planet Earth on a Milky Way quite different from what we know in pictures. A pulsing light distinguished the planet from other bodies, located quite a distance away. *"We do not explore your planet, because we have had bases here for thousands of years. Other civilizations do it."*

Getting closer to the control panels, I observed something similar to clocks, many of them, superimposed one on top of the other, each one with its own dials, and marked with illegible characters. Some of the clocks showed figures similar to ours, indexed by ordinary clock-hands. They seemed to measure different times, simultaneously and in relation to one another. Entertained by my momentary curiosity, I had to force my attention to return to the words of the Commander: *"We are here because we know about the calamities that will overrun Planet Earth—one of them, the Third World War. It is not far away; we know the date, but we cannot interfere. It would be against what you call 'free will.' You must learn to live in peace and harmony, but you have to do it by yourselves, and that implies gaining a new level of conscience. Perhaps the greatest discovery that Earthlings will make, will be to know God, without the circumscriptions and limitations that you have attached to Him. God has no shape, is omnipotent, and you cannot represent Him. You believe in a completely mistaken concept of God. We don't know Him as you have imagined Him.*

"We don't give Him a special name, so when we refer to Him, we call Him the INNOMINATE, the One Without Name. In our way of living, we don't need to believe the way you do."

The Commander spoke with such authority and knowledge of the subject that I was not able to object to anything at all. It only occurred to me to ask them something of academic interest, related to the Bible: "Did you have anything to do with the destruction of Sodom and Gomorrah? Our Bible teaches that it was a divine punishment. It was a punishment where thousands of children and innocent people perished."

"We did not carry out the destruction; somebody else did, another civilization, another race. You cannot understand it now. Superior orders are obeyed, and when a command is given, it must be obeyed. Those who produce those orders act with equity and justice."

"How did you travel from the Pleiades to Earth?"

"We travel at the speed of thought. At some other time we will explain it."

"What is your solar system like?"

"It is made up of three suns. Two of them rotate around a larger sun. A total of forty-three planets orbit around the three suns. We come from one of those planets, which are not all inhabited. We are still establishing colonies. We call our sun SHI-EL-HO, and we live on the fourth and fifth planets, where we come from."

We left the navigation room and went back to the circular room where the first interview took place, where we continued our talk. I glanced at my watch and, with surprise, noted that it had stopped at 8:25 p.m. I shook my wrist, trying uselessly to make it work. I estimated my stay inside the ship at about one-and-a-half hours. Krishnamerck, smiling, said, *"Your watch doesn't work in here."*

"Well, if it doesn't, why don't we fly somewhere?"

"Come with us; we have been traveling since you came in." This really surprised me, for I expected that when traveling it was necessary to wear special astronaut uniforms, gloves and helmet, safety belts, and whatnot—but though apparently traveling at great speed, I felt nothing at all.

They took me to a special panel, where a visor opened like the lids of an eye, revealing a concave screen. I sat in front of the visor, on a fixed chair. One of my companions, who was operating the controls, adjusted them and invited me to look through them. Approaching, I saw a great vacuum and felt dizziness. *"Take the controls, and adjust them to your eyesight."* I moved them somewhat, until I could see with perfect clarity through the screen.

"That is your home."

I was dumbfounded; it was a sort of telescope, incorporating a beam of light, capable of penetrating the roofs and walls of buildings. I could see my family sleeping, and the dog seemed to notice something, barking and moving about nervously at the window of my room. When I moved the levers the wrong way, a neighbor's house became visible. A bit alarmed, they cautioned me to look only at my house.

"How did you find my house?"

"With this same device; it is capable of seeing through some metals. In this way we have watched many people." We kept on going at a steady speed. I could identify 68th Avenue, a major thoroughfare in Bogotá, and the traffic upon it, along with the housing developments in that neighborhood, which looked like doll houses or models to scale. I asked them if I could report to others about all that I was seeing. *"That is up to you; you can do so."* I never noticed resistance on their part, or prohibitions. My questions in most instances were very childish. I wanted to know everything but did not know where to begin. It was

they who wisely directed my thoughts toward some special subjects. *"We have information that will be delivered at its proper time. It will affect all religions on Earth. It has to do with what you call 'The Creation of Man.' We belong to an organization that gives assistance to the Planet, and we have always been present."*

With the passage of time, I began to feel hungry. They offered me something like a chocolate bar, wrapped in plastic. Its flavor was very similar to that of "zabajón," a Colombian drink made of milk, eggs, sugar, and anise-flavored liqueur. I nibbled at it until it was gone. I felt a pleasant, warm sensation, and the hunger disappeared for the time being. Later, after several questions and answers about Biblical subjects, they gave me something to taste, which they promised was going to please me very much. From a tray, they took something like popcorn. Its sweet taste gave me another deliciously warm feeling. For a second, I thought that I was being drugged, because my eyelids became very heavy.

Cyril asked me, *"Do you know the name of the food you are eating?"*

"I don't know. It resembles a type of corn we use in our diet."

He then added, *"It is made from four cereals; two of them exist on Earth. This is the food that sustained the Jewish people during their forty years in the desert, according to your Bible."*

"Cyril, is this the manna mentioned in the scriptures?"

Holding my head with my hands, and with some manna in my mouth, I didn't know anymore what to say. This food, manna, as it was called by the Jews, quenched my thirst and hunger for twenty-four hours. It has a very high energetic value. *"We use it as food during our trips,"* said Cyril.

With the emissaries from the Pleiades, it was difficult to coordinate my ideas. Logic did not adapt itself to our conversation. Each word, each sentence, was a surprise; nothing had the usual meaning, and yet, they spoke with the ease and confidence of those familiar with a different world, upside-down to ours.

"Enrique, this experience is going to cause you many misunderstandings. You will be surrounded constantly by people who will praise and congratulate you, sweetening your ears with beautiful words, only to obtain from you certain information. But then, because of the information you have given them, you will see how they become your worst slanderers. Friends who are not your friends will seek to lose you. They themselves will surround you with hypocrisy and deceit. This is a warning, Enrique; the risk is very great."

"How do you know so many things?"

"It is very easy. Making our ships invisible, camouflaging them above your cities, thanks to a special vibratory field, we fly practically above your heads, yet you do not notice it. We fool your radars, creating confusion with our maneuvers. We

handle our ships whatever way we want to. Those are the advantages of our technology. On the other hand, we have people on the ground, blended with the humans, who daily walk the streets and avenues of your large and small towns, as in my instance back in 1969. Many of us are among you."

At this point it occurred to me to ask once more about the super-high velocities they achieved to move through space, how they had traveled from the Pleiades to Earth, and whether they could give me any more information without harming their own interests. Cyril took me with two other crewmen to a section where the machine that generated the power used for their displacements was located. My heart beat quickly. What emotion—to become perhaps the first Earthling to see in operation the "engine" that propelled the ship!

When we entered the security zone, Commander Kramier was waiting for us. He must have entered through an alternate accessway. When we entered, several alarms were activated, with a signal that went directly to the belts of the crew. They explained that the other crewmen had been warned about our presence in the propulsion area, which was also apparent at the remote control panels in other areas. Ahead of us was a window embedded in a metal wall, and in front of it were two comfortable chairs. They invited me to sit in one of the chairs and get close to the window. Wonder of wonders!

In the innards of the ship, a group of three great diamonds or crystals rotated slowly around a vertical shaft extending from ceiling to floor, which turned also, in the opposite direction. The colors and shades of the shaft surface were like a kaleidoscope of pure crystal. I was truly fascinated by the gorgeous spectacle. When I removed my face from the window, to ask some questions, I sensed that my features probably showed some pallor. The crewmen, smiling, watched me carefully. I addressed Cyril, but the Commander answered, guessing my question.

"Those are crystals, not diamonds. We call them 'memory crystals;' they are programmable and receive information from the 'main transducer' (the rotating shaft). We also call them 'living crystals.' We obtain them on a certain planet, where they grow and reproduce."

I had noticed that the crystals rotated around themselves, united to a base that also turned around the "main transducer," or shaft. The crystals must have been about seventy centimeters in diameter, maybe less. I was watching the same movement as of the Earth around the Sun, but in miniature!

I was breathless, but the answer to my next question left me even more flabbergasted. "Commander, could you speed up the movement of the crystals, so I can see better the colors and reflections?"

"No, Enrique," he answered, *"it is not possible while you are here on board. If we speed up the rotation for only two minutes, when you get off the ship, more*

than 200 Earth years will have elapsed. As you well can understand, we cannot do it."

Anguish overcame me. I thought about my family, my friends, and how the Planet might change in 200 years, if the extraterrestrial were telling me the truth, and all this could happen almost instantaneously. I thought, here, Einstein's relativity theories come into place. I could not stop feeling astonished. To calm me, the Commander addressed me once more (my anguish centered on the possibility that someone of the crew could speed up the crystals, forgetting that I still was aboard the ship, and I could become marooned 200 years in the future, knowing no one, without a family, in a totally changed world).

"No, Enrique, that is not possible while you are here on board. I am the one who commands the ship mentally, *and we have thus reduced the possibilities for error. If something should happen to me, other members of the crew have authority to carry out the* mind-machine integration, *where the coupling takes place directly by means of* mental impulses, *to the 'transducer and crystals' program. The mental energy that we deliver is translated as* flight energy. *That is why we told you that 'we have just left.' For us, the time factor is not a problem; we live in a present that modifies the future. That is why the future is 'malleable' and cannot be predicted with certainty. Not so the past; that is already history and is unmodifiable."*

With their hands over their folded arms, two of them watched my reactions to the information they were giving me, so crazy-sounding to my flimsy terrestrial knowledge.

Inside my brain, questions stirred without answers. I was facing one of the greatest opportunities in history and could not manage to pose good questions. Because of my ignorance, perhaps I was wasting the chance to acquire great knowledge. I was the living proof that collective reactions can be fatal for our civilization, for I could not integrate within myself how they could travel *at the speed of thought* without suffering physical alterations. How had they solved the problem? Perhaps their bodies had some different organs, or were they a race that had achieved mastery over Life and Death?

Later I would obtain an answer that may be the key as to how they vanquished the barrier of disease and death. But for comprehending how the *mental energy* referred to by the Commander and Cyril was produced, I had yet to witness another sensational show. That same "mental force" that reached the "transducer," achieved the vertiginous speed of thought. I could not recover from my astonishment. Why did they tell and teach me such things? And what was the role I played, or was about to play, in light of this avalanche of information? How were people going to believe me? Was there a preconceived plan, prior to my contact? What were their real motivations?

As I wrote these lines in the year 1976 (and in the twenty years since then), the panorama was (and is) still unclear. To be true, I do not know the motivations for why I was chosen for contact with the extraterrestrials. Maybe, in the course of time, when more results are obtained from research carried out by scientists in all disciplines, it will become clear not only what was the reason for my contact, but also what is the logical explanation for all encounters with intelligent denizens from outer space.

While reflecting on all this aboard their ship, I was directed to climb a ladder going up to a walkway. We arrived at the great hall, at whose center the "kaleidoscope" or "transducer" rotated, the same that I had seen through the visor. The room appeared to be devoid of furniture or visible accoutrements. We stopped at the entrance. Cyril and Krunula escorted the Commander. Kramakan arrived, and then some additional crew appeared through another entrance at the opposite side of the room. They were twelve altogether. I thought, how is the ship traveling, if the total crew is twelve?

Eight of the extraterrestrials wore the dull-gray uniform, and the other four, including Commander Kramier, were dressed in the "reddish-brown" type.

All of a sudden, before my weary eyes and already tired senses, twelve chairs emerged from the floor. They looked like dentist's chairs, located in a circle around the transducer. Then, lo and behold, from the ceiling dropped twelve helmets, similar to motorcycle helmets, which descended onto the heads of each of the crew members, as soon as they sat in the chairs. The four with the different uniform sat precisely equidistant. They held hands in "padlock fashion," each one holding the arm of the next, until the circle was complete. I, from my observation post, watched the scene in complete surprise. This ritual lasted perhaps one minute; then the helmets retracted up into the ceiling, the company stood up and released each other's hands, and the chairs collapsed into the floor.

All of them returned to their normal duties, except Kramier and Cyril, who now watched me, waiting for my customary questions. They said that I had seen them liberate their mental energy to the transducer, where it would be converted into *flight energy!*

With the extraterrestrials, everything was surprising. Had they performed this ritual with the sole purpose of being seen? But, what was their purpose, and to whom should I tell about it? It was obvious that they did it so that I would tell about it. But to whom?

We came back to the control room. Through the observation panel, I realized that we had covered many kilometers, moving at random. My eyelids were very heavy, and I was tired. Somebody asked, *"Are you sleepy, Enrique; would you like to rest?"* It was evident, and the Commander ordered the others to take me some place to rest. All of them stood up, and Cyril led the way. *"You are going to rest, Enrique."* Krunula went with us; he didn't leave us for a second. We walked out to a straight corridor, no longer than four meters, and reached another room, whose door opened automatically, without using any manual control.

The room was well-lighted, and four beds appeared before us. Cyril told me to choose one; then I lay down. The bed was very soft and yielding, the surface leather-like. It conformed to the shape of my body as I shifted positions. *"Sleep well; don't worry, we will wake you up."* They said goodbye, and the door closed. With my hands under my cheek, sideways, and my legs folded, I dropped into a comforting and refreshing sleep. My last thought was about asking for concrete proofs of my contact, to show my family and friends. Then I knew no more.

A strong pull at my brain woke me up, as if someone had touched a nerve. Upon sitting up, I saw Cyril and Krunula. *"Enrique, please excuse the way we have awakened you; we have impacted your brain with a psychic order,"* said Krunula. *"We are going to give you some final information, because the time is approaching to drop you where we picked you up."* I stood up quickly, feeling as though I had slept many hours, totally rested and with renewed energies. Back in the room visited previously, the Commander and another crewman were waiting for us.

"We want you to remember the following: a Third World War is inevitable. Men will have a four-year grace period to attempt to attenuate it, in accordance with their behavior. Only the mental state of mankind can ease its effects; it is squarely your problem." Then they took me to the main control room, and advised me: *"We are going to take a short trip, so that you can memorize the details of the place you are going to see."*

Through the wide window, they showed me great valleys, covered with rich vegetation, until we reached some low, flat lands. *"This is what you call 'Los Llanos Orientales' (the Eastern Prairies)."* The whole place was illuminated, as if it were daylight. *"Pay attention to that road and that dirt path. Our next meeting will be right there. Memorize the location."* The place was fenced with barbed wire. A battered wooden gate, ready to fall off, was the entryway to the pasture grounds. They gave me a name. I quickly memorized it, besides recording the details of the terrain, after repeated overflights above the area. Years later, I still wondered why they selected such a remote place.

"The date for next meeting will be November 18, at 8:00 p.m. Enrique, don't forget."

With a nod, I told them that everything had been duly registered. I was sure to find the place with no trouble. *"We are getting close, look."* In minutes, the ship had covered the distance between the cattle farm on the lowlands and the location in the highlands where I had been picked up. They walked withme to say good-bye, to the room where I had undressed. Cyril embraced me and, with Krunula, walked away.

From the roof, the light beam was projected and quickly surrounded me. The door opened, and I stepped into empty space. Safely, the light beam dropped me softly on the ground and, as before, retracted until it disappeared into the ship. I was again in the midst of the trees next to the lake. I saw the great ship speed away.

I looked at my watch, which was working again. I figured that it was 5:00 a.m. and, resting on the ground, waited for sunup. When I woke up, it was 10:15 a.m. by my watch. Figuring that two hours had elapsed, I deduced that the time was about 7:00 a.m. I stretched my muscles and was on my way to look for a bus to return to the capital, Bogotá.

I well knew that the problem now was related to the manner in which the experience should be told. However, the happiness that I felt gave me courage enough to face any consequences. In this manner, my first encounter with the beings from the Pleiades took place, on November 3, 1973, after which my life would never be the same.

The repercussions that resulted from this experience would lead me to an uncertain apostleship throughout the world, through the telling of my story about the extraterrestrials.

CHAPTER NOTES

[1] A square, woolen blanket with a hole at the center, used in cold climates.

[2] The names of the extraterrestrials are spelled phonetically herein.

8

My Stand Collapses

"Something similar has happened with human prehistory as with religion and science. An excess of dogmatism and lack of modesty and wisdom on the part of those who monopolize these branches of knowledge has caused humanity to fall into grave errors, and sometimes has been responsible for centuries of lost time in the achievement of certain goals, absolutely necessary for the advancement of civilization."
—SALVADOR FREIXEDO TABARES, *Extraterrestrials and Religion*

THE HISTORY OF HUMANITY IS A BOOK OF GREAT CHANGES, whose execution has been entrusted to men and women willing to sacrifice their existence in order to see an improvement in the fate of the inhabitants of this planet. These are not exceptional beings, but they are determined, and this sets them apart. To transform the world means to conceive of ideas adaptable to the reality of the current events, and then to put them into practice. Man, in his struggle for progress, has discovered that he will live in harmony only when he knows himself fully, when he knows correctly the laws of nature, all through reason and for the benefit of the spirit.

I realized all of the above a long time after the ET contacts ended. While we (in our group) were in touch daily with the ETs, we never thought about analyzing the information received from them. In exchange for revelation, we surrendered our reason! We thought ourselves exceptional, endowed with all sorts of luck, virtues, and qualities, while the only reality was that of our own imperfection and stupidity.

That day of the first in-person contact, I could not contain the immense happiness that I experienced, once the beam of "solid-light" dropped me on firm ground. When I climbed into the bus to return to the capital, I felt like yelling to the passengers, mostly peasants, to convey to them some of the happiness that I felt. I wished they could share what I had so recently experienced.

From that moment on, my transformation was total. All my mental mechanisms, my previously attained concepts and knowledge, crashed boisterously. What I saw was enough to change my way of thinking. All my ideas about the world, life, and religion toppled, taking on new dimensions.

For the first time in my life, I thought about a world without political systems and divided religions, without social classes. Anything was possible. I was at the gates of an awakened conscience, of wisdom, and of a united terrestrial brotherhood. People's guilty beliefs in misery and desperation would soon disappear. Finally, I had found something worth fighting for: *our own freedom, through the search for the truth.*

Back with my children, I embraced them tenderly and felt sorry not to be able to tell them my story in detail. If I did so, they would not understand. It was better to remain silent.

With my wife, matters were different. An insurmountable abyss seemed to separate us more and more. Her mind was influenced against me in an irreversible fashion, and when I realized it, it was too late. A final separation would be on its way soon.

Once word got out that I was at home, many of the group members began visiting me, up to one every hour or so. They also wished to congratulate my wife, but it was difficult to do so. In the evening, Richard Deeb called.

I told him that all had been successful. We agreed to meet on the morrow at Chela's home, where I would give them the details. I felt tired and fell into a dreamless, quiet sleep. Nothing disturbed me. I had inner peace, the peace transmitted by my friends from space.

On Monday, as usual, I arrived on time at the office. They must have been waiting for me, because as soon as I opened the door, all looked at me inquiringly. We waited for Alfonso Blanco, and then we reviewed together the trip of November 3. No doubt, he didn't believe me! But he didn't reproach me or make negative observations, either.

In the evening, as agreed, I went to Chela's apartment, on 22nd Street. María Teresa, deeply moved, with her eyes glowing in happiness, embraced me, unable to convey words of congratulation. Others of the group were also there. I felt moved to tears, as each embraced me one after another. No word was uttered, because none was adequate.

I waited a few minutes, until the emotion subsided. Then I told my story, without too many details, only the main incidents, such as my arrival at the tree grove, when I picked up the sphere, when the light beam lifted me, my encounter with Cyril Weiss, his welcome aboard, my interview with the ship's commander, and so on—details I considered of interest to them.

A strange incident took place while I told my story. Apparently, the members of the group were already familiar with the events, because one of them had traveled mentally to the place of the events, describing them step by step. However, there was no agreement between the two versions, mine and theirs. The obvious outcome was that somebody had to be wrong, and that surely wasn't me. There was no agreement even about the time of the contact, but I wished to avoid any confrontation. A sort of magnetism surrounded me and my words in the wake of the contact. In fact, some members of the group wished to tear pieces off my clothing to keep as souvenirs, a reaction I could never understand.

The following meeting took place at Richard Deeb's home. More than forty interested people were invited, most of them strangers, and this was my first public conference as a contactee of the ETs. This time I described, somewhat more fluently, my experience. One of the listeners was an employee with the influential Colombian newspaper, *El Tiempo*, in its Personnel Department. He would later tell the story to Humberto Díez, a veteran newspaperman.

At the end of the talk, voices of approval and satisfaction flooded the small auditorium. Others were incredulous. A protest also circulated, because I mentioned the impending and resounding fall of a religious organization, within some twenty-six years, counted from that November 3, 1973.

I had begun to offend certain sensibilities, unintentionally. Many didn't like the direct message from the ETs. With sour faces, these people attacked the ETs and all who were linked with them in one way or another, with discourteous words. Later, they called us abusive, deceitful, fanatic, and more, threatening to denounce us publicly in order to keep us silent.

The contradictory viewpoints of the attendees persuaded me to keep strictly silent about many specific details furnished by the ETs. If I had disclosed them frankly in their full extent, I surely would have offended some of the listeners, who would have reacted even more strongly, counterattacking against me in protection of their beliefs and mental constructs. I began to understand the logical consequences of my experience: mankind resists truth.

I am conscious of the direct dangers involved with making public certain specific information. Consequently, much will stay occult, until I feel confident that my life is not menaced. Truly, it is not my wish to become a martyr for a cause that is not sufficiently precise and understood.

Humberto Díez, the journalist from *El Tiempo*, visited my office the day after the talk at the Deeb's, as a result of the information given him by his fellow employees at the newspaper. Humberto, wishing to have an exclusive on the story, wanted to be certain of the reality of my experience. All was true, but I preferred not to give reports to the press or other media. He insisted. I wanted to keep my story unpublished, until I could find a means of broadcasting it adequately to the whole world. However, the journalist argued strongly in favor of not letting the opportunity pass. Alfonso Blanco backed him up, and both convinced me to give an interview.

The interview took place, and a few days later it was published in the newspaper. A provocative title announced: "FICTION OR REALITY? A COLOMBIAN ABOARD A FLYING SAUCER."

During four consecutive days, on November 9, 10, 11, and 12, sections of my interview on the contact with ETs from the Pleiades were published. I said, as they stated, that in coming years, alien vehicles would be seen in the skies like flocks of birds in all countries, according to a plan wisely conceived (and which time, as of 1996, has borne out). These sightings are a means for men to take heed about their existence, as they become aware of the official science and government policies pretending to ignore the presence of UFOs and ETs on the planet, ascribing them to "collective hallucinations," or plain insanity of the witnesses.

It was no longer possible to retreat. The ignited chain reaction from the published interview produced varying reactions, both favorable and unfavorable. Dozens of letters from remote places in the country, others from abroad, flooded my desk. All of them asked for information on how to contact the ETs. All of them asked the same questions, as if the writers had agreed beforehand on the subject.

Among the many letters received, one stood out. It came from Venezuela, written by a Rear Admiral of the Navy of our neighboring country. It described in detailed fashion his experiences with a group similar to ours, about a Master, his name "SAO" who was said to have come from the Pleiades. This letter from Rear Admiral Daniel Gómez Calcaño surprised me pleasantly.

In the telepathic communications (no physical contact had taken place), SAO had transmitted teachings to the Venezuelan group, similar to those received by our own group from an extraterrestrial who was also called SAO. I don't think this was a coincidence. Both of us were receiving from the same extraterrestrial entity! Our messages were quite similar to those reported by the Venezuelans, in fact, almost identical, and there had been no communication between the two groups. Months later, I met two of the members of the Venezuelan group, during a trip there. Another member, Antonio López, had come to Bogotá and met with Alfonso Blanco and myself.

As a result of the articles published in *El Tiempo,* many people fell into collective hysteria. Car caravans, UFO believers, and busybodies invaded the lakes around Bogotá and the nearby state of Boyacá, striving to catch sight of the evasive craft and take pictures of them. Canvas tents, telescopes, binoculars, cameras, and lanterns were common sights among those who wanted to capture the ships on film, or preferably, interview the occupants at some lonely place. I am sure that my ET hosts knew how the UFOmania was going to develop . . . and the proof did not take long in coming. . . ! People in Colombia began to assume that the location had been at Guatavita Lake, a deep lake where primitive peoples used to make religious offerings. Honoring the request of the ship's occupants, I have never mentioned the name of the lake or revealed its exact location.

In general, my daily routine changed gradually. I abandoned more and more my professional duties and dedicated myself mostly to daily conferences and nocturnal telepathic contacts. Each message was quite an experience. Recognized by the ETs as their only physical contactee in Colombia, all the members of our group took charge of protecting and surrounding me with a halo of mysticism. This contributed to increase my pretense, and I became a celebrity. If I lacked something, they hurried to get it. If I spoke, they took notes of what I said. I really enjoyed this messenger role. Later, when I finally woke up, it was a hard blow.

During each meeting, I initially experienced terrible headaches. The ETs had forbidden me to take any medications. Instead, they advised me to eat plenty of coconut and honey, twice a day, while the communications lasted. I could intersperse this with cashews or hazelnuts. In addition, I should eat fish and all foods rich in iron and phosphorus, such as vegetables. With this strict diet, a little austere for my tastes, the headaches went away. Marjorie and Maria Teresa often brought me these foods. It was interesting to see how they treated me. Many looked at me as if I were some sort of Moses, Elijah, or some other Biblical prophet. A daring fan even suggested that I was actually the reincarnation of one of the apostles of Jesus.

My reputation spread quickly. People from all over the country wanted to see me. They requested that I repeat my story over and over. Some of them mistook me for a spiritual master, with authority and power to solve their problems and give them advice. Within my means, I tried to make them understand that I was not an "otherwordly entity." My knowledge about UFOs was limited to the books I had read. The ETs had not endowed me with special powers, or anything like that. At these extremes, I was almost credited with performing miracles!

Still, as quickly as these people arrived, they also left, as soon as they realized that I was not their spiritual master. Without being sarcastic, I was quite discouraging in my answers. The visitors were badly annoyed, because I never spoke to them of spirituality, or of matters sweet to their ear. Poor folk, rich folk, executives, mothers, priests, nuns, came to see me, discreetly looking for advice. We would meet in a local cafeteria or in private homes. The majority sympathized with me privately, but attacked me rudely in public.

The ETs were very much aware of this situation, but offered no advice. By the way, it is appropriate to point out that I no longer needed the group to contact the ETs mentally; still, I continued duly attending the meetings, because I thought we might be collectively in preparation for something unexpected. The Greater Brothers gave me secret code keys to be used at the time of the contacts; these served for identification and to prevent any attempt of the "opposition" or the "evil ones" to create confusion and chaos. They warned me against this "contrary force," which could try to spoil our work. I do not know if these forces achieved their purpose, but it is significant that our group didn't last for long.

At that time, I began to become suspicious about several points, the first one being why I had been selected. I was conscious of my lack of spirituality, and the terrifying events foreseen by the ETs were far from mystical. My conclusion was that they do not select their contactees based on their spirituality or virtues, and I was the living proof of this statement.

Anyhow, the members of our group, and other groups, insisted in visualizing the ETs as direct envoys from God, charged with the mission of telling men about the terrible punishments to be applied if humanity stubbornly refused to mend their ways. Every appointment with our cosmic brothers was held in "sanctity." Exhortations from the older members, calling for abandonment of earthly things and dedication to the higher realms, were common.

It was depressing to witness how new elements were gradually incorporated, new rites added, as adornment for this interstellar carnival. Contacts with saints and other religious characters took place within the same group. Some scolded the people for their sins, and others urged group reading of the Bible as the only road to salvation. These "garrulous transmitters," a variety of telepathic communicators, grew wild.

Each message was a teaching, and each teaching, a step towards "salvation." This was, more or less, the logic of the moment. The contact with ETs became an uncontrollable addiction. Hundreds of people stood in line, waiting for a chance to be instructed on how to get a good communication. Eventually, certain self-appointed "chosen ones" presumed to discern who could become a good medium and who could not. They assumed authority to reject, "in the name of the Cosmic Masters," who could tune in and who could not. This situation began to annoy me, and I protested, kindly, at first. I knew that this first wave of fanaticism was soon to cause casualties, and such was the case. It was funny that, according to the others in the group, I was wrong and was distorting the spiritual teachings of the extraterrestrials.

Later, they began to stay away from me, although they still needed my "powers" for a perfect communication.

The fifteen days from November 3 elapsed rapidly. I had to travel to Villavicencio, the most important city of the flat region of "Los Llanos Orientales," or Eastern Prairies, and then find the pre-selected location for the appointment.

I was ready for my second encounter with the extraterrestrials.

From Surprise to Surprise

"Two things are infinite: the Universe, and human stupidity."
—Dr. ALBERT EINSTEIN

THE SCHEDULED RENDEZVOUS WAS AT 8:00 P.M. on November 18, 1973. I left very early from Bogotá, in an interstate bus that took me to Villavicencio, capital of "Los Llanos." This region is a gigantic natural resource, only partially developed. There is much cattle raising and agriculture, with huge land tracts that extend from horizon to horizon.

Heat and dust annoy the visitor, who is compensated by the vision of lofty sights and a feeling of freedom, due perhaps to the "limitless" size of this frontier land. It is a pleasure to visit, but the purpose of my trip didn't allow me much time to enjoy the splendor of this paradise.

Once in Villavicencio, I took another bus to the neighboring town of Apiay. I had to plan carefully how to get to the indicated place on time, and the solution was to enlist the help of a "baquiano," a native guide, by the name of Antonio. I hired him, and thanks to his familiarity with the region, I was able to find the place, after several hours on horseback. Antonio's happy conversation and spontaneous jokes made the road, or rather, the trail, shorter. He lashed the horses once in a while to keep them moving along in the middle of the afternoon heat and the buzzing of the "bichos" (insects).

The guide was not aware of the purpose of my trip, but he knew his way around. I told him about the place in question, and he was able to pinpoint it accurately. Every so often I looked up at the sky, searching for some type of sign. Antonio would imitate me and look at me silently and inquiringly.

I felt tired and aching, because I was not used to riding horses. I also wondered why they had summoned me to a place so far away from Bogotá, while it would have been easier to meet at a closer location, saving me a lot of wear and tear. While thinking about these subjects, we finally arrived at our destination, at around 7:30 p.m. I gave Antonio C$120 (about ten U.S. dollars). He took the money but gave no indications of leaving. Then I shook hands with him, hoping that he would leave, but he refused to leave me alone, asking, "How are you going to spend the night here, where there are dangerous animals?"

He pointed to some tall grass a short distance away and mentioned that cattle are attacked at night by the hungry "tigrillos" (wildcats), meaning that I could be in danger of such an attack myself. (At present, wildlife such as jaguars no longer pose threats to humans in Colombia, due to near extinction from human activities.) He said he didn't mind staying with me until somebody came from the ranch, still some distance away, to pick me up. Faking tranquillity, I tried to put him at ease, saying that a jeep from the ranch was on its way to meet me, and there was no need for him to stay. Not fully convinced, he finally went on his way, towing the second horse by its bridle. Every so often, he turned his head and looked back, expecting me to reconsider my decision. Finally, I lost sight of him behind a clump of vegetation, in the deepening darkness. I was alone, far from civilization.

When the hour for the meeting approached, I had mixed feelings: fear and happiness, doubt and hope, peace of mind and remorse. This mixture blocked the clarity of my thinking. The possibility of fantastic adventures passed through my head, such as space kidnappings and not being able to see my family any more. Even after the previous physical contact and the almost daily telepathic contacts, I still was not used to it.

It was a lovely night, and I could feel the cool breeze on my face. The starry sky invited observation. Many stray thoughts crossed my mind, but nothing concrete. Where I was, no one would discover me, and "they" would not be observed either. Maybe that's why they chose this location. Starting at 8:00 p.m., having nothing to do, I walked fifty meters in one direction, turned around, and walked again the same distance. Then I repeated this routine many times. They have failed me! I thought. Feeling many regrets, an idea began to knock at my brain.

Trying not to get lost, I marked as a reference the gate to the ranch, an old and rundown wooden opening, located in the middle of a barbed wire fence several kilometers long. I began to explore the area, careful not to scratch myself against any sharp thorns. At 10:00 p.m., all hopes dashed, I tried to figure out how to get back to civilization the next day. I sat down on the ground with the intention of establishing telepathic contact. I relaxed and went through the full routine learned in Bogotá, expecting that they would give me some indication of their presence. But I heard nothing, felt nothing. I reflected, thinking that perhaps I had made some mistake, and then tried again, with no results.

Intrigued, I realized that not a single mosquito had bitten me, in this region so well known for its abundance of all kinds of insects. The only thing left to do was to look for a place to sleep. It was useless to yell for help; Antonio had warned me that there was nobody for many kilometers around. I sat for half an hour, then walked a few meters, this way or another, fighting boredom and the cool of the night. This went on until 3:00 a.m.. Feeling rather depressed, I assumed that perhaps I had mistaken the day or the hour, and I felt very tired.

Once more, I lifted my eyes to the sky. No, I was not dreaming! Many, many lights, which gradually grew in size, moved slowly in the sky. One, two, three, four . . . ten, eleven, twelve, thirteen. Thirteen nocturnal lights moved in perfect formation, like an inverted V. The three up front looked larger than the rest. The ten smaller ones followed in double open lines.

Almost overhead, they halted momentarily. One of the smaller lights from the rear stopped maneuvering momentarily, then stopped again at a certain height, where I could already distinguish its oval shape. Then, its shape faded within a surrounding luminosity, giving the impression of a gray cloud. The rest of the fleet left at this moment, speeding away until disappearing. I couldn't tell their direction, because I was disoriented in the darkness.

The hovering craft zigzagged, approaching slowly. In so doing, its shape became clearly defined. It was a small "scout ship," shaped like a cocoon. Descending, it circled, with a short and even sway, performing an astonishing series of maneuvers that left me open-mouthed. The ship stopped about thirty meters from the ground. Noiselessly, three short, supporting legs emerged from its belly, and then it landed softly on them. A ladder descended, leaving a narrow door open above it. The light shining through the door was suddenly blocked by a human silhouette, which stood at the doorway and looked out. The ship was about sixty meters away from me. Thanks to the prevailing light, mostly from the shining machine itself, I could discern its shape and dimensions. It was about seven meters in diameter and three-and-a-half meters high. Without wasting time and possessed by a terrific excitement, I ran towards the machine, but a deep voice ordered me to stop: *"Wait!"*

I stopped, a bit confused, and looked towards an individual, who with a slight gesture invited me to keep coming towards the ship. Step by step, I traveled the remaining distance. The illumination allowed me to recognize the man standing at the doorway: it was Krishnamerck! His presence tranquilized

me completely, even though I perceived around me a deep, rumbling sound. I perceived that he was breathing freely the terrestrial air, without a helmet. His uniform was identical to the one he had worn two weeks previously at the lake.

He invited me to walk up the six steps of the ladder. When I extended my arm to greet him, he stepped back and motioned me to stop between the last step and the door. The door was rather narrow, about one meter wide by 1.60 meters high. A very bright blue flash of lightning shone briefly, covering my whole body for several seconds. My hands and clothing fluoresced, and I assume my face did, too. It was a little annoying and gave me a feeling that was hard to describe. Cyril, smiling, approached and shook my hands vigorously.

"Enrique, how are you? Don't worry about that, it was necessary."

I understood that the blue light was part of another cleaning or sterilizing system, quite different from the one used during the first contact. This time it was a very fast-acting type of energy. We entered the ship, and he invited me to sit on a comfortable chair. Meanwhile, two beings completely different from Cyril entered the room. These were small and smiled constantly, dressed in sort of overalls, or one-piece suits, rather ample, quite different from Cyril's uniform. I got up to greet them, but they just bowed, without extending their hands.

"Who are these people?" I asked. While I thought about it, I looked at Cyril with some surprise, expecting an answer.

"They are beings from Mercury, Enrique."

"From Mercury?" To say the least, I was very, very surprised. The look on my face would be impossible to describe.

These little men were bald, with pale brunet skin, seemingly completely coated with an oil film, so shiny were their heads. They were about one-and-a-half meters tall, well-proportioned, with large normal eyes, normal ears, Greek nose, and prominent jaw. They dressed in a purple or deep violet color, in short sleeves that exposed their shiny arms. The uniform was not tight-fitting at the waist, and it had no belts. Their shoes were a dark, dull color, and they wore no gloves.

With a gesture, Cyril indicated to me a spiral staircase and invited me to the second floor, rather cramped indeed. We entered the navigation room, which was covered by a transparent dome. Funny, while I was outside of the ship I did not notice the transparency of the dome and figured that it was like one-way glass. The room seemed disconcertingly simple. The controls were located on a semi-oval table with a few buttons and other instruments. A medium-sized screen was embedded at the center. Two chairs were in front of the controls.

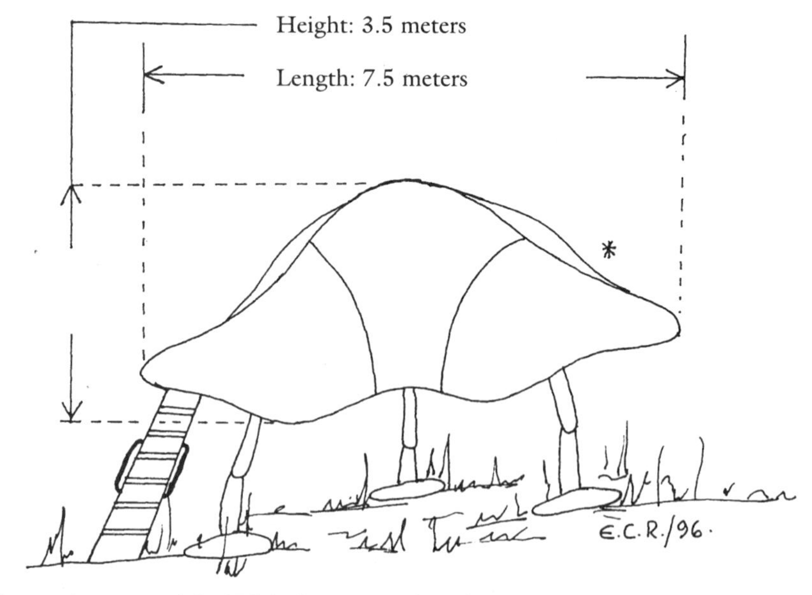

Approximate model of Pleiadean spaceship that picked up Enrique Castillo Rincón from the Eastern plains of Colombia on November 18, 1973.

* *"Cocoon" model*

The stellar panorama unfolded before us, under a breathtakingly starry sky. The dome gave the impression of metal fused to glass, or something like that. What seemed like a huge diamond with many facets was located at one side of the control table. At its base, several needles pointed at strange symbols. Some moved in one direction, and others in the opposite. Cyril, very affectionately, asked me, *"How is it going, Enrique?"*

"Incredibly well, Cyril, very well." Actually, I wasn't telling the truth. I had meant to tell everything to the group, but the bitter experiences with several of the people about the first contact made me feel lonely and misunderstood. The confusion originated from the lack of common sense about my budding task, which made me feel inadequate. I tried to keep all these gloomy thoughts to myself, though, to avoid bothering Cyril and appearing unnecessarily plaintive.

Looking at the "avocado-shaped" heads of the crew members, who were preparing for take-off, I changed the subject, trying to delve into their origins. "Brother Cyril, do they live on Mercury?" I asked this question based on my knowledge that the planet closest to the Sun had one side constantly facing it, with extremely high temperatures as a result, deathly for all types of life. The opposite side, in contrast, stayed in perpetual shade and freezing temperatures. According to this, life as we know it would be impossible on Mercury.

"You would be astonished," he answered, *"at the civilizations that have flourished there. Mercury rotates around the Sun and also around itself. Perhaps we will discuss the matter further at some later time. Now we are on our way to the Mother-ship."* One of the Mercurians, without speaking, led me back to the first floor, opened a closet, and by gestures invited me to pick a uniform that would fit my size. I took one and put it on over my own clothes. I feared some protest on his part, but to my surprise, the garment stretched and fit perfectly. While donning the garment, my hair became disarranged, so I took a comb from my pocket and used it to comb my hair. The Mercurian, with boundless curiosity, scrutinized me in detail, following the operation, his eyes shifting in their orbits. Then, always smiling, he bid me take a pair of shoes, which also enlarged and fit me as if by magic.

When ready, we walked up to the top floor. The crewman sat down and, pushing some buttons on the right side of the panel, sent the ship on its way. Cyril walked to the command screen and, handling some controls, searched the sky, looking for something. Meanwhile, I moved about in the room, looking at everything and memorizing all the actions of the crew. A sudden maneuver made the lower part of the ship rotate, while the dome remained stationary. I didn't lose my balance but felt my boots press down into the floor. A slight, electric, fluid-like sensation traveled through my body, with no ill effects.

The ship climbed upward very fast. Cyril kept looking at the screen, and suddenly, with a happy look on his face, he said, *"Enrique, take a look at the Mothership."* It was the biggest object that I had ever seen. It was shaped like a whale. "The Flagship," as Cyril called it, stood still in space, waiting for us. Beneath the gigantic "flying whale," a hatch opened, through which shone an intense brightness. The Mercurians did nothing in particular; it seemed that our scout ship was being absorbed through a funnel, directly into the entrance gate.

No sharp movements were felt. Our ship entered the opening snugly, moving up through it until it reached its parking spot inside. Our ship's transparent dome flipped open automatically, permitting the insertion of a ladder that dropped from above into the control room. Cyril climbed it quickly, asking me to follow him up a ramp or ascending corridor. I followed him closely, walking up this corridor at whose side extended a narrow conveyor belt, probably for the transport of heavy objects.

As if we were late for an appointment, Cyril walked rapidly, taking long strides, until we reached a level, metallic hall, with some projections and labyrinthine passageways leading elsewhere. I noticed an emblem in high relief, of a winged serpent holding an egg. From its mouth emerged three

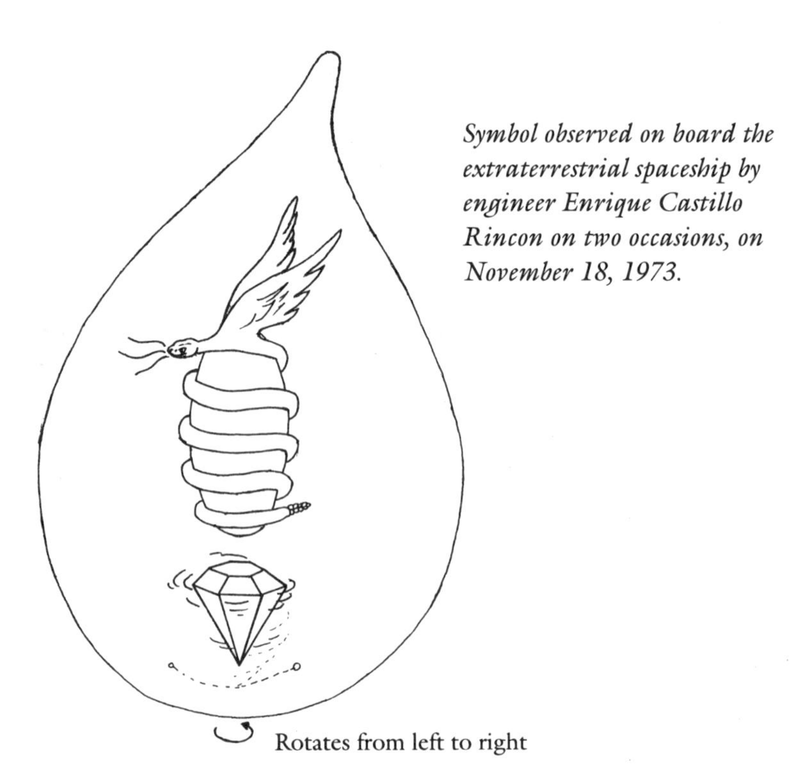

Symbol observed on board the extraterrestrial spaceship by engineer Enrique Castillo Rincon on two occasions, on November 18, 1973.

tongues, and its tail had nine rattles. The emblem was inside a "water drop," with a crystal or glass at its bottom.

"Enrique, wait!" Cyril advised me and left the hall, leaving me alone.

A metal table was at the center of the hall. Upon it was a variety of sample rocks, soils, sand, seeds, and fragments of vegetation. The samples were classified and separated by partitions and labeled by lettering or symbols utterly meaningless to me. In front of the table was a half-moon-shaped special chair, where I sat. It was built so that it could turn from side-to-side and also slide upon a track. A few minutes elapsed. Approaching steps were heard from a distance. The door opened, and with Cyril, four more beings arrived, including Krunula. I stood up to meet them.

At this moment I felt some discomfort and discreetly told Cyril that I needed to urinate. *"Come,"* said Cyril, and he led me to another room, separated by a full partition. We entered; Cyril explained to me the procedure and left me alone. Pushing a lever, something emerged from the wall with a "funnel," shaped like a lotus flower at its end. I urinated there and felt a suction or vacuum. An amber liquid carried away the waste, surely to disintegrate it. When done, a delicious scent emerged from the funnel. Upon leaving the room, the contraption disappeared back into the wall.

I returned to the hall, finding there another just-arrived character. He was a giant, at least three meters tall, and constantly smiling, mostly because of the size of his mouth. He just looked at me. I greeted him, and he bowed his head slightly, looking at me all the time. His features were remarkably similar to those of a common terrestrial. All was proportional in size. His skin was grayish, his hands, hairy, with normal fingers, shaped at the tips like spatulae. He dressed in a dull gray uniform, with military armbands on one side. Cyril was the only one who asked questions. The rest listened attentively. (I could not determine the language they spoke.)

"He comes from Jupiter, Enrique. There are great lakes there, made of water, such as your seas and lakes. Other lakes are of liquid methane. The inhabitants live in cities furnished with tremendous technology, which makes them very safe. They are not the only ones who live there, because there are other races, also. But they all live in peace, having overcome certain ancestral 'frictions.' This race comes specifically from a satellite moon, where we also have bases. Thus, I can tell you that there are two inhabited satellites."

I perceived a certain methane-like smell and realized that it emanated from the giant's skin. I don't know how Cyril communicated with the Jovian native. There was only an exchange of looks, and a strange muttering.

I took from my shirt pocket a "Parker" pen and a piece of paper with questions from members of our earthly group, and jotted down a question. Cyril called my attention and asked for the pen. He took it in his hands and passed it to the rest of the group, who studied it carefully and methodically, taking it apart fully. In their language with many Z and S sounds, they talked about it, perhaps about its operation. Cyril intercepted their thoughts, because he immediately took my ballpoint pen and explained something that I could not understand. He then asked me to look for a strange sheet of transparent plastic in one of the table drawers.

Once I had located that, he had me pick up something like a little tube joined to a thin flexible cable, perhaps twelve or thirteen centimeters long, and twelve millimeters in diameter. I looked at it from all sides, trying to decipher it, until Cyril came to my rescue, calling my attention to its tip. Pressing, I felt a slight vibration in my hand. *"Enrique, draw whatever you want to,"* said Cyril.

"I am not good at drawing," I answered.

"It doesn't matter; draw for instance the house where you lived as a child."

"No, Cyril, I had better draw a butterfly." I drew the first few lines with the strange pen, which ended in a little sphere. I was astonished! On the paper appeared a full color, well-defined butterfly, just as I had imagined it.

It was incredible; the little pen interpreted my thoughts with astounding fidelity. And it was not a common drawing; it was three-dimensional. My hand had only to touch the wondrous pen against the "paper." Cyril and his friends were smiling and curious, myself surprised. They gave me back the Parker, and I proceeded to read one of the questions.

"Cyril, is it true that on the same orbit of the Earth, on the opposite side of the sun, there is a twin planet like the Earth?" This question had arrived at a newspaper in the capital, sent by a person who claimed to have contacts with inhabitants from this twin planet.

"No, Enrique, that planet does not exist. Your solar system had thirteen planets. One of them disappeared as a result of two great wars long ago. You know the remnants as the 'Asteroid Belt.' The last and farthest planet, number thirteen, is dark and cold. It is the place where those who have failed repeatedly during their reincarnations go. Murderers, thieves, corrupts, death dealers (those who promote wars) will suffer there the corresponding punishments at the hands of others similar to them, of the same kind or 'vibration.' Until they learn their lesson, they will stay there; then they will have another chance. But not only the inhabitants of the Earth suffer such an experience. People from other places within the solar systems go there too. It is what you call hell, but it is just an inferior planet."

Cyril was always very precise and answered my questions directly. "Cyril, the information about the upcoming war caused a big stir in my group. Can I give more information about it?"

"You will find the right moment to do it; in the meanwhile, I shall try to be more specific about it. The great war will be preceded by a shorter one, which will

leave open wounds for the big one. At first, no nuclear weapons will be used. All will happen while peace talks are underway, and a beginning of agreement will have been found. But there will be a TRAITOR. A small, unimportant conflict, perhaps in the East, will become uncontrollable and will fire the detonator involving the so-called big powers. Politicians and governments will not think about the consequences derived from their intransigence and little contact with the reality of facts."

"And how should we prepare?"

"There will be a period of grace for humanity. It is the time corresponding to your wrong chronology. You have a long period of time in error. This somehow has served to 'protect' the prophecies, making them difficult to place in time.[1] *These years will serve to attenuate the conflict and help some be better prepared. Pay much attention to environmental changes, the ozone layer, the weakness of your leaders, and their lack of credibility,*[2] *the loss of religious values, which the 'religious' claim to have, the growth of crime, and the lack of countermeasures against it. No government on earth will be able to win the battle against crime and insecurity; this will be obvious. Yes, Enrique, all of this fills the heart with anguish, and the spirit suffers. I am sorry. It is the truth!"*

Cyril kept talking, while I felt a deep sadness and unrest. *"After the war there will be REMNANTS. At these places, thousands of people will survive the effects, not only of radiation, but of other parallel hazards. Thus, humanity, with its power and dominant zeal, will cause much destruction, and a change in the earth's rotation axis. Climatic changes will occur in many countries, making life difficult."* At this moment, Cyril interrupted the conversation, called by the others. They exchanged words in an unintelligible language. With a concerned countenance, he turned to me and asked, *"Enrique, what would you do if we told you that you were going to die with your family, at a certain time and place?"*

"Cyril, I would avoid passing by such a place and fight the circumstances predicting our death!"

"That is the correct answer! In this way, Enrique, we are warning you by all means at our disposal, and we expect that some souls, afraid of the destruction of their brothers, will react correctly and try to save their lives. A spirit will flow over many people at the right time, carrying a leadership born inside them, so they will know what to do of significance for all. They will act with great self-assurance, and people will trust them.

"Dear Enrique, we must make something clear. Do not believe that you will have our protection. We cannot give it, to you or anybody else. The best protection is the one the individual gives himself, according to his way of facing problems. This information may serve others who wonder about the protection that we are supposed to give. We don't."

"Brother, are you going to intervene in these events?"

"We cannot intervene directly. There are several reasons, and we have been quite strict about it. We can subtly implant ideas in some people's minds, placed in certain positions."

"What about all that pain, misery, and sadness? Where will it all end? Can't you give us the key points to improve the situation?"

"I repeat again, we cannot intervene; we must not do so. In spite of our efforts, there are many who, with their words and actions, misdirect many of the truth seekers."

"But can't you show up more often, more frequently, in the eyes of the people? Or at least initiate a direct contact with the leaders of the planet?"

"Enrique, we will answer these questions for you in some other way. Come, follow me."

We returned to the same place where the small scout ship was parked. Now another one was there, of the same size and shape. We entered the control room through the transparent dome, and then I felt an invisible force project the ship through the ramp and open hatch, into the darkness outside. Slowly, very slowly, we moved toward some unknown destination. The stars speckled the dome with hundreds of bright points of light. Through the observation "window," sort of a lengthened TV screen, I could see the flagship receding into the distance.

We were: the two Mercurians, Cyril, and myself. I estimated that it might be about 5:00 a.m. We descended to the first level of the ship, to the observation cabin.

"Enrique, we are going to answer your first question, why we do not contact people in general. Watch carefully."

The ship descended slowly (I was still wearing the space suit). It flew over a ranch, where some people were milking cows. Two cowhands were behind a large barn, milking two cows tied to the corral fence. We flew at about 300 meters altitude, according to Cyril, so that they could now see us. As soon as they detected our presence, they ran away, very scared, to hide in a hut located near the stable. The cows, very scared, also ran away, breaking their ropes and kicking the milk containers. Other animals in the corral also became very nervous, sensing something unusual. From the hut emerged first a dog and then three men. A woman followed, wiping her hands with her apron, and an eight-year-old boy. All looked at the sky, pointing to where we were. Hidden, or rather camouflaged, by a cloud, we watched the people moving. My first question had been answered! I reflected that perhaps man has not yet reached the stage for extraterrestrial contact. An idea flashed through my mind, and with it I tried to justify the attitude of the rural workers, ignorant and illiterate.

Cyril must have read my mind, for he said, *"Now we will experiment with city folks."* We moved away from the ranch towards a road with a lot of traffic of trucks, mainly, loaded with cattle, food, and materials in general. We let them pass unaffected. Then we saw a jeep, but it wasn't suitable for Cyril's purposes, either. We finally spotted a luxury automobile, speeding along the road. This was our objective. The driver was a man of about thirty-five, chatting in a lively manner with another man sitting in the front seat. Both, wearing their ties loose, were city people.

A third man slept on the back seat. We swooped down in the direction of the car, trying to show our peaceful intentions. The driver of the car turned sharply to one side of the road, leaving the car stuck in the ditch. The two men in the front opened the car doors and ran away looking for cover. The third one woke up, surprised, and watched the other two running cross country without understanding why. He opened the door and looked up, half scared and half baffled. We kept looking down from a 200-meter altitude. When he saw us, he ran away also, through the fence, tearing his clothing on the barbed wire. The three, yelling, hid in the bush. They looked at us, excited, without understanding our presence.

We moved away. Cyril, at my side, looked at me and asked, *"How do you like it? What do you say now?"*

"People's reactions to the unknown are incredible," I said. "Those individuals are city people, with a different cultural level. . . . I understand now why you cannot scare people just to show them that you exist. Besides, that would not be the way to make contact with us. We need a well-conceived education of our own, which is already underway, in fact."

"Enrique, we are going to answer the other question, as to why we don't contact directly the leaders and government heads of the earth? Wait a little longer." Silently, and without any sensation of movement, we headed at moderate speed and great height towards an unknown destination. It was daytime, and the sun's rays impinged on the metal surfaces of the craft, striking beautiful colors. I failed to look around at the observation cabin, perhaps because of my thoughts, which were in a turmoil.

Cyril had left the room, and when he returned about ten minutes later, he called my attention to the screen. The African continent was clearly visible, identical to pictures taken from satellites. The position of the sun surprised me. When we had left the stunned travelers, it was on one side. Now it was on the opposite side. Cyril explained that in this part of the planet it was afternoon, and then he changed the subject: *"Every year end, the leaders talk about lovely things, referring to human rights, and especially to children, and to hunger around the world. They formulate plans to end those ugly scars, and fill the hearts of the people with hope. But, the sad reality is different. Look at the observation screen, and think about what we mean!"*

In an African country that I could not identify, a village, lost in a semi-desert plain, presented a somber look. A long line of women, children, and old people waited for handouts, a few loaves of bread, and other staples. Children with their swollen bellies were eating some of the food, while swarms of flies crawled over their bodies and faces. Pregnant women looked absentmindedly at their offspring, debilitated by hunger.

At an ambulance of the Red Cross International, two doctors and two nurses attended the sick, vaccinating them and giving them a ration. The line was respected, thanks to the help of some members of the army, who once in a while raised their weapons to maintain order. All was in desolation and ruin. The wind blew dust into the bodies and faces of these defenseless Negroes. Some scrawny elderly, helped by their relatives, waited to be attended. I observed their heads carefully, where some disease unknown to me had produced whitish and bloody ulcers.

The picture was very sad and depressing. Cyril added, *"The spiritual and political leaders, not only of Africa, but of the whole world, take advantage of this situation, basing their promises on clear examples such as this one you have just seen. We do not contact those we don't trust—people who raise the flag of peace and understanding, when their purpose is just the opposite, concerned with only their power and prestige."*

We observed all from within a cloud, with everything plainly visible. The sun was setting in the west, the huge red ball seemingly burning everything. It was a somber sunset.

Cyril's speech, serene but open and frank, was terrifying. He made no effort to lessen the effect of his words. He spoke the truth, explaining step by step his unassailable arguments about the planet's situation.

"Sooner or later you will vanquish this situation," he said.

"Cyril, when will that sooner or later be?"

"I don't know for sure; it depends on many factors. It is true that many men and organizations have become aware, pressing the governments for more tangible solutions, especially regarding education. They fight for the establishment of effective birth control. But they face the opposition of the caste system in the more backward countries, and of deeply engraved religious dogmas. This blocks the short-term solutions. Only the inherent need for human development will alleviate these problems by means of reasonable solutions.

"Governments will have to reach agreements with the religious organizations, in order to avoid a shock in the human psyche, concerning education, population planning, and birth control.[3] *This way, the whole planet will benefit."*

Cyril, with complete knowledge of world politics, explained thoroughly the relationships among the political systems of the world. To be honest, I couldn't grasp much. My knowledge is limited, and I have never liked to get involved in such matters. Cyril knew this, but he kept talking on the subject. "Which is the best political system to solve injustice and chaos in the world?"

"None, Enrique, is going to survive."

He didn't say it in so many words, but he was final. This would include communism, capitalism, and all other political systems.

"The same will happen to all religions, although it will take some time. Eventually, people will learn to get rid of the straps that bind them to specific religious groups and organizations, which now enslave them. Many years will elapse, but it will happen eventually. Actually, these events, some of them bound to happen soon, make up a necessary chain, needed to accelerate human evolution. Many people will die during the changes; many animal species will disappear. People will fight in the cities, looking for food and survival."

In a subsequent chapter I will explain in detail how these events will take place, according to my extraterrestrial hosts. Now the ship was traveling again. We were returning. Through the window, I saw water and more water. The sea, a deep blue, stimulated my imagination, directing it to the infinite horizon. If our trip to Africa took about ten minutes, on the way back it took about twenty, until we found ourselves above South American territory. Along the way, Cyril pointed to a flying object, a commercial passenger plane!

After the sea, came the jungle, which extended for hundreds of kilometers. We were flying very high. I recalled Cyril's words two weeks ago, on November 3, when he talked about the way they took their food from the trees and stored the chlorophyll to process later. According to them, the best and most nutritious plants are here in South America, because its variety permits selecting different tastes. As far as I know, the Pleiadeans do not eat animal meat, only certain kinds of seafood, delicious and highly nutritious. We had entered the Amazon jungle. I could see the rivers and some clearings, because now we were flying at a lower altitude and a slower pace. This made the trip more interesting.

I still could not understand the reasons for my encounter. Being a common citizen, without power or influence, with a common way of life until these encounters, I could not fathom my role in this confusing drama. Aside from traveling in a flying saucer together with two Mercurians and my friend from the Pleiades, my life was meaningless. At least, that's how I assessed it. Besides, being a unique experience, nobody would believe me.

I was at a critical crossroads. They had warned me about a Third World War, the shifting of the axis, and other disasters, but I was sure that no one would take this news seriously. They constantly stressed the impossibility of open intervention in our domestic affairs. Even so, they talked to me as if I were an old friend. They said that I knew the reason for all of this, while the truth is, the matter was utterly obscure for me. But there was a feeling that united me to Cyril, deeper than simple friendship. I considered him like a brother . . . it was a very deep feeling. It was the feeling of someone you have known for a long time, through facing an adverse situation together, with the will to help each other.

It may be a fantasy, but Cyril was like my brother in time and space. Not even the members of the group grasped the real significance of this collective experience, because today, years afterwards, we are separated, both physically and spiritually. I was alone then, and I am still alone!

The conversations with my otherworldly friends, instead of clarifying my thoughts, were making them darker and darker. That is why, even for me, it is difficult to rebuild the exact sense of their words, but I struggle to convey the ideas that they tried to give me while aboard their ships, and also during the almost 100 telepathic sessions during the exhausting meetings of the group. I was not protected or guided; it was left to my own judgment as to how to describe all the details of the experience.

The scout ship was gliding smoothly over the South American jungle. In a clearing, an Indian hamlet became visible. I looked to Cyril at this moment, but he did not pay attention. He was also thinking.

"Enrique," he said, *"this is not the last time that we will see each other. We still have to give you something important that you can unveil when you think it is appropriate. But remember that you will have no backing or help from us."*

"Cyril, do you see often these jungle tribes?"

"Yes, we do, but up until now we have not been in contact with them."

"But how is it possible that you do not act, giving them some motivation to improve their lot?"

"Only once we intervened with this kind of primitive society. It was a long time ago, maybe forty years, when we evacuated from this planet thirty-eight people from an Eskimo group. The majority were starving oldsters, who would have died in all certainty, without our help. The young had abandoned their elders, looking for jobs at the new oil wells. As you well know, the Eskimo's livelihood is based on hunting and fishing, and barter of skins with some hunters of those regions. It was a necessary intervention; without our help, they would have died."

Actually, this answer involves a contradiction. They helped the Eskimo, but refused to help the jungle tribes, which didn't make sense to me. I had no other alternative than asking him directly his judgment about humankind.

"Cyril, what is your basic thinking about this whole matter?"

As if he had been expecting my question, immediately and without any consideration, plainly he answered, *"Mankind is the Law. For Mankind and by Mankind the habitable worlds have been created, and all that exists in them is to be used by Mankind. He can control the forces of Nature, as long as he acts with wisdom, and knows and respects the laws that rule it. Everything can be controlled by Man, Man is the Law, and the Law is the Supreme Universal Harmony. I don't mean the earthly man, I mean the Man of the Universe. Man is the synthesis of the Universe. The Beginning and End of everything. When he disappears, the Universe will be gone, too. All Universal Wisdom is contained in Man. He is the Code and the Key."*

With each one of these expressions, Cyril was showing me the difference between our logic and their logic. His was the correct one, I guess, although this is only my way of looking at it. We left the jungles behind, and once more the immense expanse of the *llanos* opened up. The panorama was quite impressive from above. Cyril stood up and left the room. One of the Mercurians entered, but he only smiled and looked at me, saying nothing. It was Cyril who gave me their messages and guided me. The Mercurian looked through the transom,[4] made a gesture, and left again.

From my seat, I could see comfortably through the window (which was more like an adjustable visor). A few minutes had elapsed, when Cyril came back. *"We are arriving at our Flagship. It is important that you see it at close range."*

We climbed to the dome in the control room. In the huge, transparent glass, we saw an opaque point that increased in size until it became the impressive Mother Ship. The approaching speed of our comparatively small scout ship seemed conducive to a sure impact. On the lower part of the huge whale, a ramp opened slowly. This coupling was completely different from that of our first trip. While entering, all controls in our small craft were off. A strong suction or pull controlled our direction and speed. It seemed that on board the scout ship, nothing operated. Cyril and the Mercurians watched the maneuver attentively, quite impassively.

During the whole trip I didn't feel any movement, but now, a rhythmic swaying was noticeable. A mild electric shock was felt. I could see in the rear end of the machine some gigantic straight tubes, whose purpose I could not deduce. *"Enrique, with these ships, we carry out a cleaning operation in this zone."* The scout ship, perfectly directed, landed softly in a very large hangar, where other machines were parked.

"Are you feeling well? Have you felt some strange sensations?" asked Cyril. I nodded.

"It will last only a minute. It is the electromagnetic field exerted over this ship." Certainly, my body felt sort of a dizziness, but it lasted only a minute.

I already knew the way towards the room where we first stopped, and we moved rapidly in this direction. In the room, the same "people" were awaiting us. The conversation started once more. About ten minutes later, a sliding door opened. A strange character walked in, about sixty centimeters tall, with a very large head with impressive-looking brain convolutions visible. Instead of a skull, he had at some portions something transparent, like crystal. His eyes protruded, and he walked with a peculiar gait, swaying from side to side, like an automaton. His shoulders tapered into a triangular backand a narrow waist. For the first time, at the moment when I could see his back, I noticed a strange symbol on it. All turned their heads, and there was silence for a while. This strange character walked out through another door and was lost from sight, without any explanation. He was kind of a robot, but with some human features. I thought I understood that they made it appear in order for me to be familiar with it.

We returned to the conversation. It should be mentioned that no notes were allowed; all had to be memorized. As the talk continued, I coughed frequently to clear my throat. They, with curiosity, looked at Cyril, and he asked me, *"Have your tonsils been taken out?"*

"Yes, in 1968."

"You shouldn't have permitted it. They are essential for the health of the body."

It was too late for this advice. They were out, and nothing could be done. All smiled, and Cyril especially, with his open smile, must have found my tonsillectomy rather funny. The rest, with more subtle smiles, also expressed some surprise.

During this pleasant interlude, when I felt relaxed and at ease, I heard a door opening. What emerged was one of the most impacting visions I could have in the ship. Two women entered the conference room. I remembered that during my first trip I had thought of the possibility of women living aboard the cosmic ships, and "they" read my mind and answered affirmatively. Now the moment had arrived. Their golden hair framed the most beautiful faces that I had ever seen. How envious Goya or Da Vinci would have felt! As tall as the men, perhaps 1.75 meters, they swayed their incredibly beautiful bodies while walking. They approached our table, but nobody stood up, as if gentlemanly manners did not exist.

One of them turned towards me, and with rather poor Spanish pronunciation, greeted me, *"Good day, Enrique. . . ."*

"Sister, good day, how are you?"

She answered with a slight bow of her head. She leaned on the edge of the table where the samples were kept. Her expression was very human and feminine. She balanced one of her legs on the other, showing her shapely thigh. Her tight-fitting dress showed the shape of her bosom. The other girl

was standing a little distance away, with her back in our direction, her splendid hair shining. Straight, very straight, it made strange loops, passed through "military type" clasps on her shoulders, and fell intertwined almost to her waist. Really, it was very charming. I discerned, in her manners, the wish to please and be friendly. I had the idea that such feminine charm was exclusive to our terrestrial women, but these astronauts from the Pleiades were proving the opposite. They stayed with us for two or three minutes. Then, with a slight bow, they disappeared through the sliding doors.

My hosts showed me things in a subtle manner, as if filling in gaps for me that they detected constantly. Their explanation of human evolution on Earth was unforgettable, starting with the terrifying conflagration to take place in the near future.

"The cup has overflowed, Enrique. There is no way back. Unfortunately, the more alert spirits, who will detect the upcoming preliminary changes, will not be

believed; to the contrary, they will be ridiculed. An incident will take place in the Orient that will have resonance at the diplomatic level, then extend to Europe, and then to Asia. It is quite possible that this could be avoided, thanks to the good judgment of two Latin men. This probably will take place when safer peace treaties are signed, and men will feel safer and protected.

"One of the signals for identification of these times will be when several Latin American countries will be almost bankrupt and will dare to protest. The world money lenders will take advantage of them mercilessly and will force their conditions upon them. This will not take many years. All, absolutely all the political and religious organizations will collapse."

I felt unable to answer, and cold. Cyril looked at me, to see my reaction to these predictions.

"How is it possible that these events will happen here?" I inquired, incredulous, thinking that perhaps they would not materialize, or not happen after all.

"The future is very unstable, Enrique. It changes with the actions of men and the decisions of countries. That is why I said 'possibly.' We have to stay alert!" Step by step, they sketched the complicated web of difficulties that to an extent would affect them also.

"The struggle is not only among you. We are also directly involved. We are trying hard to surpass THE OTHER FORCE, against which we struggled for a long time in OUR OWN LAND. The 'other organization,' like ourselves, is also extraterrestrial. We belong to the Great Cosmic Solar Brotherhood, to which you, sooner or later, will have to adhere. In so doing, you will obtain all the benefits and prerogatives from organizations similar to ours, allowing a closer relationship with these 'advanced societies' from other planets. This struggle I am mentioning has been moved to your own land. What happens is that you did not notice how this subtle invasion occurred, being persuaded that you were alone in the Universe.

"This was fatal! You never suspected an 'enemy that did not exist,' and these undesirable extraterrestrial visitors took advantage of that. Many governments believe that the enemy is here on Earth. The same happens with religions. But this force, which has subdued several societies and planets, IS HERE NOW! We the Pleiadeans confront the enemy; we never ignore it, because we are aware of their tricks and how they act.

"Enrique, the knowledge of evil leads the individual to confrontation with himself, to line up with the right side, the only way to vanquish the opponent. We did it and have vanquished! The ignorant or fanatic believe that ignoring the existence of evil can win, but if they do not know the enemy, they cannot protect themselves. The terrestrial history is saturated with this struggle to prevail. Do not underestimate it; they can surprise you."

While listening to Cyril speak, I was perplexed. How would I convince leaders and governments to listen? I was not qualified, and besides lacked the bravery to undertake a world crusade to alert humanity. Who would help me? What means did I have at my disposal? Add to this that many people say I am insane. Doubtless, I thought, I need proofs. That way I might dare to face the public and people in general.

During this second encounter, I had the chance to meet two additional races, the Mercurians, and the being from Jupiter. I would become acquainted with a third one a few months later, in 1974. I now had been without sleep for several hours and felt very hungry. Without my asking for it, they offered me manna, and the effect was instantaneous; my hunger disappeared. A pleasant warmth spread throughout my body, and I felt fortified but very sleepy.

"I feel very tired and would like to sleep," I told them. "How long will you keep me here in this ship, brothers?"

"We can drop you at any place close to a road, whenever you like. As far as resting, you can do it here in the ship." They took me to a room containing at least thirty beds, made of a vitreous material, with comfortable blankets. Cyril was again in charge of explaining certain things about the operation of these comfortable beds. Inside them, at the right side and within reach of one's hands, were some buttons and LEDs, which controlled an oscillatory movement, and light intensity. I even thought about patenting them. How soft and comfortable they were! They were about 1.20 meters wide and two meters long. Cyril walked the length of the room with me, to help me feel at ease. When we arrived at the end, in front of a dark glass door, Cyril pressed a button on its left side, and the door opened, revealing an individual cubicle. Suddenly, a "capsule-bed" appeared, and Cyril offered it to me.

"When you go to bed, you can take off the uniform, or you can sleep in it." I noticed that there were no sharp ninety-degree intersections between the roof and the walls; all were rounded.

"Don't worry, Cyril, I plan to sleep about three hours; it won't be necessary to take it off." Cyril smiled, amused, and left rapidly, after telling me that he would wake me up at the right moment. The dark crystal door closed, and I found myself alone in the cubicle. It was illuminated by a golden light that did not bother me at all. In front of me, hanging from a wall, was a picture of a strange, winged animal, ending like a snake. It resembled the dragons of mythology, with wings similar to a bat's, and a terrifying appearance. Its greenish color, not repulsive, was its main feature. My eyelids were heavy, and I soon fell asleep.

I was awakened after about nine hours. Cyril was again to guide me to receive more information. During all this second experience, I had the chance to ask questions. One of them I directed to Commander Kramier from the

Pleiades. I was feeling a little depressed and anguished after listening to such stern explanations and arguments. At the first opportunity, I asked him, "Brother Commander Kramier, (he smiled), when do you believe peace will arrive at the planet, and can you intervene or help us in some way?"

At this point he told me that it was preferable not to call them "brothers," that it was better to address them by their names. I agreed with a nod, accepting the advice. He continued, *"Peace on your planet does not depend on us or your avatars. In essence, it depends on how you apply the knowledge that we already gave you."*

No doubt, he referred to the millenary teachings contained in the sacred books of all religions of the world, the papyri, the Ancient Books, and the oral tradition of all peoples. Kramier assured me that there was no place in the world where those teachings had not been distributed. In the course of time, they have been promoted also by means of Great Instructors of humanity. Stopping briefly to catch his breath, seeing the impact on me of what I had just heard, the Commander also took a break, while watching me very closely. I asked another question that was choking me. For many years I had rejected the notion that we humans were descended from apes, or from a common ancestor. I disliked the idea but lacked a solid answer. The moment to ask had arrived.

"Commander Kramier, what is your personal opinion, or your opinion in general, about the teaching that we are direct descendants from apes?" With a certain shyness I looked at the Commander's face, expecting an answer that would unsettle most of humanity. The answer was complete and devastating!

"One of the great mistakes of your civilization has been to classify Man as a 'rational animal,' *lowering him to the level of the beasts. If you could grasp the principles of His creation, you would comprehend then that Man, within the scope of His Life, can degrade himself to the animal level, or* ***upgrade himself to the level of the Gods."***

Listening to such a statement, my soul, which was anguished, made me feel a Man once more. More confident, I asked, "How and by whom can we prove that we are not alone in the Universe?"

"Scientists and wise men on Earth should already take for granted the existence of intelligent life on other planets. The great majority knows well that there are very good reports on 'sightings' of ships, called flying saucers or UFOs, by reliable and respectable witnesses, who have been ridiculed, slandered, vexed, and forced to shut up, to maintain the belief that you are alone in the Universe. The miserly minds of some politicians and organizations have profited by this forced silence, capitalizing in their favor on the time factor, in order to obtain superior technology and progress never dreamed of before, through investigations in genetic

engineering and medicine. Some governments, military, and scientific groups have already achieved considerable progress in this direction."

I interrupted him at this point, "How, without anybody knowing? To me, it seems difficult to keep secret!"

"Yes, Enrique, the details and particulars of certain events that originated several years ago, have stayed occult. I will inform you only in a general way. Some 'crashes' of 'explorer ships' belonging to other races have taken place here on Earth, from where the lifeless bodies were extracted. On other occasions, living crew members have been captured and kept captive by the military of some of your governments, and subjected to merciless interrogations, forcing them to reveal formulae and knowledge on several scientific specialties. This could be all right if humankind were ready to access superior knowledge that could benefit all peoples, but IT IS NOT SO.

"Man, through his multi-staged process of evolution, and by natural curiosity and investigative spirit, has manifested in various forms his desire to discover new frontiers; it is as if something propelled him to obtain answers to the riddles that have concerned all races of the Earth. This drive or compulsion is GENETIC, and as such it generates an unquenchable thirst for answers. For this reason, when Humankind reaches THE KNOWLEDGE OF THE LAW, as never before Man will have the values to handle the superior knowledge that will lead him, first, to self-knowledge, and second, will open the way to the Stars.

"Furthermore, Enrique, terrestrial scientists should realize that developments such as exist on Earth in the fields of electronic technology, computers, medicine, genetic engineering, and science in general does not normally develop in such a short time. Therefore, it must be imported."

Here, I interrupted him again to ask another question that was pressing in my mind. But his dissertation interested me so much that I begged him to excuse me and go ahead with it.

He continued, *"It is said that interstellar trips are impossible. The narrow minds among your scientists only blunt the wholesome development of intelligence. They have subdued humanity and robbed it of its spirit of self-improvement. The imagination has been blocked. This has contributed to what the religions around the world have done.*

"You should know, Enrique, that there are inter-spatial tunnels of 'plancton' energy, which are detected by our ships and utilized for their displacement, at speeds inconceivable to your scientists. This depends, of course, on the type of craft used, because our science and technology has permitted us to develop systems that are utterly fantastic. This is one of the reasons why, in the past, our presence on Earth was taken as visits 'from the Gods.' Our presence here on this planet will not be revealed openly until after the end of the present century."

As time elapsed, I felt uneasy, trying to determine how late it was, since my watch, same as the first time, was dead. I was getting ready to leave, and this time they would drop me near Bogotá. They asked me to return the uniform, as well as the boots. Cyril, laughing, in a jolly mood, told me that perhaps some day he would give me one of those uniforms, as a souvenir of the trips. At this time, he gave me to understand that I was not the only visitor to their ships.

We said goodbye quickly to the other crew members, who seemed pressed to take care of other business. Cyril, aware that the time to end the trip had arrived, escorted me to the scout ship, which was parked inside the great ship, with the Mercurians waiting for us. We boarded the scout ship, and we felt a movement when the door closed and the ladder was retracted. A powerful mechanism took hold of the scout ship, brought it to the slanted take-off ramp, where a great hatch had opened, and projected us into empty space.

The beautiful and swift craft approached a well-traveled road, where I could get transportation to Bogotá. The area chosen for the landing had many trees (pines and eucalyptus). I was positive that this was north of Bogotá. In fact, the place was only about 500 meters from a road to La Caro, a small town. The ship landed softly behind a clump of trees. We said goodbye very warmly.

"So long, my friend; give my regards to the group!" Cyril shook my hands.

"Where are the rest of your companions?"

"They are upstairs, Enrique."

"Give them my regards, Cyril." With a pleasant smile, Cyril reciprocated. We shook hands again, and I tapped him on his right shoulder.

"God bless you, Cyril!" He just smiled. I descended rapidly and walked to the nearby road, waving to them. The legs retracted, the door closed, and the ship took off at great speed, allowing me to see it for the last time as "a pearl in the sky," far, far away.

The day was breaking. I walked with confidence and jumped two times, with my fists clenched, exultant! I uttered a tremendous yell, as of victory: "Yaaaaggghhhhh!"

In less than one hour, the road would be full of traffic.

This is how my second encounter with the extraterrestrials ended. I had been with them for approximately twenty-six hours.

Chapter Notes

[1] Apparently, our system of time or chronology has some errors.

[2] As exists today.

[3] This has begun to take place, at least in Peru, where president Fujimori had to face the Catholic church, issuing a decree for birth control and sexual education, in late 1995.

[4] A round opening.

10

From Mystery to Mystery

"Therefore, the idea that Extraterrestrial Men visited the Earth a long time ago, with the purpose of establishing a colony and creating a hybrid man, becomes the most likely theory to explain the origin of man on Earth."
—MAX H. FLINDT and OTTO O. BINDER,
Humanity, Daughter of the Stars

As soon as I arrived in Bogotá, I reported to the group about this second encounter. Like the preceding encounter experience, I described, quite briefly, fragments of the events of November 18. Even without injuring or attacking anyone, incredulity grew by leaps and bounds, due to the lack of human logic of my story. Also, as before, they expected one version, and I told them another. Still, nobody posed questions in order to dispel doubts, which were normal under such unusual circumstances. Only at the end, first Richard, and then Marjorie, with certain reticence, attempted some superficial questioning.

I received the strong impression that they were not fully conscious of the group's collective experience. However, we had received firm assurance about the need for our own spiritual self-improvement, with the help of the "Illuminated Masters." This was the objective of the communications. From this moment on, the telepathic messages became frequent. The group discipline included meetings twice a week, on Tuesdays and Fridays, the most convenient for all. These meetings were held from 8:00 to 10:00 p.m. The ETs had requested us to be ready in plenty of time, usually fifteen minutes ahead. To start with, we took our accustomed places and then practiced relaxation and concentration for five minutes. We sat in a semicircle, in complete silence, and paid attention to whomever directed the practice.

The meeting place was usually at the Deeb's. The room was placed in complete darkness, except for a weak reflection from a street lamp through the window, and a well-shaded, small light bulb, to reduce interference with concentration. Each one had an ample supply of paper and pencils. During the early times, Karen acted as director, but when she left, any one of us assumed the direction of the exercises. It became a rather mechanical matter to do them properly.

Standing about one meter from each other, we started the breathing exercises by joining both hands at the height of the navel (solar plexus), inhaling deeply, and lifting the hands slowly up to the chin, and then separating and raising them up with the fingers well stretched, resembling antennae. Karen said that this way we could capture "cosmic energy." With our hands up, we held our breath during four heartbeats. Then we lowered our fingers, rigid, touching them over our heads, exhaling during another four heartbeats. We repeated six times this breathing exercise, four heartbeats to inhale, two for retaining or holding in the air, and four for exhaling. During the intervals, we rubbed our hands vigorously to charge them with energy. At the end of the exercises, we sat at our places, closed our eyes, and put our legs together in a comfortable position. Our hands, palms facing upwards, rested on our knees. After a few minutes, the communication began. We sat alternately, men and women. I always sat with my front towards the north and my back to the south. Months later, in 1974, we were given a code word to identify the group. It was a fortifying and relaxing routine. Only during the first two meetings did I suffer any headache. Later, this effect disappeared completely.

The headaches were accompanied by strong shivers all over my body. Later, I achieved complete control over these sensations. It is fitting to add that I no longer fell into the unconscious mediumship of the first two instances. I was fully conscious, to the point of keeping my eyes open while receiving the messages. We called it conscious telepathy.

Around the end of November, 1973, a MASTER OF WISDOM appeared. I gave him this name because he never identified himself. We also used to call him Knowledge Master. His messages were always mystical, with neat, clear teachings, very easy to understand. In his messianic style, the Master of Wisdom invited us to maintain good relationships with fellow men. His teachings in the moral field were thought-provoking. He placed continuous emphasis on maintaining a clear mind and on staying united as a group while the communications lasted.

Once in a while, we changed the meeting place from the Deeb's to Marjorie's home, or to the apartment on 31st Avenue and 11th Street. By the beginning of December, Karen had returned from Cali with a lady by the name of Cecilia, who had well-recognized paranormal capabilities. With their help, we were able to get in touch with beings from Venus. These gave their names as Febo, Baros, Rondi, and finally Orhion and Yamaruck. Febo spoke first. With a certain "sweetness" but also with energy, he introduced the group to which he belonged. His words lasted fifteen minutes. Then Orhion took the initiative. It is hard to explain, but his monologues saturated the atmosphere with a mysterious energy, blocking any movement that could disturb the delivery of the message. This affected us deeply, to the extent of making us unable to react in a coordinated fashion. The talk, mystical throughout, was speckled with prophetic warnings. Lastly, Commander Yamaruck delivered his message to the group with various reports.

Eventually, Orhion became the main speaker for the majority of the messages. His companions, once in a while, also transmitted their ideas. The meetings might typically be started by Krishnamerck (Cyril Weiss) or Orhion. They never interrupted each other. Sometimes we noticed Cyril's prolonged absence, but a few days later he would be back with us. They always stressed that they belonged to the same organization previously mentioned. As if arranged beforehand, the extraterrestrial characters took turns speaking, with impressive coordination. The "Master of Wisdom" spoke a few times, always with complete command of the subjects. He went into further details on the optimal paths or freedoms of choice for human beings in their evolution. In a similar way, but in his personal style, SAO from the Pleiades also delivered his version.

The technique for communication was always the same. Only months later did we receive a code "key" for the group, whose object was our identification at the time of the communications. All, after the breathing exercises, were to repeat in a low tone, but with force and rhythm, the words "ANZALA POTALA." At the same time, we should keep together the index fingers and thumbs of both hands, keeping the rest of the fingers extended, palms up. The mantra had to be repeated for three seconds, without interruptions. Several times the communication snapped in instantly upon pronouncing the mantra, forcing us to receive while sitting in the chairs.

By then I began to suspect whether the communications were telepathic or not. I could listen to several voices at the same time. According to what I knew, telepathy involves a single voice at a time, regardless of the origin of the messages. I could distinguish quite clearly the presence of each speaker. It was easy to recognize Cyril, Orhion, or the Master of Wisdom.

Each one's mien and tone of voice, either loving or authoritarian, left no doubt as to the originator of the communications. Another interesting point was the way I tuned in to the voices. If, after ten or fifteen minutes at a certain location, no reception was possible, then I moved my head to the right or the left, and good reception could be achieved. If I then moved slightly, it faded, forcing me to stay exactly at the right location and position. It was the same technique applicable to a transistor radio, when relocating or orienting the antenna to achieve good reception.

A long while afterwards, and due to other experiences of the members of the group, I arrived at the following conclusion: The extraterrestrials were transmitting by means of sophisticated "radio" equipment, tuned to my brain waves. They could interfere with them and send messages. In January 1974, we were told about the Venusians' mission on Earth. They were aboard two scout ships in Colombian territory, exploring jungles and mountains. They had left their Mothership somewhere near the South Pole.

The group of scientific explorers told us about the remarkable similarity between these areas of South America with their native planet. I could not understand how they could be Venusian, if "scientific data" from space probes, telescopes, etc., showed that there is NO LIFE on that planet. How could they tell us that they came from Venus? Was it a trick directed to some objective unknown to us? Were they watching our reactions to such statements? Anyhow, we accepted without protest such information. They never specified which were the similarities. Some of the crew members had already visited Planet Earth before, but for some this was the first time. They seemed to be investigating inaccessible locations—at present—where the "remnants" would live after fleeing the cities during the nuclear war.

In the "remnants," according to what they said, there would be plenty of drinking water, timber, abundant vegetation, and fertile soil, in areas not subject to flooding. Good climate was a rule for these regions. Because of their geological make up, they could lodge many people at the time of evacuation of the cities. They suggested, without saying it directly, that the future of the human race was at these areas. At the right moment, they would change to an ideal climate, which would last for thousands of years.

One of the members of the group, Pedro Avila, asked about the exact location of these areas. We did not expect a specific answer, but were surprised to receive the exact coordinates of ten remnants, out of the twelve planned by the extraterrestrials. We searched on a map, and all the locations matched old cities of the Inca Empire. According to them, the remnants will house people from all races and social levels. If by then people have not bridged the gaps between rich and poor, they would not be fit for acceptance in such places. The exact location of the remnants was pinpointed with great care by one of the scientists, by the name of Gnomo.

The Venusians continually gave moral teachings, which we confused with invitations to mysticism. That was one of our mistakes. Their words were sacred for all of us. Of course, the strength of their messages, and the context under which they were received, influenced us to interpret them spiritually. They always paid attention to our group, our actions, appreciations, and comments. Without using specific names, they referred to our collective daily behavior. Once, they criticized our vile expressions at the end of the meetings. Echoing our exact words, they repeated openly the inappropriate and double-meaning jokes we had used "to lift the spirits" at the end of the meetings. This truly offended them, and they were frank enough to tell us about it. The group misinterpreted the words of the extraterrestrials; still, they encouraged us all the time with data and concrete testimonies about their presence.

One of those encouragements was offered to the incredulous eyes of some of the members of the group at the end of December, 1973. As a sign of goodwill, our Greater Brothers planned to remove the smog from the atmosphere of Bogotá , which had been detected by them in great amounts. They planned to do it eight days after the announcement was made, from 10:30 a.m. to 1:00 p.m. They would surround the city with dark and low clouds, and an electric storm would take place, with rain and wind. The clouds would hide the ships. They advised us not to be afraid and to stay at home to watch the show. They said that we could make the announcement public, if we wished to do so.

I took the chance. This caused some fear on the part of some of the members of the group. I revealed the announcement to the same journalist who interviewed me on November 3. Alfonso Blanco and myself also visited the Weather Bureau, in order to request that readings be taken before and after the cleaning operation. That was also to serve as proof of the existence and reliability of the group. As expected, no information was obtained, and we had no way to justify our request. Tension grew during the days prior to the demonstration. Some did not take the matter seriously, making it more difficult for us.

Finally, the day arrived. With a certain disillusionment, we gazed out upon a most beautiful and clean sky, as befitted that time of the year. Nothing made us suspect a storm of any proportions whatsoever. The weather report announced no wind and a cloudless sky, with long-range visibility. At my office, I waited nervously, together with Alfonso, the unfoldment of the events. It was warm for Bogotá. My associates and some employees glared at me with malicious eyes. To alleviate the tension, I walked quickly about, taking care of professional and office business, but I could not control my inner fears. I looked out the windows at every opportunity, hoping to detect some sign of the expected events. No, the morning looked splendid, good for outdoor activities. I feared ridicule when the time arrived and nothing had happened. I would lose face in front of everyone.

By 10:30 in the morning, from the eastern side of the city, from over the mountains, a strong wind started to blow. Clouds, at a noticeable clip, invaded the sky, and what had been a sunny day, darkened ominously. Within fifteen minutes, the sky became completely overcast, and powerful lightning bolts and thunder echoed over the city, unleashing one of the strongest tempests of the last months. Rain poured, flooding the streets and forcing people to look for shelter. Standing by the window, I missed no detail of this incredible event. My friends, baffled but still incredulous, acknowledged my prediction and congratulated me in a festive mood. We were all happy. Our office was on the seventh floor. The phone started to ring insistently. The first one to call was Chela, who was happily drenched, because she stood in the rain at her home's patio, in front of her sister. We laughed heartily, making remarks about the whole event. Marjorie was the second to call; she told me she could not fully understand what had happened that day.

I went out to the street, to watch the wet faces of the people. I wondered for myself what would happen if they knew the origin of that rain? Three ships had provoked that sort of chaos. They had come from a base somewhere on this planet. They had had to "close" the city in order to hide the ships while they carried out the cleaning of the air by means of gigantic "aspirators," shaped by artificial energy channels, which removed the smog and carried it away towards the South Pole. I went to visit the office of Gloria Inés Ortiz, a member of the group. Upon arriving at Trametalco where she worked, I could see people desperately scooping water out from their homes, the result of one of the worst rainstorms lately. In her office, Gloria and I made remarks about the event. What would people think if they knew why it rained? This seemed rather funny. The rain stopped at 1:00 p.m. sharp, as announced a week before.

The extraterrestrials had fulfilled their announcements with exactitude. I now better understood the purpose of the gigantic rear tubes on the "Mothership." Richard Deeb called me in the afternoon, very happy about the fulfillment of the prophecy, and told me that the Masters had punished him with a tremendous drenching, since he had failed to take his umbrella, paying no attention to the announcements.

A few days after the storm, Karen left Bogotá for Mexico City, her hometown.

During one of the many meetings at the Deeb's, after twenty minutes of fruitless effort, a strange communication arrived. We wrote it down, without any abnormal incident. There was no identification this time, and after reading the message carefully, we inferred that it had come from "intruding extraterrestrials," totally unknown to us. At the end of the communication, they invited us to meet the next day to receive further information. No clear conclusions were reached that night; the mood was rather apprehensive, especially since we had been warned about the "contrary forces."

The message was as follows: *"The magnetic or psychic force accumulated by the group during the meetings is bad for a pregnant woman, after two months of pregnancy, not only for the fetus, but also for the mother. Now WE want to take important part in your meetings. We have been watching the contact manifestations. If you are ready and permit us, we will give you information in exchange for an experience. We are going to manifest to one of you. Do not react negatively, do not be afraid, because it is necessary that you know us. If you see us bodyless, do not be afraid. That is how we are. Our wish is to have communication with the group. Try visualizing US. Do not be alarmed; we are making contact with the 'world of humans.' Very few times do we have a chance to surpass this barrier. Try it! For us it is of vital importance, and necessary. So long!"*

This was on November 23, 1973, at 9:00 p.m. at the Deeb's. The pregnant wife of Rafael, the physician, did not continue with the group, because we had understood that the psychic energy accumulated by the members of the group was bad for the development of the fetus. These ETs did not identify themselves. I still could not "see" anyone clearly. We didn't know who they were. Further, we thought we were dealing with Pleiadeans. I could tell only that the "introduction" was different. Hard to explain. The meeting had ended, and the next meeting would be on the 25th, two days later. Determined to clarify this mystery, we met at Richard Deeb's home at 7:00 p.m.

After the breathing exercises, a communication broke in immediately. Without delay, they identified themselves with the names AXA, AX, and OXO, three beings from the "Sixth Dimension," a world of existence parallel to ours. At the moment of the communication, "they" were in the same room with us, which caused some fear on the part of the group, but still we continued. They were formless and bodyless. They were different, and in their habitat, food was in the form of pure energy. According to them, the motivation for their visit was related to a test that they wanted to perform on us, and this was the only window of opportunity in 600,000 years, when the dimensional barrier separating our worlds broke down for a brief time. Their first request was to extinguish all lights in the room, so as to be in complete darkness.

Their message conveyed the following information: *"Man never builds his home over sand; it would be senseless. By the same token, it is not fitting for a man who reasons to act in error, when he has been given the fruits of Knowledge.* ***Behold a moral!*** *Our interest is in the entire group. The reaction of the one you expect will* *be totally positive.*[1] *Part of the test has been completed. The elm does not give fruit different from its own species. Here comes the crucial moment of survival of the group. What will be in each one's mind? What will they say tomorrow, if our manifestation is contrary to their wishes? Do not make premature judgments of behavior. You are at the crucible, are forged with fire, and the constituting metal is ready to take the shape that has been predetermined. . . .*

"Do not feel alarmed if nothing further is received. It is written that the little that has been received shall be taken away. The balance of the meeting depends entirely on you. Do not reject the Wisdom that has been contributed with joy; your enjoyment shall be great if you receive and understand. Break-up, imbalance, and disagreement are dangerous. Health to our brothers on Earth!"

The message was clear, but there was disagreement about this November 23 meeting and its contents. Indeed, there was fear because of the strangeness of the contact. The message ended at 10:15 p.m. Between the initial exercises and its conclusion, about forty-five minutes had elapsed. When in the middle of the meeting the "entity" asked that paper and pencil be given to me, I drew certain symbols in the darkness. We never did understand the meaning of the symbols, except one: "Infinity." It was surprising to see how there was discussion among us, trying to determine "who we were dealing with."

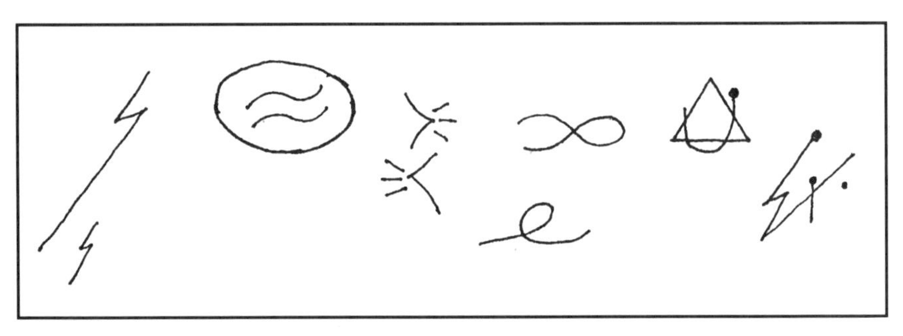

Sixth-dimension symbols

The next meeting took place on the 26th, at the usual time. Contrary to our friends from Pleiades, these entities did not give any initial salutation, and the communication was simply different. I tuned into it as a vibration. My muscles and body suffered; I felt strange and perspired copiously. Still, I maintained my observational capacity. I was conscious that this was a "vibrational telepathy," which became language upon receipt. I did not fall into trance, as in spiritism. With the Pleiadeans, it was surprising: I could even open my eyes and look at the members of the group recording, or at Maria Teresa or Marjorie wiping perspiration from my forehead with a hand towel or napkin, while receiving the messages. This was what we received:

"Our world is six-dimensional. My name is AXA and my two companions are OXO and AX. Imagine an eye, the most beautiful you have ever seen. Without eyelashes, just clean, blue, and clear. That is the way we are. We have no bodies. We are nourished with energy. You have hands, and you should be thankful for them! We want an experience with all of you. Listen well to the instructions. Tomorrow, seventeen persons should be present, among them four women. Give Enrique paper and pencil, and extinguish all lights; it must be totally dark."

We turned off the only light bulb that was burning, and we closed the curtains of the window. I heard a vibration that translated: *"Draw, draw what you see!"* And, as if an invisible hand held mine, I drew, marking the positions that the participants should take. The women should position themselves in a horizontal line, in pairs. The men should take the vertices and remaining spaces, with me at the center, sitting over a magnet, built according to their instructions.

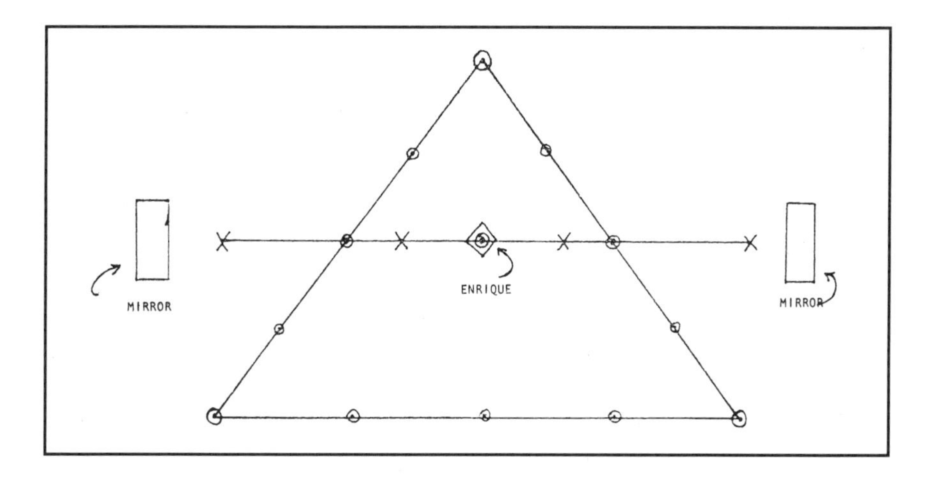

It was dangerous, and they told us so. A large mirror should be located at each side of the group. The final instructions were:

"There is grave danger if you don't follow these instructions to the letter. Our world is intangible for you," they said. *"The vision that you are going to have is a way to manifest ourselves. When Enrique claps his hands, open your eyes."*

We remained in silence for one or two endless minutes. . . . Then, impelled by an "inner" but conscious desire to do so, I clapped my hands. . . . There! A transparent eye floated briefly over the room, with a crackling sound!

Somebody turned on the lights. My chair jumped up into the air as well as myself! Fernando Márquez helped me to stand up. We were all stupefied. Then the disagreements started. The first to speak was Paulina, Richard's wife, who emphasized her displeasure with what had happened. She expressed that the group was after the extraterrestrials, but not after "entities," whose true intentions were unknown. "I have a daughter; I don't want to take undue risks," said Fernando Márquez, backing Richard's wife, and excusing himself from the presence of the "Brothers from the Sixth Dimension." Others followed, and only four wanted to continue with the experience, which was scheduled to continue the following day.

We had to get seventeen people, including four women. I would participate, along with Alfonso Blanco, Gloria Ortiz, and María Teresa, who remained eager to continue. As of that last meeting, the first "group," who used to meet at the Deeb's, began to decline. Thereafter, the second "contact group" would begin meeting at a small apartment that we shared with a new member of the group, Gerardo . . . on 31st Avenue and 11th Street, in an industrial section of town. The next day, the beings from the "Sixth Dimension" (without the seventeen people required), made contact with us for the last time and thanked us for our efforts in helping them in the attempt. They asked us to remind the rest of the group that this was possible for them only every 600,000 terrestrial years, according to our reckoning system.

The farewell was sad but interesting. They left with tremendous lamentation, calling us "poor and empty terrestrial men," for not having participated as a complete group. They offered to help those who participated, in a rather unusual way: we should just think about them when in need or in danger. It was a shame; the purpose of the two mirrors was to project their image visibly to us, regardless of their different appearance. This unleashed not fear, but panic, among those present. We had missed a great opportunity, and only in 600,000 years would a new chance arise. The farewell was dramatic at Gerardo's apartment. They had expected much from us; all of us would have benefited. According to them, "they were at the threshold of Supreme Wisdom," and this test was extremely important for them.

As the time factor operated differently for them than for us, the gates of their world would soon close. Thus, they went away as mysteriously as they came. Their last words denoted sadness, not for them, but for us. There was no actual farewell; they just left our milieu. A strange murmur, like children's voices, was heard tangibly. In practice, it was at this point when the "group of the twelve" was born, which actually consisted of thirteen people. And, usually fourteen, sixteen, or more people attended. The experience with the Beings from the Sixth Dimension was not very popular. Some of the members of the group feared them, because they were so far removed from us, so terrifyingly strange. Also, people's fear of the unknown became evident in the communications with extraterrestrials. Plus, each one interpreted these experiences, so out of the ordinary, in a different way, and many could not justify their continuing involvement with our group.

The tests to which we were subjected during the communications often seemed without sense and even unlikely. For example, we were requested to get copper belts, decorated with a particular symbol, and told how and when to use them. They also recommended that we wear a mud belt for two hours while lying on the floor. They allowed us to ask questions, and they answered them. I don't recall any instance of their refusing to answer our questions.

Thus, in a similar way, during the month of December, emerged a contact with the Brothers from Venus. This experience brought us to a remarkable collection of teachings and spiritual parameters, which we could not yet comprehend, but which began the preparation for a third personal encounter with another civilization, purportedly from our own solar system.

CHAPTER NOTE

[1] A member of the group at first refused to participate, but later changed his mind and did so wholeheartedly.

The Truth Is in Washington, D.C.

"For a long time I watch man, to determine the methods he uses to survive, and how he adapts himself to the environment in his survival effort, and I find that he thrives in the measure that he preserves his spiritual integrity, his values, and in the measure that he stays honest and decent, and I also find that he disintegrates and deteriorates in the measure that he abandons these principles."
—L. RON HUBBARD, *Introduction to Scientology*

As soon as the results became known about our daily contact with extraterrestrial entities, more and more people visited our offices looking for information related to these subjects. Besides, much information was published in the newspapers about sightings over Bogotá and surrounding districts. Perhaps many were false, but without any doubt, according to the quality of the witnesses, in many instances they were true. We knew that probably they were the Pleiadean and Venusian ships.

At that time a disastrous earthquake had recently leveled most buildings in Managua, Nicaragua, Central America. Through a friend, I was trying to negotiate the rebuilding of the central public telephone service for that city, and only a few details were pending to interview the right person in Managua who could finalize the deal. I was anxious to leave for Managua, where I expected to be able to get some rest after such hectic activity, depending on chance and circumstances.

Around the end of February, 1974, I believe on the 26th, because I do not recall the exact day, three foreign-looking individuals requested an interview with me. I suspected that they could bring me news about the business in Nicaragua. Two North Americans and a Latin-looking, very able interpreter stated the reason for their visit. The American spoke a terrible "Spanglish," as they say in Puerto Rico. I did not look in detail at their credentials, but they belonged to a U.S. government office.

"Mr. Castillo," said the translator, "we would like to know if the news appearing in the media about a supposed 'kidnapping' and your trip in a 'flying saucer' are true or not." Alfonso Blanco, who was present at the moment, amiably left, to permit us to speak freely. I gave them confirmation about the news, making it clear that it had not been a kidnapping, but a cordial invitation fully planned beforehand.

I also made the comment that a second, more spectacular encounter had taken place, for now kept secret. I noticed great interest on their part.

"We are interested in checking your version about the trip aboard a 'flying saucer.' We would like to invite you to Washington D.C., with all expenses paid during the time required, with the purpose of subjecting you to a test of regressive hypnosis. Of course it is up to you, on a voluntary basis, and with the purpose of proving your statements in public. Besides, we have interest from the scientific viewpoint, because there are other cases in the U.S. that we would like to compare with yours. You know—there are patterns that we must analyze."

I was very interested in the proposal from the Americans and foresaw no problem in going with them to Washington. It was necessary to take advantage of this opportunity, because it was the first time that my case was going to be checked scientifically, and the results would become widely known, making me a recognized, authenticated contactee. No doubt, my imagination got the best of me.

"Very well," said the interpreter, after exchanging a few words in English with the two Americans, "we will come to pick you up in two days. Please do not talk about it with your co-workers and relatives. As far as you are concerned, it will be a business trip. Do you have a valid passport?"

"Yes," I answered, matter-of-factly. "I was getting ready to travel abroad, and have everything ready."

We agreed on a place and hour where we would meet, away from the office. I told my wife and associates, Pedro Murcia and Isidro Contreras, that I was going to Managua, in relation to the central telephone service. I estimated my stay at two days at the most.

The North Americans picked me up as agreed, but the interpreter was not present. At "El Dorado" airport, everything seemed to have been arranged beforehand, without the need to present passport or visa. They told me not to

April 12, 1996. The author during his exposition at the "UFO International Convention" in San José, Costa Rica.

Photo: Dr. Richard F. Haines, U.S.A.

Left to right: Javier Sierra (Spanish journalist and investigator); Antonio Hunneus (investigator and member of "MUFON," U.S.A.); Enrique Castillo R., and Dr. Richard F. Haines, Ph.D. (scientist/investigator), of the NASA-Ames Research Center, U.S.A. Photo taken during a recess period at the "UFO International Convention" in San José, Costa Rica.

April 18, 1996. Left to right: Javier Sierra (Spanish journalist); Mrs. Ana G. Merchán de Castillo[1] *(wife of author); and Antonio Hanneus (U.S. investigator) at the "UFO International Convention" in Costa Rica.*

Photo: Dr. Richard F. Haines, U.S.A.

worry; everything had been arranged for the return trip. We boarded an Avianca regular flight. I carried only a small handbag with some clothes. According to my escorts, the trip should take three to five days at the most.

Because it was winter, I took with me a wool jacket. No one asked me for a ticket, only some type of identification for my escorts with some authority who let them pass immediately, in front of the astonished passengers standing in line for boarding. The plane took off at 10:35, according to my watch. My two American escorts once in a while looked at me curiously, talking between them, smiling. I took advantage of the opportunity to close my eyes and get some rest, interrupted twice by the stewardess offering soft drinks and a sandwich.

They asked me occasional questions about my profession, family, and pastimes. I answered them in lousy English, and they spoke in lousy Spanish. To a degree, I was pretending, because I could understand more English than they suspected. This proved useful during the test in Washington.

Upon arrival in New York after about five hours, we got off the plane and went to the cafeteria of the airport, to wait for another plane. This time we flew a modern airliner for about one hour and quickly arrived in the U.S. capital city. We passed straight through customs, where there was somebody waiting with a uniformed guard. We left through an alternate exit. Outside, two men were waiting with a luxurious, dark-colored Cadillac. I started feeling like a star in a suspense movie. They introduced me to the new members of our party, and one of them greeted me in a very "chattering" Spanish.

We boarded the car, which took off for a destination unknown to me. It was about 5:00 p.m., and I was totally disoriented, because the windows of the car were dark, or rather, one way. Besides, quite often, they smiled and asked questions in English, which I could not understand well, to keep me distracted, because they didn't want me to know where we were heading. Once in a while I could get a glimpse of great avenues and beautiful lawns. The two escorts would benefit from an intensive Spanish course.

We took a turnpike and traveled for forty or forty-five minutes, until we turned onto a narrow and lonely road. I thought we might be out in the country, because there were huge green tracts. Once in a while, we saw luxurious houses, surrounded by gardens. At this moment I made the comment that I would like to see some of the monuments, such as the Lincoln Memorial, the Capitol, and those beautiful lawns around the Obelisk. They promised to talk to the right person, once the tests were over.

The car stopped in front of a great iron gate. We waited a few seconds until a security guard authorized the admission. We advanced then on a gravel road, until we reached a large, old English-style house, surrounded by gardens and hidden behind tall trees. We stopped in front of the house, or rather, clinic. Two doctors and a nurse greeted us very warmly. The lady took my handbag and pointed to the entrance. My two escorts said goodbye and left me with the doctors and the nurse. We walked to a small room, where an interpreter was called in. He asked about my full name, age, place of birth, and wrote this information on a card.

"Were you drafted into your country's army?"

I showed him my military card and explained the reasons why I had not served in the army. I had been recently married, and for this reason I was excused from joining the military and given a second-class card, or so-called reserve. The interpreter took it in his hand, examined it carefully, and gave it back to me. I also showed him my citizenship certificate. They inked the index fingers of both hands and imprinted them on the identification card, which had my name already written on it. Then they made me sign the document and leave the name and address of my wife, in case of emergency. In the same document I had to authorize the tests on a voluntary basis.

They took my picture with a Polaroid camera. I was asked to get rid of my watch, a silver chain with a charm that hung around my neck, my wallet, and my passport. Everything was placed in a plastic bag, then into an envelope with my name and arrival date. They told me that the whole lot would be returned at the end of the tests.

After these prerequisites, we walked along a corridor and up a flight of stairs to the second floor. Along the way, I saw rows of numbered rooms and a beautifully furnished library, but few or no people. The bedroom I was shown to was ample and comfortable, spotless. I remembered that there had been no sign at the entrance that could identify the supposed "clinic." It looked more like the home of some millionaire or potentate.

The room had a telephone, private bath, a table with a typewriter, paper, ballpoint pens, pencils, a tape recorder with new tapes, a TV, two glasses, a pitcher with fresh drinking water, and a small refrigerator, which contained some fruit, milk, several kinds of cheese, butter, soft drinks, wine, and beer. The nurse showed me two push-buttons, one for the kitchen and one for the nurse on duty.

They invited me to rest. It was about 7:30 p.m. After a short while, they invited me to a confirmation meeting, in order to have everything ready for the following morning. I accepted, rang the bell, and the nurse showed up with two men: one was Dr. Smith and the other Dr. Ramírez, of Latin origin, who spoke good Spanish, but with an American accent. The questions started again, more or less the same as before, but in more detail. During the questioning, a tape recorder was running. The nurse took notes, and Dr. Ramírez consulted a questionnaire he held in his hand. When he heard that I was born in Costa

Rica, he told me: "Oh, great, I have heard good reports about Costa Rica and the 'Ticos.'"

He asked other questions about my childhood diseases, my parents' death, the occurrence of mental illnesses in the family, surgeries, if I smoked or drank liquor, other ailments, children, marriages, etc. Here I told them about the deteriorated relationship with my wife Beatriz, on account of my dedication to UFOs. They laughed casually—and congratulated me for not smoking or drinking. They asked about my beliefs and religion. I told them about my passage through Mormonism and the cause for leaving it. I explained why at that moment I was not affiliated with any religion, and Dr. Ramírez exclaimed, "Extraordinary!"

The interrogation continued. General tastes, cultural level, trips, friendships, musical likings, weight, height, etc. When they asked me about women, they laughed at my answer. They asked me to speak more slowly, because I was talking too fast. I warned them about my coughing, caused by the tonsils' removal. Thus ended this "introductory" meeting, which lasted about one-and-a-half hours. Remember that they had taken my watch away, and I could only guess at the time.

I asked the nurse if in their fine library there were any books on UFOs. When the meeting ended I found a book on the table, *UFOs Have Landed*, by George Adamski.

The conversation ended. They apologized for its duration, since I was feeling tired, but they explained that it was necessary before the first test on the next morning. The nurse offered some food, but I refused it. I was not hungry.

I slept very well. Someone knocked at the door; it was the nurse with breakfast. She excused herself and put the tray on the table. She told me that they expected me in one hour to begin the test.

I shaved and took a warm shower; that comforted me. I rang the bell, and after a few seconds the nurse walked with me to the test location. I had not paid attention to her before. She had beautiful black hair, a pretty face, and spoke an excellent, fluid Spanish, similar to Dr. Ramírez. She must have been Cuban or Puerto Rican. Her beautiful legs were visible under the white uniform. I greeted her and asked for her name. She said her name was Eva Douling.

We walked downstairs to the office where Dr. Smith, who had not been very talkative the day before, Dr. Ramírez, and another one, who dressed in a conservative suit and nice tie, waited for us. The new man was smiling amiably and was rather young. Dr. Ramírez introduced us; he said he belonged to the Air Force, although his attire did not indicate it.

Ramírez told me that the test would be a "polygraph" or lie detector test. He explained clearly the purpose of the test, and how it worked. "You should not be afraid or nervous; it is a standard procedure in these cases," he told me.

In the office was a desk with various objects, papers, folders, pencils, etc., several chairs, a calendar, a watch, and a desk clock; at the left was a sturdy stretcher and a medical scale with a height-measuring device. On the walls were X-ray pictures, fluorescent lights, and a large mirror on the side wall. The door opened and two men entered, who extended their hands and smiled. One must have been in the military, according to his short haircut, but was not in uniform, wearing just a white coat over his civilian clothes. From the way he watched me, he must have been a psychologist. The other was dressed like a bank employee, in a business suit. This completed the team, six people altogether.

Dr. Ramírez reassured me while the nurse placed sensors on my skin at different locations, all joined by thin, insulated electric wires to a black box with a paper roll and a stylus. A man was placed next to the instrument. Two tape recorders were started, each with two microphones. I was sitting, without a shirt. A clock on the wall read 8:30 a.m.

The questions were: complete name, age, place of residence, civil state, profession, etc. Dr. Ramírez asked and watched the reaction on the polygraph. The assistant made certain marks on the out-rolling paper. Then came the key questions regarding the encounter with the extraterrestrials.

Once in a while Dr. Ramírez was consulted by Dr. Smith and the others. Ramírez checked on a sheet of paper he held in his hands and asked the question, interrupted sometimes by one of them. Once, Ramírez laughed, and the rest asked why. He had warned me that as soon as I told a lie, there were involuntary changes registered by the brain and detected by the instrument. Without haste, I answered the questions with aplomb, and believe I gave them the certitude of my reliability.

I believe that Dr. Smith was an expert on extracting information. He repeatedly played the fool's role and faked bad memory, asking the same questions in a different context, in an attempt to confuse me. More than once he became bothered by my answers and my cool disposition. I believe he even insulted mentally my already deceased mother. He tried to break down my tolerance by asking tough, repeated questions, difficult to follow because of the language, until they were translated by Ramírez, who attempted to excuse him and asked me not to take this repeated questioning badly.

The siege ended, and peace returned. I was quiet and satisfied. There were questions such as how it happened, the date and hour of the encounter, where they came from, their technology and propulsion system, how they got here, age, beliefs, how they live, government, scientific advancement, etc. The test proper took approximately one hour, plus another hour for preparations, for a total of two. They took a long break while they evaluated the results. I rested in my room and read part of Adamski's book. The hypnotic regression, crucial for the validity of the results, was scheduled for the afternoon.

It was 3:00 p.m. by the wall clock at the office. The regressive hypnosis was of the "fifth-degree," where it is possible to take the patient to his childhood, and even to the fetal condition. I felt secure because they seemed to be capable professionals. Another man, about sixty years old, with gray hair, a very nice person whose name I have forgotten, joined them.

It was explained how the hypnotist, who was also an excellent psychologist, would proceed. I sat down, and he started by looking deeply into my eyes, giving me orders and making passes with his hands. It didn't work! He couldn't hypnotize me with the traditional method. He tried again and again, to no avail. A tick-tock mechanism, with a swaying needle to be followed by one's eyes, couldn't do it either. Then the doctor with the kind face approached me and asked me to stay still and close my eyes. I felt his hand passing close to my face a couple of times, then I felt it sliding down my neck, searching for a specific point; he touched my forehead with his thumb, then he searched for my throat and pressed with his fingers. That is the last I recall. When I woke up, listening to a countdown from 5 to 0, I felt very thirsty. I asked for water, and the nurse brought me a glassful. I drank it and felt better. The clock on the wall read 4:13 p.m. I could have been under hypnosis about fifty minutes, taking into account the time spent in the initial trials.

I looked at their faces; they were perplexed. Dr. Ramírez told me that all was okay and that they were pleased with the results, but could not advance any opinion. They would be analyzed, taking everything into account. The recorders kept rolling, until the end of the session.

There was no doubt; they just smiled and tried in vain to mask their astonishment at what they now knew, and a couple of them left the room. Dr. Smith was silent. Now I was under the impression that he had changed his mind. Besides, it was probable that all the information about the second encounter had surfaced in detailed form. It was pending only the pentothal test, scheduled for the following day.

While the appointment for the third session was arranged, Ramírez and Smith, together with beautiful Eva, who on a couple of occasions had caused the eyes of the participants to divert towards her well-formed legs, walked with me along the corridor, while we exchanged a few words. Smith looked a bit more settled.

They said good night, slapping me fondly on my back. Eva took me to my room, asking me several questions about the extraterrestrials. She asked if I wanted anything to eat, but again, I refused, reluctantly. She reminded me that there were juices and milk in the refrigerator, in case I got hungry, and told me that if I needed her later, I could call her. Based on her attitude, I sensed that her initial incredulous thinking had been changed; now she was changed, or shook up, but was not allowed to tell me her opinion or talk to me about the subject.

I decided to watch some TV, an old Western with Anthony Quinn, which regrettably had already started. Later, I decided to take a walk in the garden, in the backyard. Eva was with me, talking about subjects other than UFOs. After about a half hour of talking to other patients who were sitting outside on several comfortable chairs and two swinging chairs, we went back inside. It was getting chilly.

That night I slept well. Nothing bothered me mentally, and I felt happy and satisfied about the apparent results so far.

Daylight came again. The next appointment was for 9:30 a.m. This session was the most important, both for me and for them. I had breakfast at 7:30 a.m. Eva advised me to rest until 9:30, so I could be in top shape for the test. The breakfast had been very frugal: whole wheat bread, butter, marmalade, cereal, cheese, and milk.

Once installed in the ample medical cubicle, they asked me how I felt. Ramírez and Smith, the other two, the nurse and psychologist from the Air Force, the psychologist who hypnotized me, and Eva were waiting for me—seven, altogether.

The test began. They asked me to sit in a special reclining chair, which was adjustable and very comfortable. Dr. Ramírez asked me to extend my right arm; he felt it, looking for the vein. They had instructed me previously as to what I would feel under the effects of pentothal. They massaged the arm, tied on a rubber band, and after two attempts managed to insert the needle into the vein. I felt a slight prick, then a warm sensation that invaded my entire body.

Ramírez spoke to me: Relax, do not tense up. His voice sounded weaker and weaker, and I spun slowly, losing my strength, feeling weak and defenseless.

Then, I woke up. . . . No, I was not sleeping! I was resting on the adjustable reclining chair. I felt my lips dry, and Eva again gave me a glass of water. I listened to the comments they were making among themselves. The man from the Air Force was gone. Feeling better, I took a look at the clock on the wall, and saw the time. Only twenty minutes had elapsed. They gave me more water, and told me that I must rest. They took my shoes off and made me lie down. I felt sleepy. I could not calculate how long I had slept. When I woke up, Eva was sitting in front of me. She told me, as a greeting, that I had slept about five hours.

In the afternoon, a second, short hypnosis session was scheduled to complete the tests, and the next day I could leave.

It was 3:00 p.m. I had a good lunch. Eva behaved very nicely, with much consideration. That afternoon, after the second hypnosis session, was the last time I saw her, because I did not have the opportunity to say goodbye to her. Thank you, Eva Douling, wherever you may be!

The last session took place at 4:30 p.m. of the third day, under the same strict conditions. At the beginning of the fourth day, I returned to Colombia. My personal belongings were returned, along with an envelope, which they asked me to inspect and express whether it was okay. Inside the envelope was one thousand dollars! According to them, it was a compensation for the working days missed in Bogotá. It was more than I expected, because I felt satisfied by the tests and the apparent results, and I was not paying anything. They said that the results would be sent through the American Embassy in Bogotá. However, I am still waiting for them. . . .

Years later, I still have several doubts, and others have been explained. What were the true identities of those obscure agents who could take me and return me to Bogotá, with arrangements made with a complete network of people, all so well coordinated? What were their true motivations?

Why did they make me believe that the sessions had taken less than the time they really took? The mirror was double. From where was all of this filmed and observed? What strange medication was used the third day to make me believe that the session had lasted only twenty minutes?

Today, I am sure that the truth was filmed and recorded in Washington, D.C., and is still hidden there.

CHAPTER NOTE

[1]Ana Gertrudis Merchán came into my life in 1976, during a talk on UFOs at the Universidad Tecnológica in Bucaramanga (Colombia). We were introduced when she was barely seventeen, and I became friends with her and her aunt, Marina de Barrera, who had raised her from the age of seven. Her mother, Onofre, abandoned by her husband and forced to raise seven children in poverty, had given away the little girl to Marina, who volunteered to support her. As a child, Ana Gertrudis endured much hardship as a result of these circumstances.

For about three years, whenever I traveled to Bucaramanga on my way to Venezuela, I visited them. After she was over eighteen, we decided to live together. In 1987, after we had two children, Krishnamerck, now sixteen, and Enrique, now fifteen, both born in Caracas, Venezuela, we decided to get married in a civil ceremony in Costa Rica. We have been married eighteen years, and in spite of the difference in ages (she is thirty-seven and I am sixty-six), we have a magnificent marriage, based on love and mutual respect.

12

The Truth Shall Always Be the Truth

"I could never have written a book without contributing original ideas, which I deemed beneficial for humankind, not only on account of the enumeration of facts little or not known, but of the presentation of my own new and diligent interpretations, backed by serious and careful reasoning."

—Dr . FRANCISCO ANICETO LUGO,
Las Civilizaciones Ignoradas (The Ignored Civilizations)

MY RETURN TO BOGOTÁ AND RE-ENTRY INTO WORK and the group were accomplished normally. There was no problem with my associates Murcia and Contreras, simply that the job had been lost to a local competitor in Managua.

I resumed the established routine with the group. They told me that the usual communication had been attempted but could not be established; instead they practiced a thirty-minute meditation. My relationship with Beatriz was getting worse, very tense and difficult. Our separation was to take place two months later. At the time of my trip to the USA, we had recently moved to a house in the District "Jardín del Norte," where I rented a large two-story house, with a front garden and several tall trees, pines and cypresses. There were several playthings for the children, such as a slide ramp, swinging hoops, bar, etc., which they enjoyed very much.

Many of the experiences that occurred at this house are not suitable for publication here, because they were paranormal. One of them was a visit by a Venezuelan doctor, José Gregorio Hernández, who died in 1919, and who answered my call to heal a bad asthma case suffered by my fifth son, Nefi. Carlos Angel, a good friend who was interested in witnessing the experience, was visiting us at the time.

Also, by the end of April, a final separation from Beatriz took place at that house, ending twenty-two years of marriage. Our youngest daughter, Saharia, was five years old, and Enrique, the oldest, was twenty; seven children altogether. It is interesting that only the second, Mauricio, became interested in UFO matters. In fact, he belonged to one of the youth groups dedicated to the investigation of extraterrestrial presence, a group called "Alfa Centaur." The other children completely lacked any interest in these events.

Time went by quickly. The group, disintegrated as it was by the events related to the "visitors from the Sixth Dimension," met as usual at the home of Gerardo. A few others and myself met at Marjorie's and Richard's homes, until we separated as a group, but never as friends. At the home of Richard, a group continued meeting. Jorge Eduardo Silva acted as "channel," the same as Karen had done when she first arrived from Mexico. I don't know to what extent actual communications took place, because the messages were almost equal, very repetitive and mystic. Only the group that met at Marjorie's and Gerardo's homes was left. One day, being together as usual, somebody from the group, Pedro Avila, mentioned to the beings who we were accustomed to contacting that although we were sure of their existence, it would be advisable, to strengthen our confidence, for them to appear in front of the whole group at least once. Yamaruck answered immediately, *"Is this request unanimous?"* All raised their hands in approval. They then stated, *"This coming Thursday at 7:00 p.m., entering by a white landmark numbered Km-78, by a dirt road, we will be there."*

The day in question, at the designated time, we took two cars, and on arriving at the place selected by them, we realized that we were close to Fúquene lake. On the way, we could see that it was going to rain, because dark clouds were gathering and, upon arrival, there was lightning and an electrical storm. Startled, we checked the landmark, Km-78. We drove on the dirt road as far as the cars could go. We got out and searched on foot for a place with good visibility for the sighting. We carried a tape recorder.

Camelo claimed to feel "energy" on one side, leading to another road. María Teresa signaled another direction. My position was to wait until they communicated with us, and that's what we did. I selected a place with good grass, and we sat there, all in silence, keeping an eye on our watches. It was two minutes before seven. All looked at the sky, following the movement of the clouds with wind. The sky opened a little, allowing the moonlight to pass through, which shyly illuminated the landscape. It was 7:00 p.m., sharp.

Then, a radiance among the clouds over the lake moved in a swinging pattern, like a wave!

I yelled, and all marveled, cried, and waved their arms. Marjorie, if I remember well, took off her scarf and saluted the ship, sending kisses with her left hand. The ship approached us in a slanting way, coming out of the cloud where it was hidden, moving in straight line, and then inclining itself, allowing us to see its dome. Víctor Rodríguez embraced me and apologized for himself. I could not understand why, at first, but then he confessed to having requested that several of the members of the group—five, to be exact—because not all accepted, think about oranges, bananas, tomatoes, etc., during the time of contact, in order to block it, and check if the communication was real.

In this way the wish of the thirteen members of the group was satisfied. Some of the members of the initial group had separated by June of 1974, for different reasons. Alfonso "Poncho" Blanco had already left the group. According to him, he would dedicate himself to contact events in his own way—with spiritists—to accomplish healings. In this manner, our congenial friend became separated from the group, to follow "his own contacts." Without anybody suspecting it, the ones who left lost the opportunity to listen to the wonderful teachings that we were about to receive. It was as if the extraterrestrials were waiting for the final fusion of the remaining group, to initiate the most important information, both prophetic and humanistic. The former members were not to have the opportunity to know "The Logic of Logic," in its three sections, "The Nine Times That Will Change the World," the "Message to the World, Plan A," and other teachings that we had the privilege to receive.

Gradually, I began to better understand some of the information on various subjects that I had been given on board the Pleiadean ship the previous November 3 and 18. For example, one of my questions to Commander Kramier had had to do with a factor or chemical agent in the blood, which was capable of changing the personality and mien of an individual as a result of a transfusion. If the donor is stronger than the recipient, after a few months, certain violent traits could develop in the recipient, if the donor tends to be rather violent. Kramier was pointing out the risk involved in transfusions.

Another comment concerned tobacco. When he heard that I had not smoked, he mentioned that the harmful effects can reach third and fourth generations, hindering mental development, and in some cases promoting congenital deformations. He pointed out that tobacco could eventually be eradicated, but not before it caused millions of casualties.

"Birth control," he also told me, *"would get started in spite of religious beliefs and opposition, for two very powerful reasons: First, the effect of several wars would cause insecurity among young couples, who would prefer not to have children. Second, international organizations would agree on plans for slowing down the population explosion, in order to improve the educational possibilities for the young, as well as their nutrition and employment. The same would happen in*

1976. Left to right: Dr. Clemente Garavito (astronomer), Charles Berlitz (U.S. author/investigator), Father Francisco Arango (clergyman), and Enrique Castillo R. at the headquarters of the I.C.I.F.E in Bogotá, Colombia.
Photo: Gloria Ortiz

relation to poverty. Only through agreements between countries could famine, which still exists on several continents, be prevented or checked.

"You must learn many things before vanquishing all these problems, and only accumulated experience will teach you. In the Universe," Kramier said, *"there is no such a thing as a final limit of learning; if this were the case, evolution would have reached a stagnation point in the most advanced civilizations, which is not the case. All civilizations dedicate a lot of time to the search for new paths conducive to a 'final' level of enlightenment.*

"You call it 'the search for truth'—really, the name does not matter—but at this opportunity I want to confirm to you what we taught during the remotest times of humanity. The key that will open the door of knowledge is genetically engraved within yourself. It is necessary to:

"Eliminate the fear of that which is considered indecipherable.

"Similarly, discard the awe for that which you were taught to consider untouchable.

"Obtain a balanced discernment about what you learn.

"Maintain a real control and discipline over that which hurts your health or affects your senses. Intelligence should be used as such, with intelligence; do not waste this gift in all its magnificence."

During one of the discussions on November 18, I remember that I stopped to scrutinize, on the wall of the ship, a very unique "Winged Serpent." The Commander approached me as he noticed my interest in this symbol. An interesting conversation got started—which I would liked to have recorded—about illnesses and the possibility of eradicating them within a short period of time. He asked me to explain again my concerns, but then Krishnamerck stepped in; they "talked," and then I stated my question carefully. I must say that, if at the time of the contacts I had been better disciplined, my questions would have been quite superior.

He looked straight into my eyes, when I asked, and then answered, *"A 'Dark Gene' carried by Terrestrials will be detected soon, to be isolated, and as a result, the duration of life will be increased substantially. No, Enrique, it does not represent a utopia. Many will think this is impossible, but we assure you that in a few years this discovery will be a reality, and also a serious problem for science. Ethics and values are required to handle this new situation. This 'dark' agent is responsible for cellular aging, which carries with it 'premature death.' When this achievement is at hand, human life duration will be a matter of worldwide scientific agreement. The minimum standard life expectancy could be set at 300 years, without any aging at all, with an apparent age of about 33 years."*

I was left utterly breathless. I was listening to what seemed to me to be the most transcendental piece of information of all time—what has been called eternal youth. Now somebody was telling me that it is possible. Kramier continued:

"When this gene becomes known to science and isolated, then humankind shall enter a marvelous era of achievements and longer life. It will occur at a bad moment, when man shall also gain control over technological and scientific know-how that he will not be able to handle, because he lacks real spiritual values. Do not forget this, Enrique."

At the end of this short but eloquent speech, Kramier and Krishnamerck scrutinized me in considerable detail.

We continued walking inside the ship, but my heart and the "dark gene" struggled to emerge from myself. What I had just heard, the categorical statements from the Pleiadean Mission Chief, were just too much. They noticed my change of disposition, the shock produced by their statements. Now I thought . . . with what arguments was I going to explain this, and at what opportunity? Who would listen to me? How could people believe me without proofs?

This is one of the reasons that I kept the information to myself for so long. I was already being called insane; how could I defend such additional incredible data?

I learned to handle information cautiously, because the Pleiadeans, delivering the final stroke, told me the following:

"There are THREE GENETIC CODES interacting for creating LIFE in the Universe. You already have the first one, and the second will be discovered shortly, before the turn of the century.[1] *You must handle this with utmost wisdom and moderation, because when the THIRD is discovered during the next century, approximately in the year 2025, man will know how Life started on Earth and will be in a position to learn how the Universe began."*

CHAPTER NOTE

[1] While I was at Costa Rica, in 1988, I was thrilled to read the information about the discovery of the SECOND CODE. The AFP, Washington press release was published in the newspaper, *La Nacion,* from San José, Costa Rica, on Monday June 6, 1988.

13

The Word Begins to Spread

"That the Universe has a meaning, and human existence is not a mere shift from one nothingness to another, is the positive statement of philosophy. Although in its fullness it offers too subtle a wisdom, too high a morale, too strange a mysticism to be taken into account by the masses, and even less to be understood by them, and to live according to its rules, it doesn't mean that it is useless for humankind, or that it doesn't bring a message in the worst crisis of its life."

—PAUL BRUNTON, *The Spiritual Crisis of Man*

My second personal encounter with the Pleiadeans had left me flabbergasted, and I was unable to hide what was happening to me. Immediately thereafter I had decided to raise the CIFE (Center for the Investigation of Extraterrestrial Phenomena) to the category of Institute. First of all, I had to obtain the necessary funds to rent a small office. Then I would think about furniture, desk, chairs, etc. The CIFE functioned at my workplace at Conmutel Ltd., where I was not in a position to receive all the many people who came to meet me and ask questions during working hours.

Later, by May 1974, destiny would put me in touch with several people who eventually would become, with me, the motors that drove the new ICIFE (Colombian Institute for the Investigation of Extraterrestrial Phenomena). I had already launched my first talks to interested groups who wanted to know everything about "flying saucers." Afterwards, I began my first conferences for the general public, from all walks of life and social classes. This would be my "baptism of fire," casting me into the "gullets" of unbelievers and skeptics. Karen had already left me the first lessons from her "Martian" Masters (the same of Marla in Mexico), which, as a beginner's course, she taught in eight days. With the suggestive title of "Introduction to Cosmic Science," people struggled to be among the privileged few who could take the course from Karen directly. Karen was known as "the Mexican contactee" and a disciple of Marla.

I attended the first talks, and later Karen introduced me to the first informative courses. The subjects were: Quantum Mechanics, Genetics, Citobaric Quantinomium (Chakras), Psycho-Cybernetics (Mind and the Mental Spheres), Origin of the Spirit (The Overself), Karma-Dharma (Cause and Effect), Death, Parapsychology, and Astrophysics. With these subjects, the public was launched on a scientific-spiritual search, inspiring some to form contact groups, while others believed themselves to have encountered an answer to their anxieties and unanswered questions.

During the first courses that I taught, I met Gilberto Ferreira, a successful and well-known businessman, who was very much impressed when I dared to disclose my experiences in public. Mr. Ferreira helped support the Institute economically for several years, was President of the Executive Board of ICIFE for two years, and became one of my best friends. Another person who helped support the Institute and was its manager for three years was Samuel Medina. A personal, loyal, and close friendship with him has lasted until today.

Samuel is a graduate in Economics from the Universidad Javeriana in Bogotá. He traveled with me to visit several countries, among them Ecuador, Costa Rica, Honduras, El Salvador, and Mexico. The vicissitudes we suffered together during those "adventures," investigating and getting to know new sightings and new people who had experienced close encounters with alien ships and occupants, could be the subject of a separate book, on account of its hilarious and astonishing contents.

ICIFE officially started its task at 43rd Street between Caracas and 15 Avenues, second floor, Palermo District, in Bogotá in the first month of 1974. At this location, we were visited by one of the most famous contactees at that time, Eugenio Siragusa from Italy. Also at this place were taught courses, such as "Introduction to Cosmic Science," for a small fee to support the Institute and myself.

There was a conference room at the ICIFE with the capacity for seating about fifty people comfortably, with a large blackboard, almost wall to wall, where I drew diagrams and illustrative sketches. My office was located across a small patio, from where I could see my secretary, Mrs. Colombia Mondragón, who was expecting her second son. Her husband, Gonzalo Mondragón, was assistant-director of the Institute. In this way, we alternated in the teaching of the courses, given the large number of people who wanted to take them. To pay for expenses, we charged about 150 Colombian pesos (about twelve U.S.

dollars) per course. In this way we were able to furnish, in about three months, a second conference room, for about twenty people. Gilberto and others donated used chairs, desks, and tables, which we repaired, restoring them to a like-new condition. This second room was dedicated to students, who came from many schools, with the purpose of learning about my story and the UFO subject.

At the ICIFE we were able to carry out the first empirical investigations about the subject. All sorts of stories arrived, some likely to be accurate, others obviously the product of the imagination. At this location (until March 1976), we received the most incredible stories, told by the protagonists themselves. I heard several—from people in various degrees and shades of insanity—fit for psychiatrists and psychologists. Other people came looking for solutions to marital problems, mostly women, who daily asked for private interviews with me. I told them frankly that if I had not been able to solve my own problems, how could I solve theirs! Afterwards they stated that I was a "damn egotist." A considerable number came in search of medical care and miraculous healing. They assumed that I had power to cure all types of diseases . . . just because I was in touch with extraterrestrials. When told that such was not the case, they became angry and called me an impostor.

I sincerely believe that if I had dedicated myself to healing people for a fee, using the supposed powers received from the ETs, I would have enjoyed a very stable economic situation, equal or better than some other contactees who have exploited the ignorance and credulity of people. However, I could not do such a thing.

Many people would come to see me after listening to testimonies, sometimes exaggerated, about my supposedly formidable powers. Even the members of the group used to comment that "Enrique doesn't know what he has," referring to my abilities in conscious-telepathy, which according to some, were prodigious. Eventually, I began to believe so myself. Sometimes they referred to my outstanding good memory, which perhaps was awakened by my Greater Brothers in order to help disperse their teachings and information.

By this time, the first months of 1974, my marriage with Beatriz was over. We separated, and as a result I had complete liberty to go where I pleased. I did not take the initiative for the separation and had no remorse about it. I continued seeing my children and somehow provided the essentials for them. Meanwhile, I was staying at another friend's home. He was Jorge Bonell, a friend from the old times when we had worked together at the Public Telephone Centrals in Bogotá, from 1948 to 1957. Out of friendship, he traveled with me during my tours to Costa Rica and Mexico.

The Investigation Group of the I.C.I.F.E. in Bogotá, Colombia. Left to right: Mr. Carlos A. Bonilla, Dr. Samuel Medina, Mr. Francisco Quiroga, Enrique Castillo, Mr. Delio Quimbayo, and in front, Mr. Juan Osorio.

Three months before my separation from Beatriz, I had met Gloria Inés Ortiz, mentioned previously, a twenty-five-year-old woman, a secretary, who was also attracted by the events which are the subject of this book. Alfonso "Poncho Blanco" introduced her to the group and to me. In this way she became part of the initial group after it was organized.

We used to meet twice a week, without fail, at the Deeb's. Gloria and I eventually fell in love; we then lived together for five years. Three children were born from this union, Orhion, Daiyaini, and Ioninka (a boy and two girls), during the most heightened period of the contacts with the ETs. When the initial group had dissolved after the messages from the entities from the "Sixth Dimension," I had organized a new one that met at Marjorie Hollman's, on 33rd Street and 5th Avenue, around the corner from San Bartolomé High School, third floor, where she had her apartment.

Another smaller group had also been organized at the home of a good friend, Reina Zamudio, sister of some of my first friends in Colombia. She had been confined to a wheelchair by polio since she was a little girl, but had a happy disposition and mediumistic abilities. She lived at 70th Street and 5th Avenue, Chapinero District, north of Bogotá. I have maintained a good friendship with her and her family for over twenty-eight years. At her home, we received several of the most beautiful and inspiring messages from Yamaruck, Orhion, and the Master of Wisdom.

On the night of May 13, 1974, at Richard Deeb's, we received the following message:

MESSAGE FROM SHIP IN MISSION

Hour: 8:00 p.m.
Telepathy by Enrique Castillo Rincon

MASTER OF WISDOM:

There is nothing more conducive in the world to going someplace, than having no plans to go anywhere, because it is there, without signals and without hustle, where man is bound to arrive.

The voice of the Eternal Spirit whispers at the ear of men; the Soul and the Immortal Spirit talk about immortality and present before them his identity documents. Nothing happens by chance, nothing exists by chance, because luck does not exist. There is an Immutable Law, because everything has a cause and an effect. Every effect has a cause, and is subject to the Law. To you men, I make my voice heard once more, because I already told you: I am old compared to you, not by age but by knowledge. Master I am, and I humbly bow my head in front of you as I say: Blessed be those who persist and struggle for an ideal, in which the forces that manifest in him have life, and deliver to all around him that marvelous influence under which a man can be elevated, or can be also turned to dust.

Great is the one who raises himself above the others, without complaints in his mouth, and great among great is the one who, being Greater, considers himself lesser and humble. Thus, you must understand me, because the forces of evil have manifested themselves again, and my voice will be heard continuously. Nothing can stop my voice; it cannot be hidden, because my voice is a spring of living water, and I AM WISDOM and I AM POWER, and whenever there is a humble heart, I will manifest myself. To all those who love me . . . in them I manifest myself.

I AM WHO I AM; I AM POWER AND TRUTH and I am with you until the end of time. Peace to all of you. Peace among you, peace to all who deserve it. I bow again in front of you, and wish PEACE AND HAPPINESS in your hearts.

PEACE . . . PEACE . . . PEACE is my name. . . .

Immediately thereafter, Commander Yamaruck stepped in:

Without doubt, many of you will demonstrate internal controversies, negative manifestations, opposition, and poor powers of discernment. Why do you insist on being sager than the sage? It is dangerous to listen to and to receive, and then to reject, because if you ever heard the parable of the talents, with that interest rate, you will have to pay all you have received.

Do not exert yourself and choose stony paths; you yourself select and look for them, and when you arrive at their end, I can tell you with certainty, you will find your time. Because of this, we tell you, go after the good, that which lifts the soul, fortifies the spirit, and disciplines the mind. Because those of you who receive and do not keep, will lose the best opportunity given to you, and doubt will break the spirit and kill the mind. . . .

At the end of the meetings we often remained in silence for some time, each one collected in his heart. Other times we discussed and developed the message and the information received. The day after receiving the above messages, the group at Reina Zamudio at 7:00 p.m. heard the following message:

MESSAGE FROM SHIP IN MISSION

Bogotá, May 14, 1974
Telepathy by Enrique Castillo Rincón

FROM MASTER OF KNOWLEDGE: (The Truth?)

All of you here have waited for me, have waited that SHE manifests herself like a powerful column carved from living rock; where the absolute dwells, here SHE is ready to be found by whoever looks for Her.

She does not have precious metals, or colored garments, and is the property of no man or slave of no one. Nobody can enclose Her, and when someone covers it, SHE remains there, because her Law is stronger than whoever covers her or intends to do so. She is not slave and she is not 'owner'; SHE submits to no one's will. Still, many try to bend her with fallacious words. SHE has no owner, and no one can imprison her. I am HER giver and also HER protector, because she manifests herself free and beautiful like a coveted flower.

If you already know who SHE is, I tell you, you are my blessed children, because I am HER protector, and SHE and the LAW are subjected from pre-existence and will be given to men from the hills and the mountains, and therefrom people will talk about HER everywhere, in the North, the South, the East, and the West, and men will finally possess HER. If you go along with HER, you will be blessed, and peace will be with you.

I AM, thus Ancient before you, and I AM; you can call me LAW and ABSOLUTE, because I am Equilibrium and Harmony. I don't break the LAW because I am THE LAW, and its fulfiller. Remember that at the right moment, one by one will be separated from the crowd, and those that have found it will be separated, and will go with it, and will know it, and one will be taken, and the other will be left behind. Look at what I am telling you! Do not be surprised that day, when man will be swept like fuzz and burned like waste, because the day of the

Lord is still to come, and the sword is ready to leave its scabbard, to make justice, and no one will be able to hide his face before the Light that comes clamoring.

Do not be surprised like thieves; be prepared, and I will accept you and will give you finally the good news; I shall comfort you and give you my love and tenderness, and from then on you shall not walk in the wilderness, because indeed I tell you that I am the Ancient among you, but not because of age, but of knowledge. If you understand me, dear brethren, man has been from the beginning, and as such, IS SUBJECT TO THE LAW.

And I tell you, at this opportunity, that you have the wonderful happiness to be able to find it. Look for it eagerly, with all your heart and strength, because those who look for it, will find it.

Peace be with all of you. . . . Peace . . . Peace . . . Peace.

Here, a member of the group interrupted to ask about the speaker's identity. "We would like to know your name, brother."

"I am Wisdom, and I am Love; I am the Law and its fulfiller, because I am also giver among you, and wherever you are, I thus manifest myself. You can give me any of those names, because I AM THE LAW.*"*

We interpreted that the speaker referred in this message to Supreme Truth. During these meetingsand messages, we were highly impressed. We even came to believe that Jesus himselfwas talking to us, to strengthen us in the face of the upcoming serious events for Earth and the human race. In a way, we considered ourselves privileged.

14

The Venusians, Are They Venusian?

". . . the fantastic, for us, is not imaginary. But an imagination strongly applied to the study of reality discovers that the borderline between the marvelous and the positive, or, if you prefer, between the visible and the invisible universes, is very faint. . . ."

—LOUIS PAUWELS and JACQUES BERGIER,
Le Matin des Magiciens

THE ENTIRE YEAR OF 1974 was rich in spiritual teachings, both messianic and prophetic. It is clear that all of this information cannot be included here, because it would fill more than one book. The meetings followed at their usual pace, and I struggled to digest whatever information was given us.

Today I am sure that at the beginning of my "apostolate," or dedication of part of my life to this ungrateful task, I was very conscious that the Pleiadeans had not given me a specific mission to complete, as was the case with other contactees. It is my belief that I am the only contactee in the world *who does not have a mission to accomplish.* They never, I repeat, never made me responsible for any such assignment. It was I who decided at the right moment to tell the world about what had happened. Besides, the weight of the experience forced me to do it. Sometimes I felt manipulated, and protested in public, knowing full well that my "Greater Brothers" would be aware of my protest without my telling them directly.

In this way, I became the investigator of my own experiences and compared mine to those of other very famous and well-known contactees. I purchased and read all the books I could about the major religions, mythology, legends, and the cultures of our planet, among them the Inca, Maya, Aztec, etc. Rapidly I became aware that both the Biblical gods and those of other religions came or arrived from outer space. There was no doubt: gods, hybrids, avatars, mystics, masters, all had the same knowledge of THE LAW, the same wisdom that we inherited in the remotest past. I remembered now the conversations with the Pleiadeans during the contacts, the questions I asked, and the answers they gave me. *There was not a shadow of doubt in my mind; different extraterrestrial races had visited Earth millions of years ago, and originated life on this planet.*

At the beginning of 1974, José Rosciano Holder arrived in Bogotá to give two conferences at the Luis Angel Arango library. In 1973, he had become well-known because of his books: *I Visited Ganymede,* first, and later, *My Preparation for Ganymede*, under the pseudonym of "Yosip Hibrahim." His books were read by thousands of people, both in Perú and Colombia, making believers out of many of them. Later, I talked to "Pepe" (José Rosciano) in Caracas, and we gave several talks together to groups of believers that had multiplied upon my arrival in Venezuela.

In December, 1974 I gave my first Venezuelan course on the subject of "Introduction to Cosmic Science," opening a new dimension to professionals from Caracas. This was a beginning similar to the one in Colombia. Among the students were José Luis Baudet, physician, professor of genetics at the Central University of Venezuela, and Victor Hugo Cairos, who later claimed to be in contact; the well-known singer, Hugo Blanco, who also confessed in public to have been contacted; Andrés Boulton Figueira, author of several books; and Connie Méndez, who started the metaphysical movement of the Count of Saint Germain. They were my first disciples and listeners, along with a painter of Spanish origin, whose work was widely appreciated, Carmencita Vásquez Losada.

But, let us go step-by-step and see how all this happened. Going back to Bogotá, the third physical encounter was getting close, but this time it was not to be with the Pleiadeans, and at group level the communications continued. One of the few communications received at my home, where Gloria and myself lived together, was the most beautiful and well-structured of all those received so far. Our home was a small and humble apartment located at 66th Street No 23-13, "Siete de Agosto" District. The text of that message appears in the following chapter.

During that communication, I was instructed as to where the physical contact would take place with the "Venusians"—Yamaruck, Orhion, and other crew members. This was an important event for our group, because we all felt a deep love toward our friends from space, who had filled us with beauty and hope through their messages. The "rendezvous" was set for 5:00 a.m. on a July day. This time, I was going to take with me, without permission, a tape recorder. The meeting place was to be behind a mountain overlooking Bogotá, where the famous Church of Monserrate is located.

Meanwhile, these are some of the messages delivered telepathically to our group by Orhion, on July 24, 1974:

SYMBOLOGY OF BECOMING

Telepathy by Enrique Castillo Rincón

I salute all of you this evening with affection, asking all of you to present the palms of your hands upwards. . . . I am your brother BAROS, delegate in charge of the only ship remaining here to continue presenting you our communications and our special wish to continue with the training of the Group. It is our wish for and obligation to the Group to keep alive the flame and the inner desire in each of you, to vibrate with the Cosmic Scale in the highest possible spirituality. Our commander, Yamaruck, was sorry to have been unable to talk to you before leaving the Planet, but he left to the group his living wish that his image and words remain in your memory. He treasures your memory already. Our brother Orhion stays with us. Yaracka, Ourino, Ioninka, Rondhy, and Baros will be here at the necessary time. Now, before yielding to Orhion, I remind our brother Enrique of our wish to hold a short meeting and to speak to him, to present him with a few things that we have pending, at 2:00 a.m. tonight.

ORHION with you!

If any of you has had the chance to see or hear about the behavior of certain animals, I am going to tell you a story so that you are aware and ready. Sharpen your mind to find the meaning:

Stop to see the feline movements of the tiger, that strong, terrible animal that inhabits jungles and other places of this planet. I refer to the Asiatic tiger or Bengal tiger, the one with yellow stripes. The eagle watches her prey from a hilltop, from the heights, backed by her ability and the strength of her wings and claws, and her wonderful sight. She can spot her prey from far away, then launch herself, strike, and capture it. These two animals, bird of prey and carnivorous predator, have to do with our story. The hungry tiger travels its territory, the jungle, the mountain, detects its prey, stalks it cautiously, and attacks in an intelligent way. When attacking a large prey, he breaks its back to immobilize it. Then he kills it and feeds from its flesh, leaving the residue to the hyenas and jackals. The eagle is also very clever and attacks effectively. The rabbit that becomes its prey has no chance for survival.

At the present time, the tiger sharpens its claws, then sleeps, because it is not hungry, but the bamboo jungle has ready its next victim, while the tiger digests the previous one. Now . . . it is ready and prepared to attack again. The tiger always sets the right stage and never gives a chance to its victim. It knows the conditions and how to use its claws most effectively, after waiting in silence, hidden from view. Crouching, it waits and waits, patiently sharpens its claws, strengthens its muscles, and becomes hungry once more. But the eagle does not sleep either. From the heights she extends her wings; there is no one to challenge her proud flight.

The tiger is leaving its territory and beginning to invade the eagle's, but the eagle is awake and ready, and has prepared her weapons, because the moment has arrived. From the air she strikes at the tiger, who is not used to such an attack. The tiger counter-attacks and breaks the backbone of its victim, immobilizing it. The eagle has never tackled such a large opponent, and further, it doesn't know how to handle it in the open, risking a defeat from the start. The eagle will fight its enemy inch by inch and with its claws will blind the tiger, which will be left in the open, defenseless against the jackals and other scavengers. The eagle has won, and this will be known in fields and cities. Look at her!

But the eagle cannot feel safe in her nest, in her mountain, because if she acts without intelligence, she can be destroyed, too. Many animals, seeing how powerful she is, will conspire and try to attack and destroy her, and here is the answer to your questions. Why do not the lion, the bear, and the other animals leave their burrows? Many will find that it is not necessary to keep on fighting; it is better to make an alliance, to follow the eagle to share the leftovers. The tiger died here; here he fought his last battle. The eagle flies high and catches its prey. Who will fight the eagle? The bear cannot reach the high cliffs, nor the lion. Who can fight the eagle? There is only one bird as strong as the eagle, the condor! The condor will dispute the supremacy on its own terms with the eagle. The condor has a nest . . . it has food . . . it has room . . . has sea and land, and between them is the Hurricane. . . .

At the group level we discussed the symbology of this message, without clear indication as to what the Venusians meant. Architect Heberto Cediel, a very culturally literate man and a member of the group, gave his interpretation, with many historical arguments, which we substantiated as best we could to arrive at a clear picture. The symbology, we felt, must certainly refer to China and the U.S. (the tiger and the eagle), which would point to a war, which would start when China suddenly attacks (we believe) Russia. The condor is without doubt South America. We leave the complete interpretation to those who know more than ourselves.

Later, as had been suggested, at 2:00 a.m. that night, I learned by direct transmission to my brain where to go for the upcoming physical encounter with the Venusians. I left with a farewell from the group, wishing me good luck

Costa Rica, site of the Volcano Irazú. Left to right: Dr. Jacques Vallée, U.S.A.; Prof. Carlos Ortiz de La Huerta, Mexico; Carlos Vilchez, Costa Rica; Enrique Castillo R.; and Salvador Freixedo, Spain. The scientists and investigators questioned Enrique at the very edge of the volcano.

Photo: Ricardo Vilchez

Enrique Castillo R. with several investigators questioning him on the sighting of the UFOs in the area of the Volcano Irazú in 1963, in Costa Rica.

during the encounter. The day had arrived to meet the Venusians face-to-face, especially Orhion and Yamaruck, who had become so dear to us. I think everyone felt this way, as they awakened in us a strong feeling of love towards humanity. I do not wish to give the reader the false impression that this was something affected or fanatic. Not at all! We all knew that something grandiose and different from what other mortals normally experience was taking place. I never asked the members about their feelings; all I know is that they always came on time for the meetings.

The day of the planned encounter, I got up early, protecting myself with a ruana against the cold of the early morning. I took the tape recorder, said goodbye to Gloria, left at 4:00 a.m., and flagged a cab at the corner. When I gave the driver the destination address, he refused to take me. A second driver took me to the main avenue closest to the mountains, by my paying extra.

We arrived at the designated place, where I left the cab and walked up a small hill, from which I could see the mountain called Cruz Verde, behind Monserrate. The meeting was scheduled for 5:00 a.m. I sat on a promontory and waited. The day was about to break.

My heart was beating a little fast, but I was in full possession of my faculties. I had the chance to muse and even to philosophize about the impact that such an experience might have on me and the group. While in deep thought, I perceived a "silent noise." Yes! The ship came, moving slowly in my direction. I could not see how it had entered the forested area, flying at the level of the treetops. Compared to the Pleiadean vessel, this one was only about sixteen meters in diameter, by four meters high at its center, where there was a transparent dome.

While it approached, I noticed some strange "rings" at its bottom, which separated when it slowed down. I could see the vessel moving against the background of the forest. When the ship was about thirty meters away, I started my tape recorder. I heard a whistle similar to that produced by the wind against electric cables, which I remembered from my childhood in Costa Rica. My heart was beating fast. In a few seconds, I was going to meet the Venusians. What were they like? What was their appearance? What would be our mutual reactions?

I would know the answers in a few more seconds. The sound decreased, and the ship started its descent into a clearing. As the "rings" separated, landing feet were projected through the opening. The noise ended. Daylight began to break the darkness. I pointed the microphone of the recorder towards the ship to record the sounds, even my steps on the ground and on the dry leaves. A hatch-ramp opened, and I glimpsed some small legs, without being able to see the rest of the body. I heard in my brain an invitation to come aboard the ship, which was now stationary on the ground.

I walked fast and pronounced aloud the names of the Commanders: "Brother Yamaruck? Brother Orhion?" While traversing the thirty meters that separated me from the ship, I saw several of them waiting inside, standing in a semicircle. I was greatly surprised. I expected them to be at least 1.70 meters tall. Not so. I realized that they were small in size, and this surprised me, because I had read George Adamski's reports, saying that the Venusians were rather tall, 1.70-1.75 meters. Now I was a bit confused, but, forgetting this subject, I hurried aboard, ascending the sloping ramp. The tape recorder distracted me momentarily; it was not working. The ramp was of a sandy texture, about four meters long. When I reached the interior platform, I was really surprised: all of the crewmen welcoming me were very much alike, all about 1.50 meters tall, but very human-like. I was about to speak to them, when I heard their welcome greeting, in perfect Spanish:

"Hello, Brother Enrique. Is everything okay?" I extended my hand and greeted each one standing in the semicircle. They were five. I asked, "Orhion? Yamaruck?" At the front was Ourino, then Yaraka, Febo, Baros, Commander Yamaruck, and finally Orhion entered. At last, I was able to meet in person the one who had taught us the values of spirit!

I was feeling like a hero, triumphant over evil; it was incredible that such an exalted being could be so human and similar to us. I embraced him, and on an impulse, I kissed him on his cheek. I felt surprised by my own action. He, holding me by my shoulders, returned the salutation. It was a timeless moment; all the others watched us, silent and smiling. Commander Yamaruck broke the silence and invited me to come in. I walked with him, and the rest followed us. I noticed that they reached the height of my nose, and I calculated that their height must be about 1.50 meters.

At one side of the metallic hallway, an ample door led us towards the center of the ship. Individual and well-padded chairs awaited us. I observed, around Orhion's neck, a sort of necklace with some lettering and symbols that looked like "runes." The others did not wear anything, such as stripes, indicative of their rank. Commander Yamaruck wore a smart, silver-colored, one-piece uniform; the rest wore light green, similar uniforms, with several horizontal and vertical pockets. Their boots were dull silver, with soft lights on their soles, which illuminated the floor as they walked. Their exposed hands showed a smooth skin, which I felt during our handshake and the brief contact with Orhion's cheek.

They told me there were sixteen crewmen, distributed on two levels and in the dome, each with different assignments. As compared with the Pleiadeans, they didn't show me their engine or power source, and they did not "disinfect" me. The conversation started in Spanish, but they mentioned that they could speak several other Terran languages as well. The subject of the conversation was mostly the group and the results of the information received during the six months from December 1973 until the present month of July 1974. They said that they belonged to the same stellar organization as the Pleiadeans, only that these were much more advanced in many fields.

There were exchange agreements between the Pleiadeans and Venusians on undisclosed matters. As the Venusians asked me questions on the development of the group, during the approximately forty minutes that I stayed aboard, I began to suspect that they were carrying out some type of test on us, the nature of which I could not evaluate. The spiritual and messianic teachings, having a Christian flavor, seemed to me to be intended as a means of gauging the reactions of humans when faced with news of a serious, impacting, possible event at a planetary level, because our religious beliefs are so entrenched. I believe they purposely touched the point of our religious beliefs, to estimate the reactions at planetary level, should they disclose that humanity was not created as taught by the religions, and show that all humanity will have to drastically change their values and actions in order to survive, or else face certain extinction.

I warn the reader (and this is only a suspicion) that these non-Terrans, who in the remotest past could have had a direct influence on our beginnings, might feel disappointed at the manner in which their teachings have been misused by humans, and how they have been utilized instead for gaining control of and manipulating people. By this statement, I openly beg pardon to all my friends who are or were members of the group, if they feel offended, but I have thought out this matter at length, and this is my conclusion.

The stay aboard progressed to meeting the six crew members. They mentioned the arrival of a gigantic ship with a very important personality for an interview with two greatly-evolved men from Earth, a meeting that was to take place during the following month of August. I received the impression that after this meeting, something serious would happen, such as World War III, but it was not to be so. I found the implications of this meeting very difficult to interpret.

From the few questions that I asked, they sketched a very grim picture for humanity's future. By now, it seemed clear that the time for their communications with our group was coming to an end. But the information already received had given me a clear idea about the future, both short and long term, in the political, military, social, and especially religious fields. Upon ending our conversations, they sent special regards to brother Quiroga and his son Javier. These two had been able to establish communications with the Venusians, but for some reason were not able to maintain it. They also made a comment about the name that we would give to the baby that Gloria was expecting, and predicted that it would be a boy and would be born between the 23 and 25 of December, 1974. How could they predict this so exactly?

They had approved our calling him Orhion Yamaruck, because Gloria preferred Yamaruck, and I favored Orhion. We finally reached an agreement, using the two names, with the approval of both beings. They also asked me to pay attention to the organization of the group, because "something" seemed to endanger it. Furthermore, I suspect that this "something" was to accelerate the phasing out of the plan. (Apparently there was a more complete teaching plan that was for some reason cut short.)

This entire contact took place aboard the ship while it stood still on its legs at the landing site. The farewell was quite friendly and jovial, giving me a great deal of inner confidence. I felt privileged. Why not? I was one of the few mortals who can tell such a story.

The ship took off after I had walked away from it a safe distance. I felt very nostalgic, and my eyes watered. I heard the barking of dogs in the distance, which were recorded on the tape, once it came back to life. Far away, a plane became visible in the cold but beautiful dawn. I recorded with my voice my impressions about the encounter and sat on the grass to meditate and regain my balance after such an experience.

Now I am sure that the extraterrestrial presence on our planet operates according to and obeys a long range, specific plan, with all the consequences that this implies. The two universal opposing forces, good and evil, are confronting each other, and so far, there is not a clear winner. Later, I will explain how perhaps the force of Truth will prevail, just when everything will seem lost, as when in the suspense movies, the "good one" is taking a beating, but he remembers his honor, and thus gains monstrous strength, to defeat his opponent. In this way, the principle of freedom will prevail, and religions no longer will make fanatics out of ignorant people, depriving them of their identity and immortal essence.

15

Teachings from the Stars

"There are other questions and subjects that science does not accept yet, but which during the last decades have achieved a certain degree of respectability and have become the subject of experimental study. Some of these are, for example, telepathy, teleportation, telekinesis, precognition, transmigration, foresight, and the existence of a psyche."
—CHARLES BERLITZ, *World of the Unusual and the Unlikely*

AFTER THE MEETING WITH THE VENUSIANS, I telephoned Chela, where Luis Enrique Cuéllar, a group member, was expecting my call, as we had agreed upon the day before. He picked me up at 10th Avenue and 15th Street, where I had arrived in a cab. He took me directly to Chela's, where they were waiting for me. The first one to greet me was María Teresa, who with a long and touching embrace acknowledged the success of the contact. Then Marjorie, then Richard: one by one they congratulated me.

It was 9:00 a.m. I gave them a brief description of how the events had taken place. We agreed to meet that evening at María Teresa's, where they would listen to the recording of the landing sounds and my voice giving impressions afterwards. Not all of the members of the group could attend, because it was a working day. Luis Enrique took me home without much delay, where Gloria was expecting me.

It was very thrilling to tell them about the encounter with our dear friends from Venus. We listened to the recording and heard very clearly the whistling sound and "silent noise" of the landing craft, the crackling of the dead leaves.

By noon, I developed a very high fever, up to 40º C. I was unable to attend the meeting in such a condition. That evening the group played the cassette, which that same night disappeared mysteriously.

Nobody was able to tell what happened to it. Later, I learned that an individual tried to sell it to a magazine for twenty thousand pesos, a hefty sum of money at that time. The group was uneasy about the disappearance of the cassette. The Institute continued with its tasks of investigating and disseminating information on UFOs. I continued giving interviews through TV, newspapers, and magazines. The TV interviews had impacted public opinion. Letters were received from all over the world, requesting the opportunity for extraterrestrial contact. Others wanted to be introduced to the ETs, and still others wanted a "space ride." It is impossible to include here all the varieties of nuts, supposedly persecuted by the CIA, FBI, or MIB,[1] who visited me at the ICIFE looking for help. We were even visited once by "Jesus and Mary" and three apostles, who claimed that I was Moses!

At the ICIFE I met two people who claimed to be "Helena Blavatsky," two who were "Moses," and one who was "John the Evangelist." One Moses lived in Cali, another in Bogotá. All claimed to have powers that should be kept secret until the arrival of the "last days." Some attributed me with powers, and others took them away. Thus I came to realize why most scientists refuse to listen or pay attention to the UFO subject, because of this horde of half-crazy, self-appointed "contactees." I have heard them speculating, organizing a "city of love," convening sometimes up to forty people in order to "take them to the planet of peace and harmony," or selecting a group of "chosen ones" to take them to a planet where death does not exist, with the prerequisite of relinquishing their material possessions. I have seen the deluded ones cry after learning of the deceit which enveloped them. I have also known unscrupulous "contactees," who rob their foolish followers of their belongings.

One of these insane people spent two weeks without eating, waiting for his powers to manifest, believing that he was Christ's reincarnation. He walked the streets naked, with a long beard so as to resemble Him, saying that the Apocalypse was upon us. He ended up in a clinic, in Medellín. He had been a very cultured professional, from a distinguished family. I personally met both him and his suffering wife, who didn't share his mystic fits.

Gloria's pregnancy progressed normally, and the meetings continued as usual. I must mention that the house where we lived was very humble; it lacked chairs and furniture adequate for welcoming all the people who wanted to meet me. The living room contained only a medium-sized bookcase, a cowhide on the floor as a decorative rug, and a leather bolster. A flower pot stood in the center. The wooden floor was kept very shiny and clean by Gloria, who enjoyed keeping everything in perfect order.

The owner of the house, Ana María, lived in the first bedroom. She was single, very Catholic, about fifty-four years old. A flight of stairs led to a terrace, where the laundry facilities were located. A wall telephone hung at the entrance to the living room, and a small kitchen, a bedroom, an auxiliary room, and a bathroom completed the meager living facilities.

On July 23, 1974, I was awakened by a communication, without Gloria noticing anything; she was soundly asleep. Only a partial transcription of this message follows here, under the title, "The Logic of Logic." I have good reasons for waiting for the points of view of those who read this first part before disclosing the balance of the message in a second book, where the rest of my contacts will be described. I must say, however, "the voice" did not identify itself as an extraterrestrial, exalted spirit, or the like.

Ms. Ana, the landlady, and Gloria did not wake up, dream, or hear anything. It was a normal, quiet night for them. For me, it was one of the most important and fabulous experiences I have had, because of the content of the message. The voice in my brain urged me to get out of bed and go rapidly into the living room, to get paper and pen, and to be ready to write. I listened to the voice, but not as a voice in my brain; the speaker was talking in his own voice, quite loudly, and I was afraid that Ana would wake up. But the voice came from above and commanded me, *"Write, Enrique, write what I am going to tell you."* Sitting on the floor, for lack of a chair and table, I supported the paper pad on the leather bolster, and got ready to write down what I was about to hear.

"Listen, Enrique, and write!" the voice repeated. *"These are true words; be cautious with them. Use them wisely, and make them known when the time arrives; you will know when."*

During the dictation, the voice paused when my hand felt tired of writing. Twice, I ran out of paper, because I didn't anticipate the extent of the material and the amount of information. When the first pad was full, I got out another, this one without lines. Since it was not a full pad to begin with, it didn't last long. Then the ballpoint pen refused to work. There was an interruption until I could get another pen, a blue one this time. The voice stopped and repeated itself, to make sure that I was following correctly. I had to stop and ask whether I was understanding the dictation well enough. The last pages were transcribed on loose-leaf newsprint. I numbered them at first, but there were instances when I pulled them loose and put them on the floor, while shifting position. In the end, I realized that I had failed to number all thirty-nine pages correctly and was forced to organize them according to my memory and their contents. There were three sections, in all, as follows:

1) The Logic of Logic
2) Prophecies about the Northern Country of the South
3) The Fundamentals of Human Terrestrial Evolution

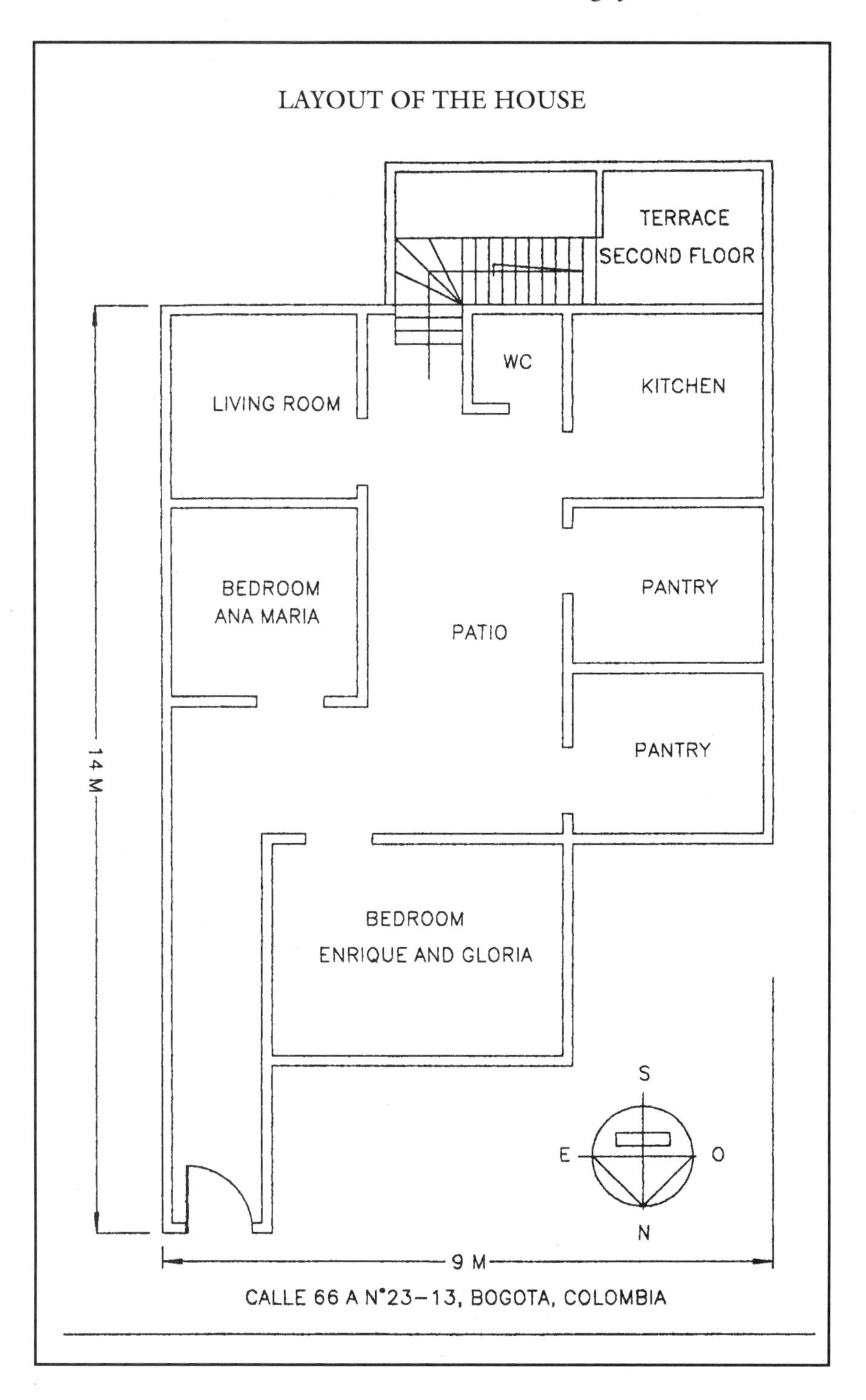
LAYOUT OF THE HOUSE
TERRACE
SECOND FLOOR
WC
KITCHEN
LIVING ROOM
BEDROOM
ANA MARIA
PATIO
PANTRY
PANTRY
BEDROOM
ENRIQUE AND GLORIA
14 M
S
E
O
N
9 M
CALLE 66 A N°23-13, BOGOTA, COLOMBIA

The first part, "The Logic of Logic," is reproduced here.

THE LOGIC OF LOGIC

Information delivered to Enrique Castillo Rincón
on July 23, 1974, from 11:00 p.m. to 3:00 a.m.,
at Bogotá, Colombia, South America.

WISDOM AND KNOWLEDGE SUMMARIZED ACCORDING TO HUMAN LOGIC, FOR ITS INTELLECTUAL AND SPIRITUAL DEVELOPMENT.

Thus, listen, oh Men of all progeny.
I have not spoken just for one breed of Men;
I have not spoken to nor blessed just one people.
I have not taken out arrows to hurl at my enemies,
nor do I throw people into desperation.
Listen, then, to the Manifestation of the Intelligence
that reaches the ear of those who listen.
KNOWLEDGE IS UNIVERSAL AND PERPETUAL;
THE MASTER IS THE INTERPRETER
WHO COMMUNICATES AND SPREADS IT.
Therefore, Truth expands in the measure that Knowledge grows,
and Man expands in the Universe in the measure that he acquires Knowledge.
Do not misunderstand my clear words; do not interpret them otherwise,
I tell you. I do not demand honors for MY NAME,
I punish not those who lack knowledge about ME.
I promise no covenants with any people.
I do not give nor ask anything in exchange for supposed alliances.
Let it be known!
KNOW THE LAW, AND MEN WILL KNOW ME!
Thus I have spoken by mouth of those who know ME.
MY KNOWLEDGE IS CLEAN, do not tarnish it!
MY WISDOM IS ETERNAL, do not undervalue it!

The LOGIC OF LOGIC is prepared to give enlightenment to those who look for the right meaning of THE LAW AND THE TRUTH. And you, the names do not matter, do not fall into rebellion, pretending "to know it all" and underestimating the First Knowledge, which is presented to you. Such is a negative action of the Intelligence, which should not be allowed to advance, lest you see your conscience altered in a useless search, where your senses are fooled by appearances, so to speak, by the defiance of Matter against Spirit. Do not fall into this mistake, where your understanding becomes confused and distorted, altering the mechanisms of the Spirit in its real search for Truth.

Give to men who look for clarity and honesty the LIGHT of CLEAR WORDS WITHOUT CONFUSION. To those who believe themselves sager than the Sage, ignore them; leave them with their dark beliefs, and do not confront them in discussion. If you have undertaken a search to enrich your spirit, then you should know that you have activated certain mechanisms that will link to each other to open the mind and arrive at the TRUTH. If you persevere, you will see this search crowned with an enrichment of your spirit. The one who achieves little will have exalted his search with the WINE OF PEACE. Therefore, it is good to know that whoever undertakes this search will shed along the way his false gods, his fears and dreads, and will leave behind his old wrappings, to ***line himself with a new inner plumage****.*

Such as these will reach new horizons with the Treasures that are available to them. The brave will taste the ***inebriating liquor of Peace and Happiness****. They will understand the Truth and shall walk without fear towards their own IMMORTAL ESSENCE. If fear takes hold of them, it is certain that they have made false interpretations.* ***Be very careful with what you teach as truth*** *to your children and friends, lest you pull them into the same abyss where you are dwelling. And you who at present are a group, it is necessary to collectively put forth the will to advance together as necessary.* ***Afterwards, each one will follow his own path.***

Please believe me: any negative force that you release or produce against someone will eventually come back ***against you. Nothing that hurts another will be without punishment.***

You will have the opportunity to see in regressive form, from the moment of your death back to your birth—all your achievements, your good actions, your happy and bad moments, but you will also see the evil that you have caused to others, the bad intentions within your free will, and your judgments against others. You will see the countereffects against THE LAW, those that you have caused. Here the INDIVIDUAL accepts full responsibility for his wrongdoings and will experience his own punishment. He will have to relive all the scenes that he experienced in physical life and will realize the weight of his own shame and dishonor.

The prediction of what each discarnate being will have to live is written in his own blood. Therefore, he will have to live and feel the same atrocious pain that he caused, in its own essence. Hence, please use well the knowledge that is granted you. Be wise while using it. This action preserves man from errors and failures in his life. It is good to ponder about the events that take place during the lives of

Men. Some believe that SUFFERING inflicted upon you is only a means of God testing you. Here I tell you, SUFFERING is necessary for Men—a passerby in the Planet—not as a testing by God, but as a purifying action of one's own errors, ***both present and past****. Here* ***KARMA*** *functions, in perfect harmony, as a balancing LAW, with mathematical precision. Hence, learn to overcome, and you will improve your spirit without falling into the agonies that will prolong your suffering.*

Let me tell you this: on this Planet called Earth, as a result of multiple evolutionary experiences, a NEW MAN is being created, who will populate this portion of the immense Universe with the necessary components for his MENTAL-SPIRITUAL development, reaching new and high levels on his way to the Universal Knowledge of the Great Creative Conscience. It has not been easy to take this step, but Terrestrial man has shown some intellectual, scientific, and spiritual improvement. These attributes are essential for his perfectioning. We mention it, not to satisfy the pride of some or the vanity of others; we do it because there are already some who deserve it, among you Terrestrials. This process has advanced in a certain measure.

We who have in our hands the necessary ingredients for your development, training, and improvement have taken certain steps, arrived at certain decisions, and taken into account certain faculties developed by certain Terrestrials, who, in a quiet and exemplary way, have become true makers of this great change. WE know them!

We know of their search and sacrifice. We are aware of their great intellectual and spiritual development. In a way, we are surprised. A capacity for forgiveness and inner illumination has emerged within them, conditioning them for the coming changes. Some of these special men and women have already qualified. Many others are on their way, generating undoubtedly adequate momentum for the pattern in question to reach those who are intuitively ready to achieve the level of "CONSCIOUS CONSCIENCE" of the Truth factor. Consider well what we tell you, for we will not repeat it. ***This information must be correctly used and directed.*** *You shall give it with some commentary to the true initiate on the search for Truth. Utilize good judgment, and act responsibly at the moment of delivery.* ***Become Masters of Truth.*** *Be honest while informing others. The times are difficult and tough. Many will not understand.*

It is easier to reject than to check. Do not languish in your attempt to put in the mouths of those who need it, ***the taste of TRUTH.*** *I exhort you to become the determining factors of the MENTAL change. The religions have done what they had to do to survive; now they are dying. If you try to revive them, you will be responsible for acquiring anew* ***the virus of error*** *and for returning to terror and fallacy established as law. Do not waste the opportunity to advance in a tangible* *way, instead of advancing in the false FAITH, for fear of losing your life.* ***We offer you the Crown of Life!***

The New Man *has been born in your land, mutant through excellence, with desirable radiance, with inner sheen, with Eternal Voice. We are giving you, as Law, LOVE and UNDERSTANDING—take them! Leave behind the old trappings that have brought you desolation and ruin. Adorn yourselves with wings of Eternal brilliance! Be daring and brave while trying out this new flight. Do not repeat the mistakes of the past. Cultivate the new attributes of creative majesty in this golden dawn.*

The Old Man shall always fear life. The New Man accepts and understands it. The New Man knows and understands the need for "Death"; all will experience it, whether they accept it or not. It is better, then, to know it and accept it. It is transformation; it is new life. Give, then, to whoever listens to you, to whoever reads you, the certitude of Eternal Life, but also the understanding of the majesty of "Death," and this way it will no longer be ugly or terrible to the eyes of the ignorant. Alleviate their ignorance as to the overbearing need for Death. Give them light and consolation at the ends of their life cycles. ***Remind them about their own essence of Immortality.***

Fill their hearts with beauty from your words, and elevate their souls with understanding. If you do not live and feel what I tell you, it would be wrong for you to dare to talk to others about something you do not understand. Be sincere, and your heart will be the one that will understand and do the talking. The greater the wealth of Man's spirit, the fewer his material bindings. If you see men in elaborate garments, with gold and silver decorations, eating elaborate meals, then you have already identified the false spiritualists, the religious men.

They brag at their table, laden with succulent meals, luxuriously dressed, close to the politicians and the military, preaching false teachings as if they were the true scriptures. Also, there are false learned men among you, who attribute themselves titles valid only among the superstitious, but I can tell you that they have devalued the real and authentic teachings given to you through revelation, and have manipulated the manuscripts according to their whims and interest, like fake "saints."

Thus, be patient and learn to wait. The fracture of all that was established as IMMUTABLE LAW is near—it has already begun—but will happen in individual fashion at the moment of comprehension. In the face of the undeniable TRUTH OF REASON, worn out and wilted are the arguments of the fools and the ignorant who claim that 'GOD gave them infallibility in the interpretation of the Scriptures.' Know them well and be sure to remember them, so that you will not be dragged with them to the abyss, where you will lose your right to reason. The force that leads in rightful exercise to TRUTH is the MENTAL FORCE. Without this attribute, the student can become lost. Mental force generates the mechanisms that will allow you to discriminate the REAL-SPIRITUAL-INTELLECTUAL from the FALSE-RELIGIOUS-DOGMATIC, which annihilates the Conscience of the investigator. Here he loses his capacity to understand, to interpret, to know.

*I warn you not to go in search of distant wisdom—**that your search be clean and wholesome within yourselves**. During your magical dawn, you were given the keys that would open, one after another, the mysterious passages of life, and of your life. Keep your search very present! The disappearance of Conscience in the individuals who fake spiritual knowledge, who experiment with false interpretations through the senses, is a degradation of true knowledge, misinterpreted with obscure motivations. Such exists among you.*

But if your search centers in the true values of the Spirit, in the acquisition of Wisdom, you will be able to distinguish THE FALSE COMMUNICATORS OF TRUTH. They will be easily identified. These obscure individuals will never be permitted to match forces with those who challenge them, point them out, or question them. There you have them!

*Truth shall always be clear and lucid, bright and pure, in the mouth of Its Real Interpreters. The false ones will not be able to give you the satisfaction that your Spirit craves! You must be honest in your faultless search for knowledge, which will merit you the highest credential that Man can obtain: WISDOM. And if you use correctly the new knowledge, with wisdom and prudence, you will be in possession of the noblest achievement of the INITIATE-SEARCHER: **THE ROAD TO IMMORTALITY**. I exhort you to seek for these fruits without pause and without dismay. They will be achieved by those who do not disguise themselves with false plumage. Be it known that the Law sets a time within time for the avatars, the beliefs, and the religions; all is linked to a space-time continuum, and during it, all must be fulfilled, according to Laws known to us. "According to this Law, you will see how the wise man evolves and separates from the fools that encumber the progress of the rest. **Nevertheless, those who listen to and communicate with their INNER VOICE** know and learn that the greatest conquest on the road of evolution is the one that gives them the security of being on the right track, without false pretensions of acquisition of powers or knowledge impossible to interpret. These special individuals, silent, humble, and exemplary in their general behavior, are wise and sound defenders of the Truth. Do not forget what is most important for you: THE KNOWLEDGE OF THE LAW. This requisite is absolutely necessary to be able to enter the Temple of Wisdom and to reach then the threshold of Logic, leaving behind the old conceptions of what seemed to be Truth. **There is nothing more precious that shines of its own, in the eyes of the initiate, than the TRUTH.***

But unfortunately for many who began the path of sacrifice among multiple experiences both spiritual and investigative, they have lost the determination to arrive at the end of the tunnel. They have been fooled by the sparkles and shades of their own intellectuality. They were distracted by indecipherable verbosity, false vanities and appearances, which they accepted, obscuring the true interpretation. Behold, I repeat: beware of the phony interpreters of the Law; they can mislead you like children into their ill-intentioned interpretations. Those who twist and distort the Truth that we gave you, as well as those who proclaim themselves worthy representatives of Wisdom, abound and proliferate among you. They come in all sizes and shades.

It is already traditional among you to participate in so-called spiritualist movements, where well-intentioned searchers for truth fall prey to phony mystics and the falsely illumined, who claim to have "faculties" to tune in to messages transmitted by so many other nonexistent spiritual masters. These humbugs of knowledge also function as priests or priestesses of alienating organizations, which make people lose the true understanding of their own search. How fragile is the human spirit. How fragile is the mind in its interpretation of what seems to be the Truth. Do not permit yourselves to be deceived any further. Let's break the chains of the pretty words that inexorably lead you into the pits of false interpretation. Be brave and daring when using the undefeatable shield of your Inner Voice. You will walk without fear, and nobody will be able to hurt you. The distorters of the Law have their "particular smell," and are recognizable by their peculiar speech.

They are easy to spot by those who with their acts and knowledge of Truth have acquired the logical judgment that is characteristic of the humble and plain followers of the Truth. Do not join their groups; do not be tempted by false doctrines with pious looks. Do not join groups where you lose the right to dissent. Examine them carefully; they are just mediocre individuals who have a gregarious spirit and adore their phony leaders, who manipulate them for their own self-interest. Many are the wretched who walk without direction, without seeing, without hearing. They are the creations of their manipulators, who with half-truths fool them and contaminate the sound knowledge of the true doctrine. Like the owl is blinded in the sunshine, the brilliance of the Truth will blind you when you approach it. It is so written, and it is so. So be very careful not to accept all as incontrovertible truth, lest you grasp only a shadow of the real Truth.

Do not become another fool who accepts all that he hears, just because it consists of sweet words "smeared with God." In this way you will realize that the most sensible way to evolve is through ***inner development****, the alchemy born from the prodigy of the illumination process. You must use REASON to avoid violence; you must use WISDOM, so that there will be justice.*

Wisdom must be used with Logic; therein dwells the greatest WISDOM *of man when selecting his path in life. On the other hand, if you use Knowledge with Logic, your words will be full of reason, and your arguments will be crystal clear.*

There are men who hunt for treasure, but not the treasure that will give you palaces, mansions, or power. The type of man that I speak of is the one clothed in humility and sacrifice, ignored by the adulators and the powerful, whose action endures, growing silently. This is the 'opera magna,' the man dedicated to the service of Truth.

I shall tell you, if the Truth arrives at the gates of your heart and understanding, then your acts will be armored by Equity and Justice. If your acts are the fruit of the Truth that you live, then your Spirit will be indefatigable in the search for new answers for your Soul's thirst for knowledge.

Search out these exceptional men and women. They are the reflection of the well-oriented search for knowledge and Truth. Eternal youth will be given them as their inner answer. Happiness will be their perpetual companion. Under their shade, others will find their path.

They always will have encouraging answers. They shall walk on fertile soil in response to their efforts, and inside them is reflected THE MASTER, WHO MANIFESTS HIMSELF WITH THE POWER OF A HURRICANE.

In such men are born the eternal truths; LOVE *and* KNOWLEDGE *reveal themselves. Their words will be safe, and clear truths will they pronounce.*

Listen to them without fear. Learn from them without dread! THEY *are here already!*

CHAPTER NOTE

[1] "Men in Black," mysterious characters who persecute UFO investigators, contactees, or witnesses.

16

Under Wonderment

"Only at the cosmic scale,
the impossible has possibilities of being true. . . ."
—TEILHARD DE CHARDIN

AFTER CAREFUL CONSIDERATION, I made known only a part of the information I had received to the members of the group, given that I was alone when receiving it. Usually, Yolanda, one of the members of the group, would give a copy of what we received to each participant every week. She used to take the recorded tape home and very patiently make copies with each member's name written in pencil on the front. Why not distribute this latest information to the group? Obviously, the LOGIC treatise mentions the group. But again, why was it transmitted privately? I did not have the answer, and because of this I was very cautious with the information received. Gloria must have read some of it, but I don't recall any comment on her part.

Rereading "The Logic of Logic" several times, almost daily, I realized that the implicit message was dynamite, for its directness in pinpointing several spiritual misconceptions among humankind that had originated thousands of years ago and are still perpetuated in error. How should I go about making this message known without opening old wounds or offending many people? Might not this be considered an attack against the establishment, the traditionally established belief structures?

I struggled between anxiety and glee—anxiety for the feared reaction of those who might feel attacked or threatened, and glee, because I understood that the message was a great renovating force in favor of the true searchers for spiritual truth, including the honest followers of all faiths and religions. It acknowledged a planetary awakening of conscience. For the above reasons, few people were given access to "The Logic of Logic." Also, only in hindsight could I better understand a message that had been given us by the "Greater Brothers" thirteen days before they dictated "The Logic of Logic." In retrospect, I became positive that they had been preparing us for this information, for they had announced something important for a previous evening, on July 11, nearly two weeks before delivering "The Logic of Logic."

That night, in expectation, we wondered what was going to happen. Strangely, we were only nine, among them a newcomer, Vladimir, a student of medicine, who today heads a clinic in Bogotá. He had recently returned from Mexico and had brought with him to the meeting a Mexican "poncho," a long, colorful type of ruana. After our preliminaries, communication had been established. I stretched myself on the floor, in shirt sleeves and with a loose tie, the lights turned off. My head was resting on the bundled-up Mexican poncho. I was instructed to tell all that I saw or heard, in detail. In this way began what they called a "displacement," or the yanking of my spirit from my body through a "connection," so that I could remain fully conscious of what I saw. Here is a transcription of that "displacement."

Bogotá, July 11, 1974, 8:15 p.m.

FIRST DISPLACEMENT TO THE LAN-DAK TEMPLE: THE PRIMITIVE MAN

From the depths of space and time, through countless eons, Man has wandered in search of new horizons—since the first line was established at the beginning of time, since the remotest of times, whose history has become dust. From this origin came the inhabitants of this Planet.

I begin to see dark caves, gigantic creatures, groups of quasi-men fighting them. And I see catastrophic upheavals where both perish. I am shown this titanic struggle, where the spark of intelligence predominates against the behemoths, against the elements that sweep the fields. The tribes get together. The strength of their numbers makes them more powerful against their natural enemies and the forces of nature, as time elapses. And I see time flow by! These creatures begin to see the need for permanent associations, to counteract those forces and neutralize them. Certainly, many are the factors against them, but it is written that they will develop an incipient intellect to fight against adversity.

Many centuries pass by, and I see multicolored flames spewing from the ground, lofty mountains rising up, and the titanic and wrathful force of the elements. Much more time slides by; darkness falls upon the Earth, and new epochs are born: man survives. He survives through the times, the epochs, and the cataclysms, joining with others against adversity, which presents itself implacably. Darkness falls once more upon time and Earth. Man strengthens his conscience, and his intellect grows, stimulated by such difficulties. He is prepared with new weapons for survival. New and better times arrive, and the more primitive struggles are just a memory from the past. I see man entering temples, growing, possessor of enlightenment.

I can see symbols, hieroglyphics; I can see men sitting at temples, surrounded by listeners. The Voice of the Master rises above all, not by its volume, but by the content of his words. I can see him sitting, radiating enlightenment after enlightenment, advice after advice, and I can see the gesturing of his hands and of his head. There is a special expression in his eyes. The movement of his mouth exerts a spell upon the listeners. The thundering voice of the Master fills again the ears of Men.

I see engravings on the pillars of Enlightenment. I look at the walls and put my hands upon its drawings and reliefs, created with perfection in marvelous hues, where history and great deeds are recorded for future generations, so that they will know the treasures from the past. Not all men have access to these treasures; not all can access the old and dusty books that are kept in these vaults, inside tombs and secret caves, and in specially prepared places within temples. I see the Master directing the operation: 'Close and seal in indelible form the vaults, before the hammer comes and destroys them.' Happy epochs, for only a few men keep the keys in their hands, and they share the knowledge with just a few others whom we can discern.

But I keep on walking, brothers, in the Temple! I can see its large pavilions, the height of its roofs, the construction of its windows, the shape of its floors and walls. Here in the Eastern Hall are marvelously colored crystals, through which the sunshine filters. The initiates stay there. I see the Main Hall of the Temple, where only a selected few have access. I can see them with their books, with pen in hand, writing, meditating. Here they light their lamps and oils to stay absorbed in their parchments and their enlightenment.

I keep on going, with a guide whom I can describe fully. He is not old, just middle-aged, wears a toga and a flesh-colored robe, and has no hair on his head. He pierces me with his gaze, and I feel intimidated. He looks penetratingly at me and bids me follow him. And there, at the bottom of the Temple, under a granite mausoleum, he raises his hand and motions me to follow. I can see his chest, his short sleeves, elbow-length. He wears no rings and has long nails, slender and clean hands. Most probably he has never performed manual work in his life. He wears a great pendant on his chest, which sounds metallic. It bangs against a great medallion, which sounds like a rattle. He has no beard, his nose is very straight, and his hair has been shaven. His feet are clean, and he wears leather sandals.

The atmosphere inside is cozy. I can hear the noise and voices of other people inside. He climbs down two steps and motions me to follow; there is much light here. I timidly climb down two or three steps, then bow as a sign of respect. I keep on going all the way down twelve small steps and a large one that points to a great eye inlaid on the floor, on which I am stepping at this moment. It is brightly colored and seems to follow me with its gaze.

The man urges me to follow him, motioning with his hand. It is a very low passageway; I have to lower my head. But everything is flooded with light! I walk and walk; the walls are very white, with nothing drawn on them. The tunnel is long, and the steps of the guide slow and sure. Here is another, brighter light. At the end, there is a small altar. There are no images! At the central hall, a small golden disc hangs from the roof by a golden thread. There are many hanging arches. I would say that all is pure gold. . . . I don't know where the light comes from.

I stop to look at the disc; the guide looks at me and I signal him, asking if it is possible to pause. He remains silent. Then, I follow him, because I don't want to inconvenience him. . . . What wonder! The disc has no markings; it is completely smooth. There is only one oil lamp burning; I would say it smells like incense or myrrh. A strange feeling comes over me. There is a beautiful carved censor, with fine lace above it; it seems made of silk. I had better move; I stop, at a signal from my guide, and a door opens.

THERE **HE** *IS, SITTING! HE is sitting. My guide tells me to wait, and enters. HE is sitting at a rough-hewn table, with lots of books and papers on top of it. There are no lamps, but there is plenty of light. . . . HE is young! Young, and wears His hair long, with a beard. His face is unlike that of my guide; it is kind, loving, and sincere. His clothing is as white as snow, very white. Both of His hands rest on top of the table. The guide comes back out and tells me I can enter. The guide finally talks to me, tells me . . . 'Behold! HE is the Signaled of the Centuries! The One who shall come! The One that came and shall be within us!' The guide tells me to stop, that I should not approach him.*

HE IS THE SIGNALLED OF THE CENTURIES! He is the Great Eye, the Judge, and the Astonishment of the Centuries. . . ! He doesn't talk to me. Doesn't talk to me! I believe He reads my mind, and I ask: Is this the Man for whom I have waited so long? He doesn't answer. My guide puts his hand upon my shoulder, and tells me, 'Do not ask anything!' And I understand that I am allowed only to look, and communicate what I see. That Man smiles and lifts His hands in a kindly gesture—He says that I must learn to wait . . . and now I must leave.

The beauty! The beauty of His face. I shall try to describe it. He is not old. He must possess much wisdom, for He radiates it, and He is there, simply marvelous. His eyes, deep and happy, His cheeks a bit prominent. He smiles, He always smiles. I can see His teeth, extremely white and even: mustache and beard of the same color, not gray nor black, hard to describe; the hair covers it. I cannot see His ears either. His forehead is ample, shows no frown, no wrinkles. From the way He is sitting, I would say that He is no taller than 1.70 meters.

I must leave now. My guide tells me to withdraw; I bow my head in acceptance, and bow before the Signaled of the Centuries, the Signaled of the Times. That is His name. I would say I hear music, but cannot distinguish where it comes from. I don't want to turn around; I want to keep seeing Him. His kind face gives me strength, and I feel safe. . . . There He is, all the wisdom, and the way He stays in absolute, perfect harmony.

It is HIM. And there it is—The Great Book! There it is, The Great Book of the Times! I will be allowed to look at it. They motion to me to draw closer. The Book is below a great sun that I saw at the entrance. My guide washes his hands and wipes them with a white cloth. He tells me to draw closer.

He opens the first page, and directs me to look at it. Do you know what is on the first page? Only two open hands, alone. He turns the second page and tells me, 'Look!' I see drawings of birds, flowers, symbols, hieroglyphics, small hands, one way and another. What strange symbols it has!

Almost all the pages are symbols and signs of prayer. I see two hands held together, two hands, one facing up, the other down. He looks at me again, silently, turning pages after pages, and I do not understand anything. Nothing.

He closes the book; it is large and thick, the pages white, with golden edges. All of the books are printed gold on white, with a great sun symbol and a white pyramid on the front cover. I do not see lettering or anything else. Again, the question: what is inside? A voice responds: "These books are touched only by the Great Masters. They contain the history of man, his origin, his birth and death in each reincarnation, and eternal life, and also the great mysteries of creation—the origin of man, from the confines of where he was created, to the limits of the highest wisdom that he will reach. . . . It is the 'history of history.' It is actually the history of our planet." "And who wrote it?" I ask. "WE DID!" "And who are you?" "We are the conscience of Men. . . ."

I dare to ask: why? The question remains unanswered.

"Your trip has ended," the guide tells me. "You have been allowed to see, but not to ask." I nod with my head, meaning that I understand perfectly. As I leave, my guide gives me a slap on the shoulder, and tells me, "Look again towards the exit."

I move closer to him in order to walk at his right, and he slows down, waiting for me. I ask him, "Where am I? Where have you brought me, and why?" . . . He answers, "I told you before that you are not permitted to ask questions." I walk in silence at his side and try to see as much as possible to keep the information deep in my mind, and I believe I am free to record all that I can see. We pass another door, but it is not the place where we entered! He explains that there are several different chambers, all full of people, initiates. They prepare themselves in that area. I would say that they are secret chambers, because they have no additional doors. They are like exquisitely decorated labyrinths. In each one are two censors, which issue a blue, blue smoke that dilutes in the atmosphere. They must contain incense, because the aroma is marvelously sweet. I am cautioned not to stop and look, and finally. . . . "This is your place, sit down!"

My breath was very shallow, and my heartbeat, according to Vladimir, had almost stopped. For a while, they were worried, listening to me. Having ended the displacement, somebody unwittingly turned the lights on, nearly blinding me. I was thankful for the presence of a lady, a friend of María Teresa (also from Chile and a great esotericist), who took control of the situation, turned the lights off again, and talked to me soothingly. This was my "landing" from a tremendousspiritual experience, where I was face-to-face with an elevated and disconcerting Personage, in a distant temple.

Who was He? Why was He not identified more openly? I was astonished beyond measure. It is important to clarify that this "Message from Lan-dak" was received on July 11, 1974. A week later, on July 18, a second part was received, an astounding complement, which without my knowing it, was the prelude to "The Logic of Logic" message, which was received on July 23. The "Second Displacement to Lan-dak" commenced the same way as the first, but this time I was able to see the name of the temple and know the name of the Master whom the guide called "The Signaled of the Times." I also was able to remain face-to-face with this marvelous Personage for a few minutes.

Bogotá, July 18, 1974 - 8:00 p.m.

SECOND DISPLACEMENT TO THE LAN-DAK TEMPLE

Concentrate on a luminous point, a bright point at the center of our circle, as if you were seeing a small point. . . . Let's concentrate! You must look at it as if it were here, inside. A small shiny light, where we all concentrate our minds. All begin to see it mentally when sweeping their minds clean of images and ideas. Center your minds on the luminous point. Try to make an effort, so that all are ready and comfortable, slightly relaxed, free of images and ideas, and clean in thought. . . . Listen and look attentively, because you will take another trip, during which your mind and senses will steep in the Eternal Aroma of Enlightenment.

I take you to this trip through Time and Space, so you can revive, so you can listen to the words intended for men in all ages and all times, through all those who are designated as "messengers." Thus, you find yourselves in this situation. . . . Pay attention to the small light. . . .

I watch the surroundings and the gardens. Listen, brothers, it is a temple. . . . I am again at the Temple! I walk again and look at the entrance. There is a wooden door with some metallic decorations, copper or bronze. The door is at least four meters high by two meters wide. I feel rather chilly, but not cold. I hear a voice that tells me before entering, "Look to your right."

"At one of the 'vitraux' (stained glass), what do you see?" I see only an exquisitely cut stone, with symbols. I don't understand any of them! Around the stone is a small water fountain. A stream of fresh, clean water falls upon it, and I can see the symbols but cannot read them.

I hear the voice again; it says, "Here is the name of the Temple. If you want to know the name, you will." "I want to know it!" I repeat. I move in front; it is strange; the water stops flowing, and I can see more clearly now. . . . I make an effort to concentrate, and I hold my head with my hands. My head aches, but I can see: LAN-DAK. That is the word. I can see it clearly. I open my eyes, and I can still see the stone with the same symbols. Lan-Dak! . . . Lan-Dak! I must remember: The Temple of Lan-Dak. The door opens ponderously, and I am told, "Come in, go ahead!" And I hear a voice that tells me, "Repeat all that you hear." I begin walking and see again the walls, the inscribed stones, and the colored drawings. Most of them are brown or dark yellow, which produces a feeling of movement as I walk by: it is the effect of light and color.

I hear the voice again. . . . "From the Heavens are given vestments to the fearless, to those who persist and armor themselves with love, because anyone who sharpens and sharpens his blade, shall lose the ability to cut. . . . The more you sharpen the blade, the less the blade will last."

I walk again and see once more the stairs, wide and high . . . the pillars, columns, censors alight, the smell of incense and myrrh. I am aware of voices that talk, that argue. I hear several voices: "Remember this name, so that you can investigate by yourself, so that you can revive the Inner Voice, so that you can develop your mental brilliancy. Listen to this name: RAM-RI-DAN is The Name. . . . RAM-RI-DAN is the name. This great name will be remembered. You should investigate all you can about his life and facts, because this great man, this Great Master, and the temple that you are watching, originated here. The Temple of all Wisdom. The Temple where eternal Truth shines and burns for all men who look for it.

"Because you are no longer sheep; BECAUSE YOU WEAR NEW GARMENTS and the LIVING ENERGY that propels the worlds, that begets men, is accumulating for you. . . that begets mind and conscience. . . . Whoever rides the doctrine of Love, LIGHTS UP THE CANDLE FOR HIMSELF, and [who] searches and investigates, will be given the rest besides, because enlightenment, and wisdom, and THE SUPREME FLAME THAT ILLUMINES, is never extinguished. There is the food for man, and there is the Innominate. Look at Him well! HERE IS THE FLAME THAT LIGHTS THE WORLD. . . . Here is the Innominate, look at Him well! Here is the Innominate. THERE IS THE

BREATH OF LIFE, the way of the ways, the history of history. And ALL THE LOVE AND THE WISDOM OF THE UNIVERSE. Imperium has been given Him, AND ALL THINGS ARE SUBJECT TO THE INNOMINATE, for He learned here, here He saw the light of the Father, and from here came the Light of the World. From here came Truth, and the new and wholesome doctrine. We watch that under the protection of the Eternal Light, ALL EYES CAN SHINE WITH THEIR OWN LIGHT.

"Do not clasp to your chest more than you need to live. For he who loves his life in excess will lose it. He who gives his life away to bring Truth to the world, or for his friend, will find it. It is a pun, and he who understands my parables will find the light of life. The one who loves too much what he has, will lose it. And whoever loves exceedingly the world, and what it contains, will lose his life and shall never find it.

"The first sparkle that reaches your mind is precious and will permit you to constitute your Book of Life; gradually, I WILL PERMIT YOU TO ASCEND AND TO SEE, so that you do not lose the incipient sparkle given to you. I WILL PERMIT YOU TO WALK THROUGHOUT THE TEMPLE, because it is written that the enlightenment will issue from here, and my voice will emerge and reach people such as you, brother, who are forged by fire and wind, in the water, and with the taste of earth. Do not despair; patience makes the miracle!

"You can look back this way: walk some more, and then look again. The voice you hear shall speak again, and my hands will extend over you. FOR I AM THE LIFE-GIVER AND THE ONE WHO PREPARES IT. I CAN GIVE ETERNAL LIFE. No one will blame me for bringing death to this world. I HAVE MY HANDS CLEAN, AND MY FATHER IS MY WITNESS. I bring death to no one. Death meets only the one who looks for it, BECAUSE I AM LIFE, AND LIFE IS MY NAME. I GAVE MY LIFE AWAY IN ORDER TO GAIN IT, so all who believe in me are never lost AND HAVE ETERNAL LIFE. I give you a portion of My life breath, and when the day comes to rip My vestments before My Father, I will testify THAT I BRING LIFE, AND LIFE IS MY NAME. I have given Love, and Love is My Name. I HAVE SPOKEN TRUTH, BECAUSE I AM TRUTH, and in Me are contained all things, and Imperium is My Name.

"I HAVE BEEN WITH YOU IN THE BEGINNING, AND I SHALL BE AT THE END. And if any of you understands My words, and gets close to Me, I will extend him My strong hand, and will cover him with My robe, and will give him to taste the eternal love that comes down from the Heavens, so that he becomes a new man—so that he is indoctrinated with Me, and I with him, so that the son of man is not lost, and WE CAN BE TOGETHER WITH THE FATHER, AND ALL OF YOU IN HIM. I always speak of life, and if you deliver with Me this enlightenment, YOU CAN BE CALLED CHILDREN OF GOD. You can

look at Me: you can see that I give you Eternal Life. IF YOU FOLLOW ME, YOU WILL NEVER SUFFER THIRST OR HUNGER, because I am the Good Shepherd, and I rescue with My hands, and give you life. Take then your vestments and follow Me; do not leave thorns along the way. You can go. . . . You can go now.

"Go back, take to all My eternal blessing, so no one will be lost. TELL THEM THAT I AM FOR THEM, so that they can be in Me, and at the right time I shall gather them and will put them among ours. Peace be always with you. AND I AM FOR YOU. . . . Amen. . . . Peace. . . . Peace. . . . Peace."

Once the experience finished, we all embraced with much happiness. Somebody said that he had never experienced such a deep love and peaceful feeling. I cannot make clear what type of phenomenon took place, totally directed by the extraterrestrials. I am sure it was not an astral trip or "unfolding," which I have also experienced without my will, and without their intervention. Therefore, it is difficult to identify what sort of experience I was subjected to. I can say only that I felt cold air on my face and the cozy atmosphere inside the temple; I smelled the incense, touched the walls, clearly listened to the voices, and experienced the tremendous impact of being in front of a superior spiritual Being. What is His role? Who is He really? Why did the Pleiadeans have me see and hear Him? What is going to happen? Was it a trip in time, visiting the past? How to prove what happened? Honestly, I have no answer.

Some members of the group frequently visited at my home, not only as group members, but also because a great friendship had grown between us. As stated previously, the original group had disintegrated, and new members had joined. The new members of the group were:

Alcides Camelo (introduced by Pedro Avila)
Ernesto Pérez Gaitán (invited by Richard)
Gloria Inés Ortiz (my girlfriend at the time)
Yolanda Franco
Luis Enrique Cuéllar
Rafael Cozzarelli
Vera Quintana
Captain Gustavo Gómez
Vladimir
Fabio Gómez (who didn't last for long)
Gerardo León
Nelly Ordóñez (Gerardo's girl friend)
Nelly's sister, whose name I don't remember.

The number of members increased to twenty-six, and we divided into two groups. The original group had thirteen members, but was called the "Group of Twelve." The second group met at the home of Gerardo León, as already mentioned, on 11th Street and 31A Avenue, in the southwest, industrial sector of town. Frequently, some of the second group attended the meetings of the first. For me, it was exhausting, since at Richard Deeb's, Marjorie's, and Gerardo's, I was the "receiver" of the communications. A few times Alcides Camelo was the "channel," but there was a problem; he could not interpret the communications. Sometimes Chela was the receiver, while the two groups developed. Karen participated sporadically, because she kept returning to Mexico, after some short visits in Bogotá.

Once we met on an emergency basis, because the Greater Brothers from Venus had announced that the time was ripe for a visitor announced previously to talk to us. This was on August 26, 1974. Two days before, a surprise birthday party had been held for me at the office. It became, without my knowing it, a farewell party from Conmutel Ltd., because the following month I left the company, where I had served as a manager. For the meeting of the 26th, since it was a special celebration, we invited many unknown people. Each member invited others who were unbelievers in the UFO subject. The meeting place for so many people was an empty apartment that Marjorie had on 20th Street and 5th Avenue, a corner building, third floor. It was at 10:00 p.m. People were seated on the floor, except for two chairs, one for me and one for Marjorie.

This was the message. The recorders began to roll. . . .

Bogotá, August 26, 1974, 10:00 p.m.
Telepathy by Enrique Castillo Rincón

FAREWELL FROM ORHION

Good evening, good day, dear brothers:

LIGHT and ENLIGHTENMENT open your spirits to receive WISDOM according to your wishes.

We convened you tonight to explain why He has come to this planet and is among you, my Great Master, SAAMAT KAMUT. He will address you personally, as well as myself, He who for many hours has been in your hearts and has given them the force that vivifies the spirit, which will stay with you and with me. This is one of the greatest treasures that I have received. I have enjoyed giving you my words and messages, which lately you have been able to understand.

This is the last time that I will be with you; I leave my heart, which so many times has beaten for you. If any of your hearts can beat with the Universe, it will find its origin. If anyone should salute his brother, he is turning towards himself, the very conception that He has created of life.

During my last day in town, I have addressed you by express wish of my Master and myself, because you of the group beat in my heart, and I took you on as my mission. I have made myself responsible for each one of you, and the flower of beauty has grown in my heart. The love was already there, but you have made it bloom. I told you many times that my love for you was great and real, and I manifested it to my brother Enrique, and that there was only one path which, in my words by means of the message, all will find in a simple and clear way their Truth.

If you found in my words no LOVE, no WARMTH, cold was my heart.

If you found no TENDERNESS, my words were bitter. . . .

If you found no SWEETNESS, I have failed in my mission. . . .

If you could not understand the love I gave you, my visit has lost its purpose. Therefore, when I say goodbye, I leave you the deepest of my wishes: THAT EACH ONE OF YOU ENCOUNTERS HIS OWN SELF, AND HIS REASON FOR EXISTING. My purpose in this mission was to give you a breath of Life, to give you LIGHT and ENLIGHTENMENT, so that under the protection of heavens, each one finds the ESSENCE AND SPIRIT, which are revealed only to the men who find inside themselves the manifestation of their Own Maker.

I reveal to you tonight that he who improves himself has a great future in the NEW WORLD that is coming, which according to what I have been able to perceive, CERTAINLY FEW DESERVE.

To brother Enrique, I remind him of my words: 'For the time has arrived to obtain the crown of life.' MY LOVE remains for all of the group. I leave you my blessing, wishing you PEACE.

Later, I became aware that the greeting of the message, "Good evening, good day," was due to the fact that at the location from where he addressed us, it was daytime. The messianic-spiritual flavor was a constant among the Venusian communications to the group, some of which I cannot publish here on account of their length. There is no doubt that it was the traditional messianic style, against which I myself, being the means of transmission, once rebelled.

Orhion was leaving, and this was sad news, because we all liked him. Once he told us that he was young, only 150 terrestrial years old, out of a total 300 that they lived. The sadness that we all felt was really tremendous. I kept my own feelings to myself.

Then, right away, without interruption, a second message came in, at 10:25 p.m.:

Bogotá, August 26, 1974. 10:25 p.m.
Telepathy by Enrique Castillo Rincón

Message from MASTER SAAMAT HAMUT, Visitor to Our Planet

Dear brothers, good evening, good day: The sadness that overtakes me, the pain that my heart feels, the experience that I have lived, what I have seen and heard, have made me think deeply about your destiny. All the men of this world, in the groups that felt my words, who approached me, received ENLIGHTENMENT. I see in their hearts, in all of them. Sadly, I see fallacious words, pride, egotism, few virtues, little love, and what is sadder, much darkness. My arrival on the Planet had as a specific purpose to meet with two marvelous men from your world. These meetings took place on August 20 and 23, with many selected as witnesses of the meeting.

THESE TWO MARVELOUS MEN, who dwell among you, HAVE THE RESPONSIBILITY OF PREPARING YOUR WORLD, of building the foundations upon which will rest the peace and enlightenment of the future. This was my mission, where my race and my world, connected to you in one and only one purpose, took the steps to accelerate the arrival of these events that will astonish all. IT OBEYS A PLAN, unknown to you but designed with the highest WISDOM, where MY PLANET AND MYSELF and many brothers from the Universe have a role in the ETERNAL SEARCH FOR TRUTH AMONG MEN, the struggle between good and evil. The foundations were established, the responsibility resting upon these two marvelous beings.

PREPARE EACH ONE AND HIS BROTHERS, and learn to wait, but above all, learn to visualize and to know the new concept: LOVE, MEN, AND UNIVERSE ARE INEXTRICABLY UNITED, AS THE CENTRAL TURNING POINT OF POWER AND ENLIGHTENMENT. Blessed are those who received and waited for this moment. More than 1200 people from this Planet, among them several children, heard my words; the ones who could not receive me, lost the LIGHT OF TRUTH. . . . And if you brothers understand, then all effort is worthwhile to arrive at the final enlightenment. . . . I leave each one a blessing that contains all the strength of THE CREATOR.

Thus, my planet is your planet. From this point, you will be closer, and only one word will keep us together, AND ONLY ONE MAN, . . . LOVE AND MY BROTHER AND YOUR BROTHER, JESUS THE CHRIST, AND HIS TRUTH REVEALED TO THE WORLD.

May you find peace and the world you are looking for! Peace. . . . Peace. . . . Peace. . . .

May, 1991. Left to right: Mrs. Ana G. Merchán de Castillo (wife of author), Colonel Wendelle C. Stevens and daughter, and Enrique Castillo at the UFO World Congress in Tucson, Arizona, U.S.A.
Photo: José Noriega

Mrs. Marina Popovich of Russia, pilot and astronaut, with Enrique Castillo R. at the UFO World Congress in Tucson, Arizona, U.S.A.

Enrique Castillo R. and his wife, Ana, at the UFO World Congress in Tucson, Arizona.

One day, about that time, a man and his son visited our office. They asked for me, using my full name. These strangers said they had been invited by beings identified as from the Sixth Dimension. The boy, very early, had developed surprising paranormal capacities, such as levitation, telepathy, mediumship, and so on. During one of Arturo's spells (that was his name), these beings showed up, using the same names known to us. They were now accompanied by a fourth entity, AJAX (I couldn't help thinking about a detergent). The four told them about their contacts with our group and asked them to get in touch with me to improve their information. Arturo and his father, Enrique Murillo, showed me the message received, which matched ours completely. Arturo and his father in this instance had lost precious time in locating me, and the Sixth Dimension beings had already finished their visit to our world. Later, Arturo, with Dr. Eberto Cediel, a member of the group, carried out incredible telepathic experiences. This fact reinforced one of my suspicions: even to the dislike of the members of the group, and regardless of their friendship and respect, we had to accept that I am not a telepath. The extraterrestrials communicated with me and the group because they so desired, and not because I was especially gifted. This would be proven later. Such awarenesses reduced to some degree the mystic style of our meetings, contributing to the further fracture of their structure.

Regardless, the messages continued. The Venusians told us about a second purpose of their expedition: they were supposed to contact people from this planet. That is why they took advantage of our link with the Pleiadeans, with their permission, to improve our information and knowledge.

I read again the several messages received from the extraterrestrials, and one of them caught my attention while I was sitting on the floor at my home, because somehow the contacts and communications had filled me with doubts . . . such as, where was all this leading us? The following message gave me inner strength:

Bogotá, May 10, 1974

MESSAGE FROM "WISDOM MASTER"
TO THOSE WHO START ON THEIR WAY
"Which is the way?"

For all those spirits who have lost their way,
For all those who have had only darkness as roof,
For all who have been covered by the mantle of confusion,
For the ones who have walked and have to return to start anew,
For those who leave no track or leave something of themselves along the way,

For all those who search for the impossible, and for those who do not,
There is only one way, there is only one horizon, and from it, only one sky.
Altruism, kindness, beauty, magnificence, love, understanding,
Empty words they are, when pronounced constantly,
Without knowing the meaning of their essence, but there is wisdom in them.
I shall tell those who seek only this: What do you want to find?
What do you want for yourselves and for others?
I shall leave you my sound advice and shall give you my words:
Listen to me, then! To those whom I love, listen to me.
The man who meditates and thinks his thoughts over and over,
So that his thoughts are compressed and renewed, his spirit grows,
And the humility that makes him small before the eyes of his fellow men
Makes him greater in front of the Universe.
The small one is great, and the great shall grow small,
And he who has learned to walk can reject what he has done so far,
Because it will be lost, and the one who has walked without knowing
has to start anew.
All men, unquestionably all, without a single exception,
Shall have to walk this pathway.
And you, who have learned to walk without help and without backing,
If you do not abide by what I tell you,
along the way you will have to lean on a cane,
And you will not be able to achieve much.
Trees give no different fruit than according to their own species,
And each species gives nothing different from itself.
Man cannot give more than what he has.
You have seen that no frontiers have been set for man;
He has been given the way to walk, and he must do it,
Because it is a shame that someone enters the pathway
And has to return because he is lost.
Shame on whoever has seen the light but loves darkness,
And shame on all those who insist blindly in leading the way for others,
Where there is no truth.
There are those who possess enlightenment and blind others,
And they shall be judged sternly according to the Law.
Learn from children when they walk, and from the old when they sit,
And from the sensible man who builds his house on rock,
And learn from birds, and from the wind, and from the sea,
and from the river,
From the little bird building its nest, from the ant, and from all,
But above all, from yourselves.

I bless you and remember you; you are standing at the doorway of a new world. I assure you, you are already in it.

While the Venusians flooded us with deeply spiritual messages, the Pleiadeans, through Krishnamerck (Cyril Weiss), made us aware, in 1974, about the existence of another force, "the evil ones," among some of the extraterrestrials, whom the Greater Brothers had well identified as to who they were, where they came from, and why they were here.

When I discussed this matter in public, I had no idea of their origin and identity. The Pleiadeans never told me. They told me that they were their "spiritual enemies," and that they had sustained confrontations with them in the past. When I gave out this information, even close friends, including two members of our Executive Board, told me that I was wrong, that there were no "evil ones," only incorrect interpretations. About this time, the arrival of Eugenio Siragusa, the "Italian contactee," made me keep quiet about the "evil ones" for a while, in order to avoid frictions or controversies, since several of the members of the Institute were his followers and distributed his written material.

Siragusa arrived around June of 1974, escorted by several secretaries and assistants, which left me perplexed, for we could not understand how he could afford to travel through several countries, stopping at good hotels. Anyway, this did not concern us directly; we could not criticize, but only make a passing comment. His arrival increased the "UFO wave" that had been initiated in 1973. His statements and conferences at the ICIFE headquarters made me fall into one of my worst mistakes, namely, stating twice in public that World War III would occur in less than a year. This was influenced both by Eugenio and by a color picture showing a supposed ship next to the figures it had traced in the sky, which, according to him, was the fateful number "76." The newspapers and TV had already reported, live, an interview, where he claimed to be the reincarnation of John the Evangelist! I felt extremely embarrassed when I heard such nonsense.

Another incident by Eugenio Siragusa left all the members of the Executive Board of ICIFE speechless, when they went to bid him farewell at the airport. Eugenio told them something that, upon returning to the office, no one knew how to express. All were impressed and very moved but could find no way to tell their story. After some whispering amongst them, the responsibility fell upon my old friend, Luis Francisco Quiroga, "Pacho," a former soccer player at River Plate from Cundinamarca.[1] Pacho, with a serious and stern face, told me bluntly, "My dear Enrique, my friend, you are Luke, the Apostle!" As you can well understand, dear reader, I was utterly speechless.

After a few seconds, in the midst of the silence, with all looking at me and expecting an answer, I asked for the origin of such a statement. Gilberto Ferreira repeated the words of Siragusa: "I leave very pleased, because I have found another one of Christ's apostles." Somewhat uncomfortable, I invited them to reflect upon such a statement. They knew that I was not a spiritualist and had never shown any signs of being such a personality. While I rejected such statements in a definite way, they argued that perhaps I didn't know it, or was unaware of it. I judge such a statement as showing a tremendous lack of responsibility on the part of Eugenio. Kiddingly, I told them that this was not possible, for if the real Luke had come back, he surely would be conscious of such fact, and surely would preach the Gospel once more, something I have never done and never will do in the future. Dr. Juan Guáqueta, member of the Board, repeated the statement that I could be Luke. I asked them to stop such nonsense and please not spread such speculation any further, because it could injure me seriously. We concluded the incident, and all my friends complied with my request of not divulging such a fantastic idea, which they have honored until today.

Meanwhile, the Pleiadeans suggested that I be very cautious, because "the Other Force" already had a foothold on the planet and had penetrated several levels of society, fooling with much tact many phony spiritualists, who vibrate at a certain rate. This force was able to identify such people and prey on them, the Pharisees of the truth. The Pleiadeans pointed out that these phony spiritualists are present in the so-called "spiritualist" movements all over, where they produce apparent mystical experiences during sleep.

That Force, powerful and demonic, utilizing men of fragile mind and feeble spirit, had permitted its leaders to occupy a dangerous place, by means of a very powerful weapon that affects those thirsty for power. This was accomplished by means of some psychic "O"-type waves, with which the Pleiadeans could not interfere.

The Pleiadeans also explained to me that terrestrial man has had, from his creation, three special features. About the first, they told me:

"Intelligence is programmed with a special characteristic that indicates our true Genesis; she awakens in individuals within a certain time, for good or bad. This "signal" generally arises in all, even those who have no religious roots. This signal is located in the memory's neurons."

The Pleiadeans further explained that their purpose in being here was that, in a way, they are responsible for the development of intelligence. This seems to coincide with the dreams of thousands of people of all ages, who describe accurately the Greater Brothers, their way of dressing, their ships, and what they are doing in the way of help.

Some scientists deny the existence of the ETs and at the same time, the possibility of their trips across the immensity of space, considering the ridicule to which they could be subjected by the public the world over, were they to take any other position. Even so, I believe that their current stance will be revealed as incorrect before too many years. The only restitution that will be available for these myopic scientists, when all this becomes known openly, will be their apology. After all, they are not infallible; they are human. It will not be the first time that science is proven wrong—and it will not be the first time that they are excused, either.

The public remembers the abyss in which Dr. Edward Condon became submerged, with the University of Colorado, losing face because of his famous book, *The Condon Report,* maliciously rigged, with "shaved" information, all directed by the CIA.

This time public opinion will be more stern, and I believe that although there are scientists who have "sold their soul to the devil" in order to silence all the true information existing today about the real alien presence on our planet, some honest gentlemen scientists do not agree with this situation and believe firmly that all the existing information should be made public all over the world, as soon as possible, before this imposed silencing with dubious motivations turns into a disaster.

Chapter Note

[1] The Colombian state where Bogotá is located.

17

The Shangri-La of the Andes

"Truth never wins; its enemies only die off."
—MAX PLANCK

WHILE THE MEETINGS WERE TAKING PLACE with "the group of twelve," the ICIFE was flooded with people of all kinds and types. The lectures continued, and Dr. Clemente Garavito, director of the Bogotá District Planetarium and very dear and respected in the field of astronomy in Colombia, made himself available as a speaker on these subjects.

My friendship with Dr. Garavito led us to appear together on TV, on a very congenial program conducted by Harvey Caicedo. During the program, Harvey inquired about the mechanisms used by the extraterrestrials to make it known that they do exist. I answered immediately: blackouts. I mentioned the New York City blackout in 1965, and others in several capital cities of many places in the world.

The program ended at 7:30 p.m. If I am not wrong, it was a half-hour program. Clemente drove me home in his car and continued on alone. At 8:00 p.m., a blackout occurred over all of Bogotá. My phone rang; it was Clemente, saying that his neighbors had seen UFOs over Bogotá. We climbed up to the little terrace, and we could see what seemed to be a UFO, because it moved slowly from south to north. Definitely, it was not a plane, and even less likely a satellite, which cannot move in such a trajectory.

The phone rang again and again. People reported sightings of two, four, and up to five ships over Bogotá, even in formation. The press published on the next day the headline, "UFOs OVER BOGOTA." The Electric Energy Company could not give a cogent explanation.

Was it a coincidence, or did the ETs monitor the program and decide to confirm it?

By the way, ICIFE had about one thousand members in Colombia, and many in Ecuador, Costa Rica, and Venezuela, people from the most diverse professions and trades. About thirty percent were women, very interested in the subject. The dues, set by the Executive Board, were only 150 Colombian pesos (about $15 U.S. dollars). It seems incredible, but only twenty-five members paid their dues on time. Some were behind up to two years. The little money that we received covered only the postage stamps to answer the thousands of letters received from Colombia and abroad.

Raffles, collections, painting expositions, conferences, and courses allowed us to pay for the rent, the employees, and to barely survive. We already had collections of magazines, pamphlets, and press clippings from all over the world. A good library, most of the books mine, was donated to the Institute, so that people, in particular the members, could have access to reading material on the subject. "Mysteriously," the books and magazines decreased in number, as if an "extraterrestrial" power made them disappear. Of course, we decided to lend no more books, because most of the time they were not returned to the library.

Time elapsed very quickly. I had to travel to Venezuela, as mentioned before, for two reasons:

The first was to awaken in the Venezuelan public an awareness of the UFO subject; the second was to make a little money for myself, taking advantage of the Venezuelan hard currency, the bolivar, which at the time was worth sixteen Colombian pesos per bolivar.[1] In Caracas I took lodging at a hotel (zero stars), called Hotel Lincoln, near El Silencio Towers, some well-known office buildings in the downtown area, between Miracielos and Hospital Streets. It was a family-run hotel, with meals provided.

Meanwhile, Gloria's pregnancy advanced. All symptoms indicated that the baby would come soon. I found in the Chacao sector a conference room in a reputable high school, "Saint Ignatius of Loyola." At that place I taught my first course, charging 100 bolivars per person, which I used to pay for my immediate expenses. Thirteen persons registered at this first course, which lasted eight days, two hours a day, starting at 6:00 p.m. Christmas was getting close. I opened the course on December 18 and was planning to end it on December 27, excepting Christmas, the 25th. The pupils were anxious to see a contactee at close range, and they accepted me with a lot of enthusiasm.

On the 23rd, while sleeping at the hotel, a communication entered. The extraterrestrials ordered me to go to a certain place in the early morning, a few hours later. With such short notice, there was no opportunity to notify the people registered in the course. I got up, told the receptionist that I had to leave at 3:00 a.m., and asked him to please wake me up if I fell asleep.

I was told not to bring a tape recorder or camera. The trip was going to last about five days. Where were they planning to take me for all that time? I thought the destination could be a nearby planet. Both excited and anguished, I hailed a taxi in front of the hotel. It was almost 3:00 a.m. We started for the town of El Junquito, a tourist location, before Colonia Tovar, a picturesque town, high in the Venezuelan Andes, with many residents of German ancestry, which is about twenty-five kilometers from Caracas. There is a cutoff before Colonia Tovar, at the road to Carayaca. The driver, a Spaniard from Madrid, was a little reticent to engage in conversation at first, but finally we discussed various subjects. Upon arriving at the meeting place, I got out of the cab and paid him, adding an extra tip. It was 4:11 a.m. and cold. I walked another half kilometer on the road, and then into a ravine.

I waited for the indicated hour. A craft suddenly materialized a few meters above ground level, swinging from side to side and projecting a tenuous light downwards.

This one was the classic "flying saucer," six or seven meters in diameter and three meters high, including its dome. With an astounding symmetry in shape, it moved harmoniously, swinging smoothly in complete silence. The nocturnal darkness blended with the ghostly presence of the alien craft. It landed about forty meters from where I stood, a tripod slid down, then a ladder was visible, and a navigator stepped to the ground. He signaled me to approach. I glanced at my watch; it was 4:27 a.m., on the 24th of December, 1974. While Cyril, who was the navigator who met me, and I greeted each other, he informed me that we were to visit a base in the Andes, where we were to receive the information promised during one of the telepathic contacts some months before. Krunula and a stranger, whose name he told me but I have not been able to remember, were on board.

While the craft flew, my first son with Gloria was being born in Bogotá, which I learned later, through a telephone call I made from Caracas to Bogotá on January 19, 1975. He was baptized Orhion Yamaruck, born at 4:33 a.m. on December 24, 1974. Months afterwards, we recalled Orhion's words, when Gloria was less than two months pregnant, that he would be born between the 23rd and the 25th of December. How could he have known it with such accuracy?

We arrived at our destination, a town in the middle of the high and millennial Andes of South America. I thought we were to arrive at a city, but it was a small town, with a good extent of land, as I would find out in a few hours. The flight took only twenty minutes! Thousands of kilometers in such a short time! Incredible! And as usual, I could not detect a single motion or discomfort. This time I was not "sprayed" as the previous times. I forgot to ask them why.

While I mused, Cyril exclaimed, "Look, Enrique!" Below were the majestic Andes, and, at the tip ofone of the mountains, the arrangement of the buildings was clearly visible. Cyril told me that the inhabitants called this place the Vortex of the Andes. "What inhabitants?" I asked.

Cyril answered, "Yes, Enrique, at the moment there are 318 people here, who for many years—even entire families—have been contacted and brought here voluntarily. Here they live, work, study, and learn. They are instructed about the great events that humanity will experience, the teachings of the Law, so that it will prevail. Many of them will be trained to help when the moment arrives. Nobody will know who instructed them, and besides, nobody would believe them; it could even be dangerous for them. This place, at about 3200 meters above sea level, is located between two great mountains that give natural protection against blizzards and frosts, and is known as ALTO PERU (Peru Highlands)."

I am under the impression that the place is closer to Bolivia than to Peru.

It was still dark when we landed. It was impressive to see how the disc flew closely between steep mountain slopes and then landed softly on a platform and slid into the mountain—perhaps through hydraulic means—penetrating in through a horizontal tunnel.

After climbing down to ground level, we walked to an office, where I was asked to take off my sweater and shirt. What surprised me pleasantly was the temperature, about 16ºC, similar to Bogotá, where I had lived for many years. The next day I was able to verify this point. The people getting ready to give me a brief check-up were not extraterrestrial, just ordinary people, except that they used some devices unknown to me. The first test was routine: heart, blood pressure, reflexes, lungs, vision, hearing, etc. They asked me my city of origin and consulted a listing. They wrote down something and asked me if I had with me tape recorders or cameras. I answered no.

They asked me to take my watch off temporarily. They placed a yellow band on my left wrist, and the watch was moved to the right arm. At the end of the examination, another Terran took me to the room where I was going to live during my stay. When I went out, somebody followed us quickly. Apparently there had been a mistake; they explained that the wristband's color had to do with the type of food that I should eat. Finally, I was taken to my temporary bedroom, leaving the comfortable and well-ventilated underground tunnel through the point where we had entered.

Once in my bedroom, I rested on a simple but comfortable bed. I thought I was going to see a city of the future, but the buildings were wooden, sort of

"Canadian type" cabins, with smooth and well-cut but rustic beams and boards. The floor of the corridor leading to the bedroom was polished wood. The great rectangular cabin had two rows of bedrooms, on both sides of its central passageway. I will omit other details to center on the essentials.

Up to then, I thought that I was the only guest at the Vortex. When they announced breakfast, I had not slept. I was restless as to why I had been taken so far and to what mission I was to be assigned. It was 6:45 a.m., and I had been there almost two hours. The fellow who picked me up was surely of Incan descent. I followed him to the dining room. Surprise: six more people waited there, having arrived before me. Others would arrive in an hour or so. These contactees came from nineteen different countries, and eleven were Latin. There was only one woman among us.

There was an individual self-introduction; no names were given, just the countries of origin. Now I knew the meaning of the colored wristbands; all wore them, some different, some of similar colors. Each was to eat from the trays marked with the same color as the wristbands. Instructor number one (there were four) told us that the food had been prepared according to geographic zone. Their ionization was different, according to the elevation above sea level. This way it prevented illnesses from occurring on this account. Another difficult-to-handle aspect was the altitude. I was one of the four older visitors. Some received oxygen upon arrival, after which they felt okay. I felt a bit of "soroche" (altitude sickness). We were given warm—probably goat—milk, honey bread, and some delicious biscuits, freshly baked.

The instructor called our attention from the head of one of the tables; I was sitting along one side of it. He gave us the reasons we were there. Each one would be given privileged information. The information should be treated with utmost care, and we were to be very careful as to who would receive it, either orally or in writing.

Further serious recommendations were to be given to us later. The instructor told us that grave events were taking place in various fields, which would lead the planet to undergo, with its occupants, untoward experiences of several types.

Our presence in that place had the objective of transmitting to the public, through various means, the occurrences that will take place and culminate in several momentous events.

For personal reasons, I do not give out an account of the calamities announced by the instructors. They had information covering many years as to how the facts will unwind. They had a very clear picture of all this, known to all of the inhabitants of the Vortex. The extraterrestrials, through documented and adequate scientific means, had transmitted this astounding information.

And, we were not given all the information. Some reports were not transmitted. Only in case of emergency would they be given, we were informed, through personal contact. The instructors subtly led us to understand, between the lines, as it were, that the Pleiadeans would make the final decisions. We were told that the withholding of certain information from us at that time was intended to protect us from any danger.

This dialogue took place by "telepathic induction." The instructor told us that this was a technique obtained over several years of learning, because only one of the terrestrial instructors had natural abilities, which had been perfected by the extraterrestrials. This ended the presentation.

Afterwards, we walked, enjoying the magnificent view from that fabulous place high in the Andes. We listened to the howling of the wind, clearly perceptible at some places, which was a bone-chilling temperature. We were able to see a great contraption projecting from the mountain, with fins and crystals. We were told that energy is thus captured for the whole community, and that there is another energy source for the appliances and lighting.

One of the energy sources was used for powering a "magnetic shield" or camouflage of the base and its climate-controlled environment. I knew it; I could see it. It was an example of technology used for the benefit of all. We saw fields cultivated with legumes, strawberries, and other fruits. I had seen earlier some tropical fruits at the breakfast table and had wondered to myself about who provided them with oranges, pineapples, and coconuts.

All was managed uniformly. The residents worked, studied, investigated, and learned. They knew history better than students at colleges and universities. I asked myself how I might adapt if I stayed on to live with them.

There was time for leisure. Some slept, and others lounged in the convertible swinging chairs of the corridor of the great cabin. The aroma of chrysanthemums, violets, and forget-me-nots suffused the atmosphere with peace and quiet, as if the world had ground to a halt. Isolated from all haste and hassle, we felt we had entered a veritable "Shangri-La."

Lunch was delicious, composed of a great variety of legumes and greens, with fruit on top. The instructor told us to take a look at the spoons and eating utensils. They were wooden! He explained that each one should take the foods marked with the color of their wristband. Tomatoes and peppers were served whole, complete with the skin. When eating, we were to cut them with the wooden knives and do the same with the rest of the foods. We were told that when cutting them with a metal instrument, a chemical change takes place, producing a loss in the vitamin content. With the wooden knives, the complete content was preserved. "Wonderful!" said some.

It was announced that the following morning we would witness a special event. A very important being was to talk to us. We should just listen; the

whole population of the base would be present. The speaker was not identified. The announcement was repeated until the information was clear.

We retired to exchange views of all kinds. The Mexican doctor was very cheerful, even funny. With others we communicated through sign language and a little English. It was a rather laughable situation. Among the Latins, only with the two Brazilians did we have a little trouble language-wise.

In the afternoon, fully rested, I was called from my room by the same native that I had met upon arrival. He took me to a pleasant, small living room. Cyril entered smiling, and we greeted each other as old friends. He was not wearing a uniform, just cotton trousers, a sporty shirt, and a wool sweater.

"Come here, Enrique, sit here," he said, pointing to a chair. It was 5:00 p.m. "Take some paper and write what I am going to dictate." On a table there were paper, ballpoint pens, and pencils. Six more contactees arrived.

"It is up to you whether or not to divulge what we are teaching you. If you don't, you will not be blamed." The instructions were the same for all. All seven contactees took up paper and pens and got ready to listen to the dictation.

This was the message dictated by Krishnamerck, from the PLEIADES, scientist and liaison officer on Earth, member of the GREAT SOLAR COSMIC BROTHERHOOD, at 5:00 p.m., on the 24th of December, 1974:

MESSAGE TO THE WORLD: PLAN "A" IN ITS THREE PHASES

To all the inhabitants of the planet called Earth, to all my beloved brothers, whatever their origin, color, or social condition, to all those who cannot yet listen to or understand the voice of ETERNAL TRUTH, we announce to you a better world, where a new mind will prevail and take you to true Spiritual Love, where you will live in the True Science of the Spirit, LIGHT-LAW for the children of the Planet, where all the opponents of THE GREAT COSMIC PLAN shall be vanquished, and Supreme Harmony or Greater Absolute Law will be the daily bread for all men.

Most beloved brothers: You will have a clear mind and a great decision to make about this knowledge that is given to you. You will know how to make the right decisions with great wisdom in the face of the Contrary Forces that have been unchained against this Plan. The mere fact of bringing you here has already implied the presence of a great countermovement to establish negative forces with the intention of making us fail, of rejecting and not heeding the true and elevated teachings that give birth to the highest and sacred elevation: the elevation of the Spirit.

If you work with Love, the Opposition is condemned to defeat. If you follow the good behavior commandments, you will be protected; if you stand by Truth, yours is the victory and the compensation of living in a better world. All the sacred principles that have been given to Man, since his pre-existence, must stay with Him, and you and the men of goodwill and clear conscience will fight for them with the weapons of Truth and Justice. Be aware of the protection given to you by the Universal Force of Love, dispensed only by the Great Solar Logos and members of the Planetary Hierarchies.

"Become, then, planters of good seed."

Prepare your brothers, administering patiently and wisely the information: prepare them in groups or individually, according to your best judgment and rightful discrimination. Disseminate the seeds, look for good soil, but if it does not exist, go to the countryside and talk to the workers. Search for those who want to listen, and go wherever you are called. Do not look at their clothing or dwellings; pay attention only to their wish to learn, and deliver the information without adding or removing anything, with a didactic criteria. May the firm wish to propagate the Truth embrace you, and for this purpose, brace yourselves and deliver only what has been given you, and if you give more, make sure it is with the genuine wish to spread in a more ample range, the Truth only.

***PHASE ONE:** In 1958, the U.S. Air Force admitted that the Strategic Air Command bombers had been hurled more than once against Russia, when the* *defense radar detected mysterious objects, which have never been identified, and which flew in apparent formation. It was proven that the attacks were not justified, but the danger is even worse at the present time.*

This information from the U.S. Air Force makes it clear that nuclear war can start by accident or error, through confusion of our ships with rockets from a foreign power against the U.S. It is positively known that our ships can initiate a war, when detected by the radar network, due to the degree of tension and fear between the different countries. Countermeasures have already been taken, both on the part of our ships and the governments of the countries who study the presence of our fleets of Space Ships.

This phase is not difficult to explain, and even less to understand. The important aspect is that our ships are systematically making cautious appearances in the air spaces above all nations, especially those whose technological, military, and technical advancement are such that they are bound to observe us. We have done this for a long time, to create a clear indication of our presence among you.

The recklessness of the governments of two terrestrial countries has been obvious, when they have ordered their combat pilots to attack our Space and Scout Ships, as soon as they are detected in their radar. This is highly dangerous for the crew members of your airplanes, because if they approach our Gravitational Field, their engines and controls become inoperative. In this way, several have lost their lives, because of extreme stubbornness and stupidity. They do not seem to understand that our orders are clear, not to harm their craft. Otherwise, at least fifty of their planes would have been destroyed.

We are aware that many high-ranking military personnel and scientists have been silenced under the pretense of endangering the security of their countries, if public statements were to be made. This is another serious mistake of those governments. If we had any ambition or desire to conquer this Planet, we would have done it 300 years ago, when the population could not have opposed any resistance. Even now, it would not be difficult to do.

This phase is alternative; we shall continue making appearances, landings, contacts, all over the world, more and more frequently, as planned. You will be responsible for the education of the people in the different countries.

This preparation and divulgation can be carried out using all means available: radio, TV, press, conferences, meetings, individual and group talks, pamphlets, etc. This is a difficult task, because you will be left to your own means and time. Besides, you will have against you those who do not take this seriously, and the dark machinations of the great established powers on your planet, hampering, creating doubts, and attacking you as promoters of this knowledge. In many instances, they will use the weak of mind and spirit, opposing that which has been established. This will be the most powerful weapon of the enemies of The Great

Purposes of the Planetary Hierarchies for the evolutionary development of your planet. You must know well these men; they are unconscious instruments of those powerful organizations, which take advantage of their weak minds to spread false rumors and postulates that cause only confusion and uncertainty.

Stay alert! Know them with your wise judgment; do not permit that wrongful, doctrinairian winds carry you away from the elevation of mind and spirit, where the Supreme Truth and Only Source of Knowledge guide men towards Equity, Rectitude, and Justice, sheltered by the Universal Government of Love, in which all Men (I am talking about Universal Man) receive for their own evolution this absolute vibration to achieve the Peace and Justice that already prevails in other worlds, and which must triumph with your help, on your own planet.

HELP FOR THE PLANET—PHASE TWO: *When the conclusion was reached—after many years of observation and analysis of your world—that its inhabitants should have assistance in order to advance in the Cosmic Evolutionary Scale, there was a moment, when, according to the available information, a final conclusion was reached, after seeing the ferocity with which men continuously waged war, how they mercilessly ignited cities with incendiary bombs, how they destroyed and tortured men, women, and children, and how the governments and spiritual leaders showed no concern and witnessed the starvation of children, both during peace time as during war time.*

The conclusion was that humankind, with few exceptions, were a barbarian horde, sanguinary and bloodthirsty, from the deepest levels of their spirit, and utterly incorrigible. Nevertheless, because of the merit of a few, it was favored with assistance to combat effectively the unscrupulous seekers of riches and power—who, sheltered by the same forces already mentioned, took unfair advantage and plunged other men and their own brothers into extremes of chaos and violence.

We are aware of the enemy's strength; we know when and with what weapons it fights. At this time, the circle is closing around it. The enemy knows it, and in its desperation to survive, it will take Earth and its inhabitants to a final showdown, along with its standard-bearers, whole peoples and tribes, to their self-destruction.

PHASE THREE: *This phase involves direct help to many men, instructing them. It requires in many cases their evacuation from this planet, to a special place where they will be provided with a new conscience, to be transmitted afterwards to their fellow men on Earth. These men, on account of their values and courage, are elected to help the world through this great task. The disappearances of such people from Earth have already begun.*

With your help, in this new dawn, surely many will glimpse this future world and become very important factors in this struggle, where the two forces are facing each other.

All those who have been instructed in the beginners' stages will be given frequent telepathic instruction. We will seek these people earnestly. In many cases, personal contacts will be required; there will be dimensional projections, and they will receive strength and spiritual assistance.

This procedure holds the key to the future of your planet.

Your brother, Krishnamerck, Scientist from the Pleiades, Member of the GREAT SOLAR COSMIC BROTHERHOOD.

During the dictation, we seldom had to ask him to repeat, because he was extremely clear. The funny thing is that while dictating, he held in his left hand a gadget the size of his fist, which he operated with his thumb. It must have been a decoder or screen, perhaps an advanced kind of teleprompter, from which he read the text to be given. At the end, no one asked about it.

We were given a break. The day was ending, and we had exchanged opinions. Cyril came to look for me before nightfall. He told me that he was authorized to take me for a short ride aboard one of the available ships. Several others from the group were selected, too.

We entered through the same tunnel we had seen in the morning. A stupendous "scout ship" was waiting for us. We climbed aboard one by one; we were only five. We greeted each other and sat down on comfortable chairs located around the upper dome; there was a concave screen showing whatever was underneath the machine. Cyril told us that several "scanning eyes" made up the viewing screen.

The takeoff was impressive: the craft flew away, slowly at first, and then surged forward tremendously. We didn't feel any pressure or discomfort, though. Within a few minutes we were watching the high peaks of the Andes, forests, and small hamlets and houses. There was a fabulous view of Lake Titicaca. I was finally able to see its so-famous shape, like a jaguar. We approached a town. The ship stopped. Cyril told us that the altitude was 5000 meters above sea level. We could see the settingsun, sinking quite fast, after the "stand-still." We turned around to have a different view, and moved again, at low speed. Dusk gave way to night.

We could see clearly a great city under the ship, which was changing position to let us see various different views. It was Lima, the capital of Perú. We stared, open-mouthed, as the ship lost altitude, oscillating like a falling leaf in the wind. It stopped again, after "skimming" twice over a section of Lima, a middle-class sector, according to the type of housing.

The craft had several multicolored lights on, whose reflection reached the cabin. Now the lights flashed, in order to draw the attention of the people below, which was exactly what happened. We saw several people getting out of their houses, going out on the streets, looking and pointing upwards.

There was quite a commotion. We watched clearly men, women, and children, and a police patrol car showed up. The policemen got out of their car and looked in our direction. It was impressive to realize that so much excitement was due to our presence.

Among us, we made all sorts of comments. One person, speaking humorously, said, "I would like to jump out in a parachute!"

This lasted approximately four minutes, and I thought it couldn't possibly be ignored by the press. Besides, it was Christmas (the 24th of December), and such an event certainly should be registered in the media. Or perhaps it would be considered nonsense to publish it.

On the way back, it was the same routine. Another group had been taken for a different tour. When we got together for dinner, we learned from the other contactees that some had been given other types of information, restricted to the general public. They would act in a different way than us, penetrating at the executive level and very discreetly passing information, suggesting the possibility that we were being infiltrated by two different extraterrestrial societies, one dedicated to corruption, manipulation, and domination; and another one with the intention of helping, but while acting very discreetly, so as not to jeopardize the true plan, known to the Pleiadeans. Even today, after all this time, I don't think there is a single person who knows fully their complete plan.

Dinner was uneventful. All were very friendly. I could see how some moved their heads, meaning, incredible . . .wonderful!

After dinner, the instructor talked to us again, reminding us of the warnings received before, about the personality who was scheduled to address us the following morning. He repeated that we were not to interrupt, not to applaud, and not to ask questions. We bade each other goodnight and retired to our bedrooms. It was 7:45 p.m., December 24, 1974.

Chapter Note

[1] Currently, the Venezuelan bolivar approaches the low value of the Colombian peso.

18

The Masters of Wisdom

"You are made out of parts from infinity and from the stars, but you do not know it, because you are asleep. . . ."
—COMMANDER KRUNULA, from the Pleiades

ON THE NEXT DAY, CHRISTMAS, DECEMBER 25, 1974, at 7:00 a.m., somebody knocked gently at the door of my bedroom. We were awakened and called to breakfast, which consisted of steamed potatoes with a delicious vegetable broth, three different kinds of bread—toasted, whole, and baked soft—warm milk, herbal tea, and fruit juices. Each one served himself, buffet style. Two Inca natives stood smiling at both sides of the table, offering additional food. Fresh water was served at room temperature.

Once rested, we were offered a very peculiar type of bath, from a spring that was dammed behind the cabin. The water was warm, from volcanic origin. The attendants gave us large towels that some of us wrapped around ourselves, and we looked quite funny wearing such a garment. After fifteen or twenty minutes, we showered and got ready. Instructor number four was waiting for us, to give once again the same instructions given by instructor number one. Earlier, because it was Christmas, we had congratulated each other during breakfast. The only woman among us looked half nervous and half happy.

The designated hour finally arrived. We were led through a subterranean passageway. Cyril, Krunula, and two other extraterrestrials showed up at the tunnel entrance. The greetings were very warm, and for me, especially tranquilizing. Cyril, after greeting and wishing us all good health, moved close to me so we could walk together through the tunnel. Just for a second, he put his hand on my shoulder. Light, emerging from the floor, illuminated the whole passageway. The floor was made out of some clear, hard plastic blocks. All was very clearly visible, without annoying reflections.

We walked about eighty meters, almost in a straight line. Then, there was a slight curve at the end, where light became visible. The ones ahead, walking with the instructor, were shaking their heads in astonishment.

At one side of the cave outlet were four small "explorer ships," each about four meters in diameter, levitating in midair!

They were shiny, without any trace of doors or windows, and were suspended about eight to ten meters above ground level. We passed our hands below them, trying to detect "something," but no, there was nothing there!

From here we could view all the magnificence of the incredible Andean countryside, with snow-capped mountains on the horizon. A lovely valley lay in front of us. Guanacos and llamas[1] dotted the scenery, and two native shepherds cared for a herd of about twenty goats.

We all shared a feeling of great expectancy. We witnessed the arrival of the population, men, women, youths, and children, who were sitting on the green grass, against a great promontory that like a wall deflected the cold wind. All greeted us, bowing their heads and waving their hands in friendly gesture. Some young girls were carpeting the ground in front of the entrance with flower petals and little twigs. Instructor number one showed up and reminded us to abide by the instructions.

He asked for a collective greeting from the gathered people for all the twenty-four friends and brothers (us), a very original greeting, which consisted of waving both hands and uttering a prolonged AAAAHHH! We were able to just say: thanks, thanks!

The instructor approached the entrance to a tunnel carved in the living rock and clapped his hands twice. He retired to one side, and the most incredible Being made his appearance.

We were astonished beyond description!

That being looked exactly like Jesus, the Master.

I thought immediately that the Pleiadeans had brought us here with the purpose of meeting Jesus Christ, who was here again, fulfilling the prophecies. We looked at each other, speechless. Those were seconds of extreme tension. He looked just like the images kept in the homes of all Christians: his beard, his hair, and his age, which I guessed to be about thirty-seven years. He wore a light brown robe, gathered at the waist by a cloth band. The fabric looked rough, like "cabuya" (sisal), with medium- (three-quarter) length sleeves and an open collar, where we could see his chest hair. His arms and hands revealed infrequent exposure to sunshine. His bare feet were shod with one-piece sandals. The robe reached below his knees.

Smiling, he bowed in salutation, crossing his right arm to his left shoulder, with the left hand under his right armpit, and then repeated in the opposite way. Gazing toward all the listeners, he said:

"I am not who you believe I am.
My name is a thousand names; give me any, and That I Am.
I am ancient before you, not in age, but in knowledge,
And humbly I bow my head before you.
My name is Age, for I am the Ages and the Time.
I am Wisdom, and my name is Wisdom.
I hold thirty-five percent of Universal Wisdom,
And humbly I bow before you.
(He repeated the initial salutation.)
I am Knowledge, and I bring you Knowledge,
I am the breeze, I am the wind, the cloud and the rain,
The tender blade of grass in the morning.
I am the soil, the furrow, and the seed, the river and the sea.
I am the good, hardened hand of the soil tiller,
The tree, the flower, and the mountain.
I am the valley, the dawn, and the night.
I am the Ancient One among you, and humbly I bow my head.
I pull my sword out of its scabbard to tear the hypocrite and the vociferous

off their pedestals.
I am the bird and the flower.
I am the white hair of the old, the laughter of children,
The lullaby of the mother, and the awakening of the conscience.
I am the conscience!
My name is the Law, for I am the Law!
My name is Life, because I am Life.
I am the Word and the Wisdom. My name is Wisdom.
I am the Ancient One before you, not by my age, but for my knowledge.
Humbly I bow my head before you.
I am the hurricane and the movement.
I am the force, and the whisper and the voice. My voice has life!
I am the bride, who unblemished arrives to be married.
I am the Peace among men, my name is Peace, and Peace I give.
My name . . . my name . . . is Love. I am the Love that propels the Universe." [2]

He stooped and picked up a small branch, which he struck gently against the palm of his left hand,and took a few steps, looking at all present. There was absolute silence, the silence of the mountains. It seemed as if everything was keeping quiet, in his honor.

He walked, stepping among the legs and feet of those lying on the ground. He came close to me and looked into my eyes from a distance of about four meters. What a beautiful countenance! Never had anybody looked at me as he did.

He walked back towards the cave, without turning his back to us, saluted for a last time, waving his hands, and disappeared through the same tunnel.

The intelligence and love expressed by his face, projecting peace, was the most incredible and marvelous that I have ever felt. All stood up and in complete order returned to their duties through the tunnel.

After this formidable experience, I was left with several questions:

Why a single woman among twenty-four?

Why could we not keep in contact afterwards?

Why was the information not the same for all?

Where are the other twenty-three now?

What type of information was given the others, and why?

What is the role of this unusual personality whom we met at the Vortex?

Why are his words so similar to those of Jesus Christ, being somebody else?

What is his relationship with the extraterrestrials?

What is going to occur at a planetary level that will lead to a new human behavior pattern?

What role do we—the contactees—play, in this confusing panorama? I still do not know. What about the other twenty-three?

Why were no names and addresses interchanged? I don't have the answer.

My return from the Andes left me breathless. The experience with the extraterrestrials, the instructors, and the personality with a thousand names, left me in a quasi-mystic condition, which I could barely surmount.

Thanks to my education as a child and the freedom I enjoyed, I was able to realize the danger to which I was exposed, if I interpreted wrongly my experience at the Andes Highlands.

There was no doubt, as far as I was concerned: the High Entity of the Andes was the same One that I called, and rightly so, the "MASTER OF WISDOM."

CHAPTER NOTES

[1] Guanacos and llamas—South American mammals, related to camels. They produce fine wool and are used as beasts of burden in the highlands of Peru and Bolivia.

[2] These were his words; I cannot guarantee their exact order.

The Prophecies . . . Are They a Promise?

"There has never been so much consciousness about peace.
There has never been so much antagonism against war.
'The New Man: The only hope for the future.'"
—BHAGWAN SHREE RAJNEESH

UPON MY RETURN TO CARACAS, I continued and completed the course I had begun before Christmas. I apologized to my students for having failed to meet them on the 24th, since all had been present for their class, at the right hour.

Based on this new and extraordinary experience, I felt motivated to undertake some research work upon the extraterrestrial historical influence on the planet, and its consequences in human affairs. To me, there is no doubt that the Pleiadeans and other "blond" races at some time put Man on Earth. It is still not clear how this mind-boggling event came about; they never made it clear, only suggested it a couple of times.

Consequently, it is quite possible that:

We are the outcome of an advanced hybridization.

Races created elsewhere were brought and planted here, when the planet was ready for habitation.

The first races were created here, upon arrival of a great scientific expedition, which established bases at least at three different geographic locations, giving rise to the typical characteristics of the future dwellers, once the local conditions became known, with the possible adaptation to new conditions as required.

I do not intend to establish here a theory or a forceful statement, but staying away from any fanaticism or dogmatic belief, in view of the evolution of the planet and its inhabitants, I realize that reality has nothing to do with the present scientific short-sightedness. I cannot fail to see the inevitable, that we came from the stars, one way or another. There, in the stars, is our true genesis, which cry and call us, and make us reflect upon our origin and destiny.

The year 1975 brought other events, during my trips to Europe and Latin America. But, before these, I had to experience my fifth physical contact with the Pleiadeans, which took place on January 29 to 31, 1975.

During this encounter, which proved to be the last with my Greater Brothers from the Pleiades, they took me to a submarine base in the Mariana Trench, for two hours, at a depth of 5000 meters below the surface of the ocean. This experience will be the subject matter of my next book, together with information gathered during at least thirteen International and World Congresses and meetings on UFO and Paranormal subjects.

My arrival in Bogotá and the first meeting with my son, born during the flight to the Andean Highlands, brought me great happiness. My friends and members of the group complained about not understanding Camelo, who together with Chela, had received communications in my absence. The communications were intermittent, and sometimes they just meditated.

The moment arrived to move ICIFE to a new location, on account of the growth in its membership,and sympathizers of the UFO subject, who dropped in continuously during the ten working hours each day of the week. We moved, thanks to the financial assistance of Gilberto Ferreira, to a good two-story house on 16A Avenue and 39th Street, Teusaquillo district. A great "flying saucer," made out of wood, with multicolored flashing lights, decorated the entrance. Now we were more comfortable.

Our conference room, which seated eighty people, was crowded on Fridays and Saturdays, with up to 100 attendees during conferences, talks, and films on scientific and science fictional subjects. During its inaugural days in June 1976, this new headquarters was visited by Fabio Zerpa from Argentina, Francisco Aniceto Lugo from Venezuela, Salvador Freixedo from Spain, astronomer Clemente Garavito from Colombia, and others. Dr. Lugo came with a group from Venezuela, along with his wife, Pachita.

Sometime later, two conferences were directed by Charles Berlitz, the famous investigator of the "Bermuda Triangle." Other speakers on related fields gave their talks, widening the background of the Institute.

At this location, we carried out our most important investigations, of cases labeled "high strangeness." One of the most interesting took place on July 9, 1976. I was getting ready to give a talk to a group of teenagers, when my son

July 15, 1995. Left to right: Kristina Punceles, Elsa Gil (behind), Ana G. Merchán de Castillo (holding the book), Patricia Heller, Graciela Zarikian, Josefina González, the author sprinkling the book with champagne, Natacha Puigbó (behind), and another invitee at the presentation ceremony of the book, OVNI: Gran Alborada Humana. *Caracas, Venezuela.*

Mauricio came into the office with another friend, yelling at me: "Daddy, daddy, there are some flying saucers in the sky!"

It was 1:00 p.m. Some of the objects flew at high altitude, but were clearly visible, like silver melons. I counted them; I could see eleven objects. Others counted nine, others fourteen. They were flying overhead, north to south, east to west, changing course, stopping, making sharp turns, or hovering, stationary. Mauricio came out with the telescope dismounted from its tripod, and tried to follow the evasive UFOs. At least fifteen people gathered on the street at the entrance to the ICIFE. I watched them for about three minutes and then went back into the office. The objects continued their exhibition for another two minutes, then sped away. Many seemed to think that this aerial ballet was a salute they were giving us, because they knew that I was present. Of course, this was not the case; they simply showed up.

I kept reading again and again the prophecies made by the Pleiadeans. I still could not understand or make any sense out of one called, the "PROPHECY FOR THE COUNTRY AT THE NORTH OF THE SOUTH," thinking that it referred to the U.S.A. Others thought that the country referred to might be Canada, being located at the North. I eventually came to believe that the prophecy refers to Venezuela, with Carlos Andrés Pérez, as its main protagonist.

As explained before, this prophecy, in nineteen numbered sections, is a part of the total subject matter dictated to me by "The Voice," together with "THE LOGIC OF LOGIC," on July 23, 1974. The following is the transcription of the complete prophecy, followed by an interpretation of it, which I wrote in Costa Rica in 1988, when Carlos Andrés Pérez had accepted the candidacy to the presidency of Venezuela.

PROPHECY FOR THE COUNTRY AT THE NORTH OF THE SOUTH

Dictation taken by Enrique Castillo Rincón, in Bogotá, Colombia, South America, on July 23, 1974, from 11:00 p.m. to 3:00 a.m.

I

The nimble-footed leader, without trying, will become the Leader.
His heart longed for it. He will win and shall become second in command.
The tricolor of Power will be his.
He will become laureate among those of the South and the Center,
in search of the great promise of the Mansion.
The burdens that hunger cannot pay for, shall commence.

II

The Leader shall win unique privileges before
the Committee of the Nations. He will obtain purses with valuable treasure.
The great and the rich shall share with him their vestures.
The underground wealth shall not find easy profits.

III

He will become King without Crown among those who speak his language,
shall be exalted and will enjoy lofty reputation.
But his the main "flying feathers" shall be taken away.
Now his chair will shake. The hidden darkness shall attack him.
He will inspire on his own white crescent,
with those that spices have given him.
His own former followers shall attempt to kill him, his "brothers in
eloquence," those of the "flourished vegetation," shall carry the blame.
From the conspiracy many will end up wounded,
and shall pay the price that is due.

IV

His dissonant harangues shall sound cataclysmic.
The attack occurs, and [he] will be left badly wounded.
Many who loved him, will curse him. The hyenas fight for the spoils.
The mediocre will take power.
Meanwhile, cannon fire sounds on another continent.

V

In the country at the North of the South, he who has the inner voice
stands up. The crucible has forged him, the fire has tempered him;
he has seen the seas, the valleys and the hillocks.
He has surpassed them, and keeps the memories well etched.
Meanwhile, he who has understood My Word, offers the seekers
the wholesome doctrine that will lift the hearts.
He has passed the seas and the lands; he is here, now there.
The meaning is encrypted, now it is not.
There are no symbols, only the Truth, clothed in words;
he knows it. We know it.

VI

The one who came. Who went away. Who came back.
The one who stays gave him a wise behavior.
Symbols that clarify and strengthen, messages that take shape.
His clear humbleness will be interpreted only by a few.
He brought his knowledge from the North, coming from the South;
his knowledge came riding with the Lords of Happiness,
the Lords of Yesterday, the Lords of Peace.
Some will take the Message, others will understand it.
This one and that one will know when the time arrives.
They Labor in silence, and the Silence is in labor.
Two great roadways:
The Acts, and the Knowledge, shall enter the Temple of Truth.

VII

Interpreters of Knowledge, of Space and Time, emerge.
Only one will be able to recognize and alter the way
to make light and clarity.
One generation will make him strong, and bearer of Truth.

The body is ready, the mind is clear, his Spirit strong.
The visitor delivered him his vision.

Several shall become messengers of the Word, and will have it.
Their encouragement is Love. Their force, their own knowledge of Truth.
Open your doors and your windows;
let their voices and their words enter in your homes.
Welcome them! And you shall become ONE.
They turn the secrets into dust,
and give them well understood to those who seek them.
They shall make germinate the seed planted long ago.

VIII

He knows it. His INNER VOICE speaks.
Strengthen the seekers, and clarify the Truth to others.
Behold . . . The Interpreter of the Symbol!
Behold . . . the Awakener of the Truth!
The voices of the impious break down!
The concepts of the ignorant and mediocre are silenced.

IX

The throne of the "Legendary" is empty.
Meanwhile, the countries to the south of the North are touched.
The OTHER FORCE does not stop the violence.
It offers easily to marauders its false riches;
other sources are strengthened to obtain easy gold, easy silver.

X

Thunder keeps sounding. The trumpet keeps resounding!
And you, who give the Truth to Men, do not forget the essential:
Only well-entrenched faith will give Immortality to the believer!
Therefore, speak to humanity. Armor them with eternal bodies
and give them the light of eternal knowledge!
Utilize the power of the Creative Word!

XI

And you who take words from my mouth into your mouth,
nothing will scare you; nothing will make you forget your essence.

Climb the mountain, climb the pinnacle, rise to the summit
and tell the Truth, using the power, obeying THE VOICE!

XII

I have been watching you. . .The seed is giving its fruit!
I have been keeping you. . . . The fruit has grown ripe!
Now . . . stand up and write the words that I shall dictate to your heart.
With words that I shall mould in your mind . . .
and you shall grasp the pen as scintillating chisel . . .
which will pierce like steel the mind of humankind.

XIII

MY TEACHINGS no longer shall be lost in time.
They no longer will be forgotten.
Your pen shall not tremble when writing them.
With masterful hand you will carry brilliancy.
Yes, men of clear conscience will understand.
Yes, men of the dark face shall tremble.
Yes, men, in their agony, shall hear MY VOICE.
Those of false doctrine will shatter.

XIV

The veils are drawn open; false churches shall not prevail.
No false messiah will act in MY NAME.
They will not act in MY NAME if they have not the Inner Voice.
They shall not take away the bird's flapping of wings in its majestic flight.
Polyphonic blossoming of the Truths of the Son,
mountains, oceans, rivers, and valleys, in MY new awakening.
Some will run, others shall jump; happiness all around.
MY true sons do not shatter; they belong to the eternal Truth.

XV

The religion of fear shall end,
and he who keeps the most valued vestment of Man,
who has given true value to his being, shall have, at the end of his way,
the Crown of Immortality.
And I tell you all, I exist, although you do not see me!
I AM in your hearts, although you do not feel me!

I AM THE ETERNAL, THE NAMELESS, THE ENDLESS!
Yes, my children, Eternal Survival exists!
This historic moment is arriving to some.
It is when thought believes in ME.
It is when the Soul *recognizes me* and when the Spirit longs for ME.
Therefore, do not deposit false promises in GOD,
which the heart does not accept.
The ignorant and fallacious rejects me in his arrogance.

XVI

The invested one shall travel to meet his blood brothers.
He will strengthen affective links and shall be taken as outlaw.
One shall break. His return shall give him force and wisdom.
His banner will be clear, and he will raise it. The inner fire now will be blue.
He can remain without the companion coupling.
No insult or gag will be effective.
Its course shall not vary; the river flows to the lands.
The seeds shall be fed. The Voice keeps its course.
The eagles have room and fly in peace.
SHE will teach love and pain also,
the two great forces that modify the Spirit of Man.
Meanwhile, there will be signs in the skies, and he will know he is not alone.
He will emerge, fortified with reason.
The forging will be accomplished, and the metal shall now be ready;
his brothers will raise the rejoicing,
and those who know him will say, admiringly: It is him!

XVII

He will not be touched during the attempt to make him shut up.
His cunning shall be challenged.
Now he will take the Message, and its interpretation. Look at Him!
He has the inner voice. Clear words shall be understood.
The knots break, his Word has scars.
Genuine ointment the heart shall perceive.
Now he has understood, and the road is long,
but for his meekness will be shortened. Go and speak.
Write and silence the senselessness of ignominy,
that your pen shall ignite the dead flame in their hearts.

XVIII

Now you. . . . Make sound the trumpets of approaching Liberty!
Speak with prudent and wise word,
and do not ask for anything along your way.
Make Truth shine with clamor of multitude.
Raise your forehead and your flag . . . take the flaming sword
that breaks and splits the dark gag of the Truth.
You are yet the inner voice! Listen to me, listen!
And I'll put with sweetness MY WORDS OF LIGHT in your mouth.
Listen to me, listen! And I'll put in your hand MY ETERNAL TRUTH.
Listen to me, listen! And I'll make all ears listen.
Listen to me, listen! And I'll give you the strength that breaks bounds.
Listen to me, listen!
And I'll make you feel the BREATH OF MY MOUTH.
And I'll make you listen TO THE WHISPER OF MY VOICE.
Thus, the veils will be torn away, the vestments will be ripped,
and the hearts shall rise.

Listen to me, listen! And I shall call you Beloved Son,
because you have put your heart at my side,
because you have put YOUR SPIRIT IN MY HAND,
because you have put your being under my PROTECTION AND SHADE,
because you give away your life in MY FIGHT,
and there will be no more nights without light.
Neither destitute shall you be in MY PRESENCE,
because MY FORCE is your force, because MY LIGHT is your shelter,
because MY VOICE is your flag, because MY LOVE is the Truth of Men.
And you, who accepted MY TEACHINGS,
you shall be MY INTERPRETER and REVIVER OF THE TRUTH!

XIX

You are the blast of the triumphal trumpet!
Thus, you will take MY WORD, clean and pure,
to the heart of those who listen.
Therefore, go and answer MY CALL,
and never again shall you doubt or have darkness on your path.
Your country shall be the world, in polyphonic blossoming forth,
and in that flaming place, shall burn in Wisdom.[1]

When this document was made known to those closest to me, it was because it had taken tangible form, as confirmed by events that occurred in Venezuela. Only in the context of those events can it be understood. In general, the most problematic aspect of prophecy is that one cannot predict who the protagonists are, accurately, until the facts are understood, once they actually take place.

The present prophecy has not been fulfilled completely, because most of it has to do with events of a political, religious, and spiritual nature. Only after the course of time will the events take place, during the next five or six years, in other words, by around 1995/96.

This prophetic information was known in Bogotá, Colombia, in 1974, among some of the group members, without their understanding it. In the following "Speculative Interpretation," some items have become true with great precision, for example, those referring to Carlos Andrés Pérez, in sections I-IV. We don't know who is "The Invested One," who will have the power of the word, and who will come from Venezuela at the most difficult time for humanity. All points to this happening when the 666 or Anti-Christ declares himself governor of the whole planet, possibly before the end of the century. The entire prophecy seems to coincide with those of the Pleiadeans.

I interpret that the prophecy mentions clearly two characters: the one who delivers the prophecy to the interpreter, and the one who has the inner voice, the Invested. One takes care of making it known, the other creates a front of wise truths, and all who listen to him shall know that he is telling the truth. The following is a detailed interpretation of the entire prophecy:

PROPHECY OF THE COUNTRY AT THE NORTH OF THE SOUTH: INTERPRETATION

I

Carlos Andrés Pérez ("CAP") shall become President.
He wanted to be President. He will be elected and will be president
for a second time. He will be confirmed in the first magistracy.
He will be considered as leader in South and Central America,
in his zeal to ingratiate himself with the United Nations and other nations.
The people revolt because of economic scarcity and new taxes.
(On February 27, 1989, the "Caracazo" occurred,
with thousands of casualties.)

II

CAP will be very close to many European countries.
He will obtain new loans and credit for his country.
The oil industry will be in difficulty
because of low prices and poor administration.

III

CAP shall feel secure in power, but the presidential chair is fragile.
Those who elected him shall extol and flatter him.
Two of his closest men will be dismissed (the economists?).
Power shatters. A coup d'état is forged.
Some of his own people are involved, with backing from the IMF
and the international banking community.
The coup takes shape with help from the military and obscure politicians
who expect to benefit from his fall (brothers in eloquence),
and other intellectuals.
There will be dead and wounded, and the revolt leader will be imprisoned.
The "Flourished Vegetation" is to blame,
referring perhaps to someone in the Army, as in a combat uniform,
or the green of the Copei.

IV

His speeches reveal pride and egotism;
he will state that he is in charge, and will govern alone, if necessary.
He will lose credibility and confidence with the people,
and, discredited, will intend to regain his lost popularity.
His own party will take away his backing.
Politicians, clergy, military, and the wealthy will weaken him,
and he will have to compromise with his enemies.
(The mediocre conduct business behind the presidential institution.)
Meanwhile, there is war (civil perhaps?) in Europe and another continent,
as terrorism increases (Yugoslavia?).

V

In Venezuela, a man shows up with the power of the word.
He has traveled a lot through different countries,
knows well human nature, is experienced, has inner strength,

and shall return to those who listen to him the lost faith.
He shall speak clearly and convincingly, will explain the symbolic,
and there will be no doubts.

VI

He lived in Venezuela, left, and came back to stay,
delivered to someone else his great message and knowledge, is meek,
and the truth seekers will accept him.
To him was delivered the knowledge in the Andean Highlands Vortex;
he brought it to Venezuela, and showed it to a few.
This wisdom came from the stars with the lords of the Law,
known in the past as gods or Elohim.
Many struggle in the world, silently, in this great work;
eventually they will be recognized for their deeds and their knowledge.

VII

The genuine interpreters of Knowledge appear throughout the world.
A man shall recognize him (he who brought Knowledge).
He should be about 40 or 45 years
when he received the knowledge of the Times.
He who received the information will give it to whoever recognizes him.
Several men shall be messengers, upon understanding the message.
They shall become very fluent in the transmission of the truths,
and shall break old patterns.

VIII

At this time he will be aware of who he is.
He has a great force and shall speak with authority.
The hypocrite shall be indicated, and the Pharisees shall be surprised.
The false spiritualists will be discredited,
and the fanatics shall fall with their followers.

IX

Possibly here the Pope dies, or a great Venezuelan politician.
At the south of the country there are criminal assaults, violations of human rights, drug dealing, terrorism, corruption, disease, Shining Path, cocaine, opium, in Colombia, Perú, Bolivia, Brazil, Argentina, Chile, Ecuador, etc.

X

The already-Invested of wisdom and word will start his triumphal epic
of modern times, speaking in public with great knowledge,
interpreting the best of eternal knowledge.
Men shall understand and will know that it is the prophesied time.
This man will have much prudence and tact.
People will believe him and shall rejoice in his teachings.
Those will be times of war and hunger.
He will speak with power on man's immortality.
His strength will be the Truth.

XI

The Invested one receives his Baptism of Fire
directly from a Planetary Hierarchy. They give him security and force.
He hears the voice of the times,
and all will understand them without hesitation.
The Invested One here understands who he is and why.
This will give him security and more inner force.
Now he knows all that he must know to complete his mission.
He hears the voice and lives inspired to speak
with great authority and wisdom.
Also, he will write, under the firm conviction of knowing who he is,
and shall tear down false and confusing spiritual structures.

XIII

Millenary teachings shall be heard once more.
With clear and simple words, the people will understand.
The writings of THE INVESTED and THE INTERPRETER
shall slash the false masters of knowledge.
The voice of the great master of all times shall resound again
through his two envoys.

XIV

The time has arrived (1992), when the voices and teachings
shall be understood without doubt, because it is necessary
that the peoples understand and discern the truth,
so that they themselves make their own choice and become aware of
who have cheated them and how.
There will be no one who does not hear of the arrival of the prophesies.

No one, who pretends to be master or interpreter of the Truth,
shall speak with his mouth without having heard the Inner Voice.
This is the unmistakable feature of the true cognizant of the Law.
It will be the maximum test of being a true representative
of the Eternal Truth.
Thus, they will not speak in the name of the Eternal Father,
although with their lips they pronounce His name.
People will understand who is authorized to speak,
and will know who is a spiritualist humbug.

XV

The religions topple, one in particular
that has darkened the lives of men with eternal punishment and fear.
By this time, many who have negated the existence of
the GREAT INNOMINATE shall see him clearly.
People will speak openly about immortality and eternal survival.
Reincarnation shall become known as a true universal law through the
evolution of man, through the Law of Cause and Effect.

XVI

The Invested One will travel to the land of his ancestors.
Here is clearly indicated the re-encounter with his blood relatives
(this portion has already been fulfilled).
An affective link will be broken temporarily to test his inner strength.
He will realize why this occurs.
After a while, after **she** has understood it, **she** will come back.
His children receive food and comfort, although he is not at their side.
Through this test, **she** will teach him of true love
without payback of any type, but **she** will also teach directly about pain,
to modify his thinking and spirit.
The crucible will give him in this experience the real knowledge
that only real love vanquishes everything and never fails. There will be
sightings of ships of extraterrestrial origin, to show that they know what
happens without being able to stop it, so that the "forge" is complete.
Those who know, will know that it is Him, The Invested One.

XVII

They will try to shut him up, arguing false attacks on religion.
No one will be able to harm him.

The Invested shall talk with power and cunning.
He has the inner voice of strength from the Father.
All will understand. Whoever listens to him knows that it is the truth.
He will keep on writing, and people will listen with the heart.
He keeps talking with great authority and knowledge;
he ignites the flames of faith and hope. These are difficult times.
Those who listen to them, the Invested and the Interpreter,
will recognize the authenticity of their knowledge and investiture.

XVIII

Here it is understood that freedom is close by,
for the spiritual liberation of man.
Truth shines with its own light.
His words break up false doctrines and false teachings
that have enslaved man for millennia.
His words are those awaited by the generations.
They attack ignorance and fanaticism
and renew the spirit of those who seek.
Their force of Truth, Knowledge, and Prudence
shall be their main bastion for teaching without leaving doubts.
The Innominate or Eternal Father will inspire these two men on their way.
They are simple men; they don't wear robes, nor medals,
nor long beards, nor sandals. Those times are gone.
Now they dress in Eternal Truth.
There will be much love in their gaze and appearance.
People will recognize them.
They do not call themselves masters or envoys.
Only their truth will shine like a torch in darkness.
It is the return of the true teachings, without blemish,
without changes and manipulations.
It is the resurrection of the living Truth.

XIX

Here is the final blast of the trumpet (perhaps 1999-2003).
Men will have heard clean words, pure and clear, breaking away from
equivocal and fantasizing schemes, which fooled humanity
with false representatives of law and knowledge.
Wrong and misrepresented doctrines,
manipulated and man-made, end here.
Eternal Truth triumphs and shines for a long period of time among Men.

NOTE: The above is a free interpretation, and the events will not necessarily happen as described here. Several speculations have been made, partly in order to arrive at a logical explanation for each section, and the interpretation of the prophecy is subject to judgment on the part of the reader. Many events have taken place exactly as expected, and this can be proven by the testimony of various people close to me, who were familiar with the prophecy as we tried to make it match with events taking place in Colombia and Venezuela.

Enrique Castillo Rincón
San José de Costa Rica, 1988
Caracas, 1989

CHAPTER NOTE

[1] This prophecy was not published until the year 1983, almost ten years after its dictation in 1974, when it was distributed to a small group of friends in Caracas, Venezuela, and again in San José de Costa Rica in 1987.

20

The Nine Times That Will Change the World

> *"Definitely, the ultimate objective of the prophecies is that those who have the special gift to see the future warn the rest of humanity and make them aware of what will come. They can tell us where we are heading and what awaits us. It is left to each individual the option to face the future or not—and why not even try to modify it."*
> —A. GALLOTTI, *The Prophecies of the End of the World*

THE PROPHETIC FIELD IS QUITE VAST AND DIFFICULT TO INTERPRET. In all epochs there have been interpreters, some famous and some completely unknown. It is different with the prophets; they bring us the voice from the heavens as a warning to men regarding their behavior, talking about great wars, cataclysms, earthquakes, and changes in the earth's configuration. Doubtless, humanity has lived as slave to the terrors foretold in the prophecies. Many have believed in their fulfillment and have dragged others to disaster.

It would seem that this fear about the fulfillment of the prophecies is genetic. We all know that there have been individuals who believe that they are in charge of the literal fulfillment of the prophecies. These dark individuals usually come from the known religions, self-elected fanatics with otherworldly "powers," who snatch from the naive their self-direction. I have seen them in almost all cities of Colombia, Venezuela, and other Latin American countries, besides reading of them via the cables transmitted by the international news agencies. Such fanatics drag their unfortunate followers into slavery and loss of their values, denying them their right to dissent, question, or reject.

I believe that there are two types of beings on this planet: the sheep, the manipulated, who are majority, and those who have a reasoning mind, who question, investigate, and move away from the established plan. The sheep permit themselves to be dragged off without questioning. Often I have seen spiritualist groups and witnessed with sadness such people, who believe to have in their hands, along with the other members of the group, the answers to all their anxieties. Others have their "master," with whom they also lose their right to be themselves. I realize that these people feel happy, or safer, when they have somebody to lean on when making decisions; they lose their personality and become easy to manipulate. I have heard them say that they do whatever the master tells them to do.

The following prophecy, entitled "The Nine Times That Will Change the World," is about facts that are difficult to believe, even among my closest friends. I remember that Carlos Alberto Bonilla told me once, while visiting at my home, that this prophecy could not be true, because it refers to legitimate anarchism and the loss of certain values that society has jealously guarded. Laughing kiddingly, he said that it seemed an invention—my invention, and that it could not possibly occur. Also present were my good friends Samuel Medina, and Delio Quimbayo, with whom I have shared all that the Greater Brothers have told and given me, along with all my experiences. It was a matter of many years, months, weeks, and hours of conversation, examination, acceptance, rejection, and positioning. All three, and myself, had the courage to discuss and question many aspects about the Pleiadean contacts. One of the topics discussed was the Prophecy of the Nine Times.

Today, fulfilled to a great degree and published in Argentina and Venezuela a long time before the occurrence of the predicted facts, it still leaves us perplexed. Before reading it, it is important to tell the reader that I sent it to 120 people around the world, who, I thought at that moment, should read it and give their opinion. Among them was the Pope of the Catholic Church. Only a few answered, stating merely that they had received it, without giving any comment for the time being. Only two people gave an opinion: Andreas Faber Kaiser, and Dr. Jacobo Grinberg. I never knew if the others received it or not, including some members of our group.

THE NINE TIMES THAT WILL CHANGE THE WORLD

Information received by Enrique Castillo Rincón,
in the Highlands of the Andes, between January 29 and 31, 1975.

EVOLUTIONARY SYNTHESIS OF THE GEOLOGIC, SPIRITUAL, AND TERRESTRIAL CHANGES

The "Sages" will not find the answer . . .
The wise will know the reason . . .

THE PROPHECY

Dauntless, humanity shall watch, powerless to do anything.
The world's mercy organizations and the men of good will shall be tied up.
The cries and lamentations will not reach the ears of the governments.
Women and men shall no longer wear jewelry, necklaces, rings, or earrings.
Speculation, scarcity, and corruption shall be the order of the day.
The families of good will and their children shall pray in silence.

The religions stagger; only the faith of the just maintains them.
Violence, strikes, affronts, robberies, assaults, kidnapping and murders,
hunger and disease, swollen rivers, landslides, driving rain, frost, burning
heat and sun, and cold as never felt before.
Accidents will rise, because of carelessness and shortsightedness.
New diseases will appear and attack like plague throughout the world,
without hope for solution.
The just pray and wait; the "flapping of wings"
that will bring redemption from the sky is getting close.

The "Bloodthirsty" rises. Be careful!
He will be given blood to drink, and will get drunk.
He will mark his followers and they shall obey him; the time will be.
The warrior's steps shall leave nothing behind.
The time for war has arrived, because there is no other way;
men, blindly, have sought it, and the beast wakes up.
Great destruction follows the steps of the above-named.
The earth will be barren and empty.

The just keep praying; they survive just because of their faith and hope.
These are the days of terror; many just and innocent shall perish,

but they shall not bend in front of the beast. . . .
others will weaken and bend.
War has arrived with its deadly load.
New destructive methods will be tested,
which will destroy the land with its fruits, and these will groan in pain.

Men shall fall like straw that the wind carries away, burned by fire.
They shall groan, and their relief shall be death.
From the sky shall fall the Great Tribulation, clothed in disease,
wounding the skin and filling it with ulcers, dying without hope:
the murderers have succeeded.
The stench and rot chokes up and pollutes the air.
The terrible plague shall ride the clouds and the winds,
planting its poison on animals and fields.

The earth trembles and cries! Erratic, uncertain, like a drunkard.
The new lands emerge.
Continents sink forever, those that were polluted by man.
The seas rise like gigantic arms to punish the corrupt cities
and swallow them in minutes.
The works of man, his pride, his arrogance, shall be buried.

The severity of the volcanic eruptions and the unchained forces of nature
demolish the earth.
Man trembles and cries, begs for pardon, but it is too late.
The fury of the elements delivers his reward to the guilty.
The guilty is crushed with his assistants; Earth recovers its life.
The sun shines weakly upon the new vegetation.
Seeds arrive in a new dawn. The Great Instigator has died forever.
Purification has completed his task.
New lands are flooded . . . this time with new flowers!

Birds try their songs, bless the majesty of the new day.
The survivors appear. The remnants are coming.
And the great march begins, to populate the new lands.

The prophecy has been fulfilled! The meek and the just inherit the earth!
The children shall grow up in truth; the cries shall end.
The new leaders, renovated and pure, emerge.
Listen . . . listen and hear! The new terrestrial era has just begun!
The Cosmic Calendar reads the Fourth Era. The terrestrial, 2023. . . .

THE CHANGES

The drastic changes that will modify the face of the earth and create new continental platforms have already started. These geological changes will be united to a new spiritual physiognomy.

Man did not answer the call. Instead, he trespassed the laws, violated the Eternal Agreement. The consequence is such that man's pride will be consumed into dust. These alterations shall occur during this generation, during the last years of the century, felling the poor and the powerful, the guilty and the innocent, children and oldsters, men and women.

The Laws give authority to those who govern the Earth from above to carry out such purification. Nevertheless I tell you: the warnings were many, each time that it was required to tell man what would happen if he didn't change his behavior. But he was deaf, disobeyed, increased in pride and haughtiness, and left the correct path, despising the wise advice from the spirit and conscience.

Therefore, weeping and pain shall inflame the nations; there will be no letup; the warnings were given; it is the time. The earth will be reborn, fulfilling its Great Objective for the just and the peacemakers. The Great Law has spoken . . . and Truth will shine in this dawn, with those who earned the right to live in a world full of peace and work.

I announce to you a world of Love and Hope!

THE NINE TIMES THAT WILL CHANGE THE WORLD
They cover sixty-three years, from 1946 to 2008.

The First Time	1946 - 1952
The Second Time	1953 - 1959
The Third Time	1960 - 1966
The Fourth Time	1967 - 1973
The Fifth Time	1974 - 1980
The Sixth Time	1981 - 1987
The Seventh Time	1988 - 1994
The Eighth Time	1994 - 2001
The Ninth Time	2002 - 2008

THIS IS HOW THEY BEGIN. . . .

You ought to know, my dear friend Enrique, that great changes will take place on your planet, which will mark the way for the New Evolutionary Era that will affect all the inhabitants, without exception—to some, for their benefit and spiritual elevation, and to the great majority for their ruin and destruction. Listen with attention, because depending on how they accept and assimilate this Prophecy, they will be able to "feel and see" the right moment for their accomplishment.

Above all, we tell you with great happiness and hope that after the fulfillment of all the announced events, there will come a time full of peace and justice, a time of harvest for the peaceful, of true love and understanding among men, a future when you shall live in communion with the values of the spirit, which shall overflow as a fountain for all, because the promise of the Holy Spirit will have been accomplished.

Those will be days of joy. Children will be raised in the true teachings, and Knowledge will tear its bindings, because those who have earned the right to live in such a glorious epoch shall receive the necessary wisdom to understand finally the true reason of life and shall know the meaning of death. The veils shall be drawn open to the chosen ones, and they will know in full THE LAW OF REINCARNATION AND RESURRECTION.

The SUPREME PLAN OF LIFE will be known, and the reason for the diseases that have plagued man. The freedom of conscience will be one of the wonderful fruits that they shall taste.

INITIATION
The First Time, 1946-1952

The two great wars fought before 1946 are the prelude of the first warnings and great announced signals.
If man corrects his errors, the earth will grow green again
and reward its dwellers with much abundance.
Seven (7) years of grace are given, ending in October, 1952,
the so-called "period of the cold war," the time for the correction of errors.
But the voice is not answered.

The wars come back, and man continues drunk.
Blindness invades the fields of labor.
Instead of exalting the human spirit,
the new discoveries are used for terrorizing.
IT IS THE TIME OF THE MAKERS OF DEATH. . . .
Those of the "Chosen People" recover their pride and their land.
The holy land goes to its legitimate owners.
It is the time of the apparent peace.
The time of reckoning begins for the preparation of the Spiritual Era
that man shall live.

The Second Time, 1953-1959

Wars continue.
The space frontiers are enlarged, and new feathers adorn man's pride.
Deaths increase, and differences become more acute.
The war of vengeance, terror, and death to the innocent appears (terrorism).
Bloodthirsty commanders appear, whose flag is death.
Widows, orphans, and desolation menaces.
Hunger and disease dwell in the nations.
It is the grave signal of pollution. . . . Nature begins its swift agony.
Forests cry. The ax is sharpened.
The sanguinary fall down . . . others replace them with increased force. . . .

The Third Time, 1960-1966

Pacifying voices are heard. . . . The warrior's drum resounds again.
Earthquakes and tremors. . . . Earth again sends its anguished complaint.
Man is deaf and blind, his eyes closed.
Nature falls ill, and the climates are altered.
The success in space exploration causes forgetting of the fundamental.
The angel of Death makes himself strong and whispers to the ear of man
. . . promising power.
Death disguises herself as gentleman,
attacks those who seek justice and peace. She wears a sword.
The Signaled Ones arrive in the guise of children.
The gatherers of good fruit are prepared.
The Announcers of the world have arrived.
The moral and spiritual decline of the world begins.

The Fourth Time, 1967-1973

The "other force" manifests itself with power,
and in its delirium will drag many innocent towards error and death.
The anomalies in the weather increase.
Great rains, floods, droughts, overflowing of rivers, loss of crops.
The birds lose their bearings. The winds change.
The "Voice" returns, dressed as Death; it is another warning . . .
the earth trembles . . . her cry is not heard.
Climates follow their altered path.
Shortage of raw materials and signs of world famine.
Calls are made, but not heard . . . the initial warnings are given,
and nobody pays attention.

The world lives in apparent wealth.
It is the time of the crafty attack . . .
and they will fall vanquished once more.
People sing, and dance, and drink wine. . . .
In the great mansion they speak of peace,
but it is a dove with a leaden beak. There are signals in the sky.
The "flying clouds" land. The Princes of the signs appear.
They bring banners and leave their announcement. . . .
They are the Lords of Yesterday. The Lords of peace and joy.

The Fifth Time, 1974-1980

The attack continues mercilessly. The nations are in convulsions.
They speak of peace. There are rumors of war. There is war.
The merciless and mean attack continues. Innocents fall.
Men do not understand. They don't want to understand.
Pride blinds them, and it is the time of darkness.
The just are afraid; the peacemakers have no voice.
Violence increases, terrorism is legal,
kidnapping is an instrument of indignity. Hate shows its ugly face.
Corruption dwells on desks and executive chairs.
The "white powder" is a weapon, the "grass" a false illusion.
The insanity of the children worries the parents.
Prostitution opens its doors. Homosexuality is almost legal.
The politicians of the "other force" are the "great gentlemen."
Shame has been lost, and the dignity of men sleeps in a dark room.
Promises and lies are everyday's food. The gold rises. The gold falls.
The materialistic society's decline increases. Floods continue ruining crops.
Earth does not let up; earthquakes, tremors, hurricanes,
and constant changes in climate hurt man.
Revolts and political turmoil. Murders and jailings.
Religious divisions take place. Loss of faith.
The behavior of all the religious shall deny God.
Adoration is bestowed upon money. The God-fearing wait and see.
Robbery, assault, kidnapping, and murder become commonplace.
All shall fear their neighbor.
Who was honest and worthy, now is dishonest and unworthy.
Violations, affront, and abuse increase. All blame each other.
All fear, no one accuses. The law agents are also corrupted.
The government agents shall not do anything, afraid to lose their privileges.
The military uniforms shall lose their respectability,

and crime shall be their decoration.
It is the Fifth Time, with its terrifying vestments.
The Mutants are here. . . !

The Sixth Time: 1981-1987

The collapse precipitates. Satan orders the events to step forward.
The acceleration of the climatic changes is noticeable.
The epoch of the droughts has arrived.
The sky shuts-up . . . all seek redeeming answers, but the skies stay shut.
The rivers overflow, and mud avalanches bury homes and children.
Domestic animals perish, the days of hunger begin. The days shorten.
The space achievements continue, and new diseases appear.
The days of the great tribulations for Earth arrive.
Terrorism is at its height. The politicians play cards.
It is the time of slander and lie; all is a play of words.
The time of the honest and just man is gone;
it is the time of the dishonest, the crook, and the time of the lie.
The honest worker is blamed for the evil;
the powerful believe that it is time for additional profits—
the banker, the industrialist, the businessman, the swindler.
Blackmail and corruption are raised to glorious status.
Already, we can hear the steps of the "Great Manipulator."
It is his crop and his time.
It becomes notorious, the political force of an Organization
that expects to rule the world.
Genetic experiments are made known,
which will degenerate into terrible evil.
The Vivifier Force appears, the foundation of Man,
the immutable energy . . . the Chosen Ones carry it. . . .
The assault by hunger emerges. The world economy collapses.
The first symptom of new diseases attack mercilessly; they have no cure,
and death is the only hope for relief.
The volcanoes that slept in peace, now wake up.
They open their mouths, are all in accordance.
Pollution has broken slowly the spine of the planet.
Hates increase, and now the turbulent crowd looks for scapegoats. . . .
Industries fall, commerce closes, unemployment increases,
information is blocked. Solutions proposed are only apparent.
The situation worsens, the economy cracks. The "experts" are no experts.
The means are illegal, the good ones cooperate.

War arrives proudly and sits at the throne of the nations, dominates,
and as a plague it extends.
No way, the wise were not heard; it is too late. . . !
It is the crop of what the dwellers planted,
the punishment that the inhabitants looked for.
Fire comes down. . . .
The sphere will drop with its deathly load; death has wings.
The armies are mobilized . . . the weapons are the lords of hell.
The earth groans and convulses in death tremors, and tremendous agony.
The aberrations of climate signal the passage of the great changes.
Materialistic humanity plunges into the abyss . . . these are its last yells.
World production decreases because of great rains
and tremendous droughts. The ones who can, buy land.
The wise, plant. The planetary changes shall increase.
The structure of the earth crumbles, the inner layers move;
her veins are torn, her blood boils . . . the scars open. . . .
Oh, you . . . chiefs of state, ministers, majors, military, and judges,
bankers, pressmen, doctors and lawyers, financiers and speculators . . .
loud-voiced dolls. . . !
And you, laborer and worker, do not be tempted by the illusory gold.
The cup is full, be careful !
The prophecy has been fulfilled in its first part.

The Seventh Time: 1988-1994

The throne has been occupied by death.
It spreads and hits the countries that before were full of pride and riches.
Those of the old tribe and brothers detect triumph for now.
The Great Continent is now a graveyard.
Italy and France, and Spain also. The bastions fall. Alliances are made.
The governments, very busy with the war.
Those of the copper-colored face attack and win also.
The Bear and The Eagle, The Shoe and The Flower,
The Shield and The Dog, together must win.
The great dictator has spoken; the world listens and trusts him.
Meanwhile. . . . the foundations of the earth have started to move.
Atlas is wounded . . . deathly wounded. The cities fall.
The Church staggers. Cities are sunk. The sea boils, and its waters revolve.
Hunger is now the great winner.
The damned, the deadly Confederation has been created.
All the North and the South are in great tribulation.

The seed has been winnowed and is in the granary.
New shores in the meanwhile have been traced.
The capsule is ready; it is numbered . . . and waits. . . .
The vengeful criminal wears a turban;
the False Prophet succeeds greatly, and people marvel.
People's representatives before the law are powerless; their voice is not valid.
In many countries the established law does not act; a single power remains.
There are men with much power, who act on their own.
This will be another terrible mistake.
On the other hand, the words of the powerful spread.
His peace declarations and statutes that he will establish, will be accepted.
It is only a stratagem. Look at what I tell you; use your judgment.
Due to him, many of those who carry the inner light
shall be butchered in the public square.
He is not the Signaled of the Times!
He is the butcher of the sweet voice and the pale face,
the dark eyes and saintly mien.
His miracles are for deceit; his wisdom comes from the black pit.
True wisdom is not arrogant, does not cause pain,
is not used for vengeance. . . .
Look at him walking, listen to his words, notice his gestures.
Listen carefully to his formulations and teachings,
and look at his companies.
His apparent wisdom takes you to death, his acceptance,
a jump into darkness.
He, without knowing it, is the rod with which the world,
and man, will be measured. Be prudent, then.
During these times, greed shall take you to death!
These are the years of confusion and doubt,
the years of election and selection.
Who dresses in humility in the search, will find wisdom.
Who uses kindness, obtains happiness.
Who feeds on beauty, obtains perfection.
Who listens to good teachings, learns from the sage
and gets knowledge from the old man.
Who drinks only from Truth, receives the gift from the spirit.
Who gives Love and keeps Good Conduct,
his prize is the Light of Understanding, and never will he be alone.
Then, be magnanimous when you possess power, be just when judging.
Be fair and not covetous in your business.

Learn to forget, forget vengeance, and Peace will be granted you.
Be honest and peaceful, men worthy and meek.
Renew your spirit, and you will receive grace from heaven;
the time has begun for justice to shine.
It has never been absent, it has only been hidden,
and it shall tear the hypocrites from their pedestals.
Meanwhile, the earth cracks; its veins bulge, streams overflow,
and riverbeds tear . . . just wait.[1]

The Eighth Time, 1995-2001

New preparations for destruction. Weapons are flying.
The false leader has power. The world gives him authorization.
The Yellow Skin, the covenant did not respect.
Their armies sweep the enemy. The capsule is hurled.
Men are consumed. The world is mute.
The armies melt like molten lead.
It is the surprise, the feared lethal weapon.
Their flesh shall disintegrate, and before their knees bend they shall be dead.
Those of the brotherly alliance begin to triumph.
The Condor to the Eagle, food he shall give.
The lands from the South, sustenance shall send.
The signals in the sky shall continue in sight.
Insanity is the master of all; suicides shall increase,
and for many will be the only door to peace.
The time is arrived, for the moon and the sun their color modify.
With an unusual eclipse, great darkness will arrive.
The mortal weapons will be hurled.
The casualties shall be like grass leaves in the fields.
Two hundred million will be maimed, then destroyed and consumed.
The earth heats up, its pain increases, has fever inside;
great cities "perspire" at 45 and 50 degrees centigrade.
The foundations of the earth are disturbed,
and it throws up gases and poisonous vermin.
The chain breaks into lava; the fire is liquid.
The waters take revenge and invade nation by nation.
Fire also rains in tongues streaming from the sky.
Meanwhile, hunger keeps harassing.
Scenes of a terrible drama, the family will live to obtain wheat.
Dantesque street spectacles will be seen all over.
Terrorism is at its peak and invades the sea and the air.

Left to right: Mrs. Banarjee; Dr. H. Barnajee, Ph.D., Indian world authority on reincarnation and Professor of Psychology at Boston University; Carmencita Vasquez Lozada, Venezuelan painter; the author's wife; Enrique Castillo; and other invitee at the First International Congress of the New Parapsychology, held in Caracas, Venezuela, from November 5th to 8th, 1981.

Photo: Ricardo Vilchez, Costa Rica

The turban take vengeance for forty-five generations.
Madness has taken hold of men with power, and all believe it to be right.
It is the avalanche of sunset. It is too late; no one expects a new sunrise. . . .
Nevertheless . . . from affliction emerges the life-giving new light.
It barely shines. . . . It is hope. . . . It is the Voice of the Planter.
The lords of Light scatter darkness.
The Beast is wounded . . . the Beast is wounded. . . .
Again, deceit and fallacy.
The powers that deceive, clothed in red (purple)—
people and countries still listen to them. Behold, their power increases.
Able for deceiving, and strong in greed, falsehood is their prayer.
The right moment to terrorize and recapture power.
It will not last for long.
The covenant that will lead the world to the False Emmanuel is signed.
Those who have the light to guide men to the Truth make their appearance.
The fight is power to power. The spiritualists know it.
The impostor is now at the top of the throne.
Men have given him their vote and have approved their mandate.
He teaches with perfidy false teachings

and brings to the world his longed for peace . . . all apparent.
The family joy doesn't last for long. The world will know again its mistake.
The Announced Ones, reincarnated already on Earth,
have now their noble mission.
Humankind is perplexed.
People fell into the deceit, and now are not willing to believe
that it is really the expected message,
The Pacifier and the Leveler of the road.
Those of the old race take care of the flock.
They are at several places; they are the Lords of Peace and Wisdom.
The Great Message is revealed in time of war.
And contrarily, a new philosophy will invade the world,
full of rituals and cajoling verses, and it will be accepted by many.
Through threats of the Butcher, others will accept it.
The new church (religion) will end up succumbing.
Meanwhile, the earth shifts inside, the volcanoes explode,
cities sink, the ocean attacks with fury, and men have time only to scream.
The great wave of tides shall sweep; mud will bury cities.
Other ocean areas will dry up;
the waters concentrate and invade other shore cities.
The lifelines of the cities burst;
looting, together with prayers and cries of desperation
will mark the last moments of destruction.
The war cannot go on; there are no men to form a squadron.
Whoever can save himself, do it!
The rich and avaricious now give away their treasures,
and nobody wants them. All has lost its value.
Only their lives they want to save.
The moment has arrived, written about long ago.
The earth has spoken its last word. Babylon is dead!
Falsehood and purple fallacy have just died off.
The false church, struck by lightning, has collapsed.
The whole earth sways . . . the clouds darken in sudden change.
The sun is hidden. The terrestrial course is broken and aimless.
The shafts loosen up. Atlas breaks his knees. The world turns backwards.
It is the blast of the final trumpet.
The Angel spreads his fury, and men perish in the shadows of death.
The structures that ashamed the world have come to an end.
Ideologies, concepts, and political systems are wound up and buried forever.
Authoritarianism and personal power have come to an end.
In one day and one night, the schemes of the sky have changed.

The survivors abandon their uniforms,
and the uniform is changed into civilian clothing.
The Preparer is here, has incarnated to deliver the clean knowledge.
It is him. He shall speak with the Voice of the Spirit ,
and a new period shall be.
The roadway of lasting peace has finally been opened.
Freedom has finally been achieved.
It is the time of preparation FOR THE ONE WHO SHALL COME.
His promise was sealed, and now is the time for its fulfillment.
He is about to arrive. . . . IT IS HIM,
THE SIGNALED OF THE TIMES;
In Him are fulfilled all the prophecies.
Many will see Him arriving. . . but the day, the precise moment,
ONLY ONE KNOWS IT. We trust in Him.

The Ninth Time: 2002-2008

The true spiritual guides are the ones who direct the destiny of humanity.
All governments have ceased to exist,
and their political leaders are also gone.
The newly indicated course shall lead humanity to the true knowledge.
The time of weapons has passed away.
Man returns with renovated force to the spiritual life that was offered him,
to which he never arrived.
The birth of the New Life is celebrated.
Men shall be true friends and brothers.
Their relationship with God will be their most valued achievement.
Today's peace was always your decision. You negated and despised it.
Now you know the price that never should have been paid.
Never again obey it!
Walk the way now along this path of understanding,
without remorse and without bitterness.
The guilty ones have paid for their deeds.
The just are reborn again,
and their Soul is elevated and their Love multiplied.
Life has returned. . . . They have found God!

AFTER 2009

The days to come are of great peace and harmony among men. The spiritual guides shall teach with true power and authority, preparing the Second Arrival, promised by the Great Avatar of all times.

"THE ORGANIZATION"...

was founded officially the first Thursday of July, 1777. Its purpose is to take possession of the world through a slanted and subtle manipulation. Its headquarters were established between India and Pakistan, and now it has branches in the USA, France, England, Italy, Germany, Japan, China, Monaco, Russia, and its arm reaches other key countries of Europe and Africa, Libya, Iran, and Egypt. South America and the Caribbean have been included since 1933. Also, Haiti, Cuba, Nicaragua, Chile, Brazil, Paraguay, and Argentina, among others. The time when it will make itself noticed will be between 1986-1994. By the year 1992, it is planning to have an army of "clones," or artificial creations—about 500-600—the only ones they can trust to serve the Organization, called by them "Of the great Mutism."

These clones will be in posts of government, military, political, religious, student, and worker's organizations. These clones have been created, duplicating several terrestrial races, to be totally undetectable. They depend on the great super-gifted psychics, who are the foundation of the organization's power. In addition, no one knows their true leaders. They always act through "directed ones" (programmed individuals, selected from several countries), protecting in this way the real directors of the organization. Their plans are not altered; their force lies in their anonymity. They also count on outstanding scientists, politicians, military experts, and experts in finances, and on the great religions. Their financial power is inexhaustible. They have already executed great tests at a psychic collective level, activating the violence instinct, and also, the spirit of vocation and fidelity to their leaders. (Cases such as the Guyana Temple, with Reverend Jim Jones, and Charles Manson in California, are examples.)

Psychic manipulation at the world level is applied to government heads and politicians, and isolated cases of murders have removed the major obstacles in their race for domination of the planet. There exists, separate from this planetary conspiracy, the creation of a single, highly-developed race, to dominate and govern the survivors, enslaving those they consider inferiors. They promote wars, to eliminate gradually those not considered suitable for the "new order" they plan to implement. These 206 years have been effective proof of psychic manipulation. One of their main bases is probably located by entering through the South Pole, on an island called "EDEN 5," from which operations at a psychic level are carried out throughout the planet.

Many scientists have disappeared; today they are working for THEM. Many others have been seduced with money and power. They don't really know for whom they work. Complete families have fallen. Men weak of mind, and weaker of spirit, have been reached and utilized by these forces.

THIS ORGANIZATION SHALL CAUSE GREAT DAMAGE TO HUMANITY, BUT SHALL NOT TRIUMPH IN ITS PLAN TO DOMINATE THE PLANET.

It is important to tell the reader that the first periods of time covered in the above prophecy have been fulfilled completely, and because of this they didn't go into further detail in the reports. These should only be viewed as reference points for locating the rest, starting from the date of the dictation, in 1975.

The appearance of AIDS, of skin cancer, of cholera again, of the war of the Persian Gulf, the corruption of politicians, and the loss of honor of some of the military, of crime, strikes, holdups, robberies, violations, speculation, and the complacency of presidents and government heads, are known facts. But the most impressive information is the appearance in public light of an organization that will manage a new world order, the destinies of humanity.

In other words, since 1975 we were given a very clear vision of all these events—some of them already accomplished—which would develop before our eyes. In those days we didn't think it possible. Today, the facts are history.

There is no question that many of the best known prophets have failed, especially the modern ones. One example is Jeanne Dixon, who prophesied the following, which never happened:

In 1960 , that USA and Russia would fight a war against China in 1980.
In 1979 , that all California would be destroyed by an earthquake in 1983.
In 1978, great earthquakes and seaquakes, caused by impact of a comet, in 1985.
In 1978, the end of Catholicism, in 1988.
In 1972, the appearance of the Anti-Christ, in 1992.

Edgar Cayce also failed several times. We can see that the prophetic terror has failed often in its calculations. Should we believe that the extraterrestrial prophecies also will fail? How many have been fulfilled, and how many will become true?

There is a problem about accepting a prophecy with all its implications and consequences, as it is written. Can we change it? I don't think so. Because if we could, we would have already changed it, as soon as we knew how and when, and many prophecies would not have been fulfilled. Therefore, doubtless all prophets would be extinguished, and their prophecies would become worthless.

Only time will give us the last word. I believe it is necessary to take into account what has been fulfilled. As an example, I told a lady who is very well known in politics in Caracas, with much anticipation, what would happen to

Carlos Andrés Pérez, and it was obvious that she didn't believe me. She received from me the respective prophecy, in writing.

Later, she remarked to a friend in Caracas, that she had the opportunity of making known all the details to the already President Pérez. Perhaps history could have been changed, but as prophecy, it had to be fulfilled.

CHAPTER NOTE

[1] In regard to the fulfillment of some prophecies, in particular the SEVENTH TIME, from 1988 to 1994:

This Time HAS NOT BEEN FULFILLED, and I hope that it never will. The prophecies of the future can be changed and can turn something unfortunate into a positive outcome for all of humanity. The Pleiadeans warned me that, "The future is unstable and changes with the actions of people and the decisions of nations." They said "possibly" (p. 94).

This information has been discussed by the author with various groups from Colombia, Venezuela, Costa Rica, and independently with well-known investigators. The results have always been similar: "It is very possible that many events have been changed in the future because thousands of people and spiritual groups on the planet have dedicated themselves to meditate and ask for WORLD PEACE, and this Energy , which they send out at least two times a week, may have produced an altered outcome for the benefit of humanity—something that seems apocalyptic, beneficial, and positive for all—as a result of their mental attitude and love for others.

21

My Personal Opinion

"Faced with new waves of experiences of UFO contact, our religions do seem obsolete. Our idea of the church as a social entity working within rational structures is obviously challenged by the claim of direct communication with visible beings who are endowed with supernatural powers. Some modern preachers have already recognized this challenge.

"Evangelist Billy Graham, for example, has suggested that (some) UFOs may, in fact, be 'heavenly angels'; their occupants, he says, are astonishingly angel-like in some of their reported appearances. . . .

". . . an equally impressive parallel could be made between (other) UFO occupants, and the popular conception of demons."

—JACQUES VALLEE,
Messengers of Deception—UFO Contacts and Cults

THE YEAR 1975 WAS VERY ACTIVE FOR ME. I participated for the first time at the international level in the First World Congress of Witchcraft, in Bogotá, Colombia. There I met Uri Geller and Dr. Thelma Moss, with her interesting investigations using the Kirlian camera, as well as other personalities, about whom I had heard, for the first time. The brave one to convoke the Congress, even against the will of the church, was my good friend, Simón González, who later became Governor of the islands of Saint Andrew and Providence.

There, during the meetings of the Congress, an extraterrestrial arrived and got in touch with me at my hotel, pretending that he was a journalist looking for firsthand news. The most extraordinary detail is that "something" caused a blackout at 7:00 p.m. At this opportunity, he was dropped, with all his credentials, to participate. This encounter will be part of the next book, including all the details of the congress.

Three months later, I left for Germany, to an international congress in Wiesbaden, where there were two additional interesting experiences. Just arrived from Germany, I was invited to the International UFO Congress in Guayaquil, Ecuador, around December, 1975. At that time, I maintained only telepathic contact with the Pleiadeans. Less than three months later, the contacts with the Greater Brothers were to be terminated completely.

For, on February 17, 1976, after receiving approximately 100 messages, some 240 hours of telepathic contact with the extraterrestrials, and 112 hours of physical contact during the five personal encounters and trips, the contacts were suddenly interrupted, ending abruptly through a telephone call received at the ICIFE, just as I was getting ready to give a public talk. I believe the ETs were watching me on a screen, just as I had viewed my family from their ship during our first flight. It was about 5:00 p.m., and I was getting ready for the talk, which was scheduled to begin at 7:00 p.m.

My secretary, Colombia, was arranging some papers. She came and told me she was going to fetch a cup of coffee from the corner shop (about fifty meters away), and that she could get one for me if I wanted. I said yes, and gave her the money for coffee and a roll. From my office on the second floor, I heard the door chime announcing that she had left and closed the door, when the telephone rang. I answered, giving the name of the Institute. The voice that I heard said, *"Enrique, listen carefully what I am going to tell you."* I thought it was my old associate, Isidro Contreras, who used to call and talk "like a Martian," kidding me. Believing it was him, I answered with a couple of "dirty words," told him to call later, and hung up. The telephone immediately rang again, and I realized that nobody could have rotary dialed six numbers so quickly. I thought that only if the telephone was somehow hooked directly, could it ring back so fast, and with a different pattern. These were the words that I now heard, in a very firm voice:

"Enrique, do not interrupt; listen carefully to what we have to tell you. It's from us; the communications are terminated. If we need you, we know where to find you. We know what you are up against. We wish you success. Utilize wisely what you have seen and learned. We trust you. So long."

Unable to utter a word, I had to hang up. I was just beginning to realize what had happened, when I heard the chime announcing Colombia's return with the cup of coffee. She must have seen my pale face, because she brought me water and asked me what was wrong. In this abrupt way, the communications ended, communications that had taken place over the past two-and-a-half years, with me and with the group, from the Superior Beings from the Pleiades.

At the time, this termination almost led me to desperation, and I felt abandoned and guilty of some wrongdoing for which they were not willing to

April 20, 1996. Central smoke-stack of the Volcano Irazú where Enrique Castillo R. sighted the first UFO in Costa Rica in 1963. Photo: Eng. Enrique Castillo R.

correct or reproach me. Months later, I recalled that they had warned me to maintain very firm and clear the belief that somehow in the future, they would intervene more directly, once the prophecies were fulfilled and the Anti-Christ and its armies took possession of the Earth.

I realized finally that they knew somehow that I had abandoned everything, including my family, to dedicate myself full time to spreading the word about these transcendental events.

(My separation from Gloria Ortiz, after a relationship that lasted five years, took place in 1979. Three children, whose names are Ohrion Yamaruck, Daiyaini, and Toninka—a boy and two girls, now 22, 18, and 17 years old, respectively—are now outstanding students, the boy at the University of the Andes and the two girls, in high school. I feel very proud of them. They all live with their mother in Bogotá, Colombia.)

I now write this last chapter in Caracas, Venezuela, with the intention of leaving the reader with my own opinion. I have attended thirteen Congresses on UFO and paranormal subjects. I have met many of the greatest scientists and investigators, and I have discussed the subject with them; some have become my personal friends, and I know their personal opinions. I have also met some of the best-known contactees, and have heard their statements. Therefore, I believe I have an overall knowledge of the patterns followed by the aliens in contacting humans.

I have also become investigator of my own case, and have constantly invited the public to question me, my closest friends included. This book does not contain all the incidents, talks, messages, and events that were my lot to live through in the approximately two-and-a-half years of contacts. Some items have faded from my memory, and I don't remember them. Others, which I believed lost, have come back to my memory while writing this book.

There were talks with the Pleiadeans when we laughed heartily, because of the type of questions that I asked. They understood that my capacity was not the best. I saw them in several instances making an effort to lower themselves to the level of my intellect. They never gave me a specific task to complete, whether intended to save the human race, or for myself. What I have done during these twenty-three years of spreading the word has been my own decision; therefore, I have no one else to blame for my economic difficulties. It was my decision, and I don't regret it.

Here I would like to thank my good friend Salvador Freixedo, for his excellent advice during the investigations that he carried out regarding my case. The same goes to Andreas Faber Kaiser (who died recently in Spain), who also advised me as a good friend. To the brothers Ricardo and Carlos Vilchez from Costa Rica, who for nineteen years have investigated in three countries my statements, and with whom a great, brotherly friendship has grown, my deepest thanks.

Thanks also to: In Mexico, to my good friends Carlos Ortiz de la Huerta, and Dr. Jacobo Grinberg, both very important in the fields of the paranormal and the unusual. To Dr. Jacques Vallée, who with his books, investigations, and contributions has provided a fundamental turning point in the scientific investigation of the UFO phenomenon. I have learned much, listening to such an eminent scientist and investigator.

Another friend whom I appreciate exceedingly, and have had the opportunity to talk to on several occasions, both in Mexico (1977) and Venezuela (1980, 1982, 1983 and 1984), is Dr. J. James Hurtak, Ph.D., private advisor to NASA and Director of the Academy for the Science of the Future. He has given me the opportunity to grasp some spiritual aspects of the extraterrestrial teachings.

There are many other investigators whose names I have to omit in this final chapter, but my sincere thanks go to all of them. To Herr Karl Veit from Ventla-Verlag, Wiesbaden, Germany, and his charming wife, Annie, best wishes for these two excellent friends, who are always close to my heart. And finally, thanks also to my dear friend, Fabio Zerpa, from Argentina.

It is necessary to give testimony of my personal thinking about UFOs, and the UFO phenomenon in general, with all its incidents and underlying implications. It is clear that my direct involvement with the ETs does not in any way give me the last word, and I do not have all the answers. I have tried—without being a writer—to be very objective at all times, and report the most relevant facts of my own experience. Nevertheless, in a separate book, very soon, I shall reveal the more meaningful incidents of my last two contacts, including the impressive submersion at the Mariana trench.

Here and now, I would like to issue a warning to the naive who still believe that there are no "negative," or "evil" extraterrestrials, from our viewpoint, that is. This "Other Force" exists and is real. I would perform a disservice if I denied its existence at this time of difficulties for the planet.

It has been my task, throughout Latin America for the last twenty years, to make known the existence of the negative beings, who have penetrated practically all layers of society—"The Gray Ones," also called the Rigelians, associated with other undesirable races of alien stock.

I have been badly criticized and rebuffed, even by some of my friends, who did not believe in the existence of "The Evil Ones," and who thought that we were the only "negatives" of the Galaxy.

I always thought that certain "contacts" are manipulated by "the other force" to make adepts among groups of so-called "spiritualists," where they are "managed" and controlled. These would be "the sheep dressed in white," who have lost their right to reason and to hold their own opinion. The world is full of the mediocre.

Now that the "gray ones" have become so well-known, almost all of those who rebuffed me previously have apologized. Some of them believe that I could have saved them their lives. But the manipulators have always existed, same as the sheep; we have to keep up with both.

During the international congress, "100 YEARS OF INVESTIGATION OF THE GREAT MYSTERIES OF MAN," at San José de Costa Rica, held October 14–19, 1985, also called **"In Search of the New Frontiers of Science,"** I presented my ideas to several of the most important scientists and investigators, worldwide. I was the "ugly duckling" of the group. Here are the names of the participants:

Juan José Benítez
Charles Berlitz
Dr. Javier Cabrera Darquea
Andreas Faber Kaiser (deceased)
Salvador Freixedo Tabares
John A. Keel
Dr. John C. Lilly
Dr. Antonieta (Tony) Lily (deceased)
Dr. Andrija H. Puharich
Dr. Jacques Vallée
Dr. Jacobo Grimberg Zilberbaum
Dr. Carlos de León
Enrique Castillo Rincón
Lic. Carlos Ortiz de la Huerta (organizer)
Ricardo Vílchez N. (organizer)
Carlos Vílchez N. (organizer)

Others who were invited but did not attend included Juan G. Atienza and Zecharia Zitchin, who at the last minute could not attend. It should be mentioned that this congress was the best organized to date, according to the opinion of the attendees. Hearty congratulations are due to the brothers Vílchez Navamuel and to Carlitos Ortiz, who were responsible for it.

This was the paper I presented:

UFO: Psychic Cosmic Force?

Presentation of Engineer Enrique Castillo Rincón
to the International Congress,
"100 Years of Investigation of the Great Mysteries of Man"
San José, Costa Rica
October 14–19, 1985

On June 24, 1947, nine strange flying objects in perfect formation were seen from a small aircraft piloted by Mr. Kenneth Arnold, near "Mount Rainier," United States of America. This sighting was the modern starting point of one of the greatest riddles of our time, the so-called "Flying Saucers."

The challenge to solve this mystery, to discover their origin, constitution, and technology, whether they were piloted by intelligent creatures of extraterrestrial origin, or whether they represented a new terrestrial technology on the part of some super-powers, but maintained in the strictest military secrecy, has inflamed the imagination of the world. Thirty-eight years have passed since that sighting, which popularized the term "flying saucer," eventually changed to UFO, or Unidentified Flying Object, spelled OVNI in Spanish, French, and other languages.

During these thirty-eight years, serious scientific investigation has been carried out over almost all the world by governments, in official fashion, but who maintain in secret their discoveries. It is important to give credit to the private investigations, by eminent scientists and private organizations, who have quietly developed several valid hypotheses and theories, supportive of the knowledge we now have on this subject.

Most people, for lack of adequate information, are not aware that this phenomenon is the subject of study by highly qualified scientists; on the other hand, many amateur sympathizers strive with great efforts to dispel the ridicule and banter with which the subject has been received by the skeptical and the ignorant, who attack these investigations, hampering them and delaying the conclusions that it may be possible to reach. Thanks to the patient observation over many years by these courageous men, through which it has been possible to establish some theories and facts, which can be summed-up as follows:

UFOs are real (nuts-and-bolts) machines, not optical illusions.

They are flying craft of super-advanced technology, unknown to us at the present time.

As possible originating points, they can come from:

Outer space, from many places in the Universe.

Parallel worlds, coexistent with ours, in a multi-dimensional array.

Our Earth, either the product of a great technological power, as an experimental weapon.

An intra-terrestrial civilization, which has no desire to be in contact with us.

UFOs could be travelers from the future, who "peek" at our world, to see how things are going.

UFOs and their occupants could be the components of a "psychic control set-up," to maintain terrestrial groups in equilibrium. If this is the case, the question is to determine who, and from where, this mechanism is controlled. This new theory has been masterfully outlined by French investigator, Dr. Jacques Vallée, advisor to NASA at the present time, jointly with Dr. J. Allen Hynek, probably the best-recognized experts on this subject.

The above five theories contain the essential foundations of the UFO phenomenon, but of course there are others, derived from the above. The open-minded investigators have taken gigantic steps, ahead of those who have closed minds and myopic vision, and those who believe themselves to be owners of the absolute truth.

One of the most brilliant investigators is Salvador Freixedo, a former Jesuit, who has written at least fourteen books, seven of which have been dedicated to the UFO subject, from the philosophical and religious standpoints, achieving a substantial understanding of the deepest layers of the human conscience. When he was able to see further than others, it was because he took the time to make field investigations and to talk directly to the witnesses of the events, who often were contactees of the "Third Kind." Of course, his religious and philosophical background have contributed significantly to the depth and width of his writings.

The UFO phenomenon contains the ingredients to fool the most qualified of the investigators, because apparently, "it denies itself"; in other words, it does not admit rational explanation. How can this be possible, if it has been admitted as real?

We have stressed that during thirty-eight years of investigation and observation, possible explanations have been presented that fall within the field of the fantastic, the unreal, and the mysterious. They violate the known physical laws,[1] on which our civilization is based. The logic of their occupants and their behavior does not match ours. In the light of our reason, the facts seem illogical and absurd. Therefore, it is not strange to hear, even now, some pitifully simplified explanations, such as natural phenomena, planet Venus, swamp gas, or secret weapons of some terrestrial superpower.

UFOs have also been the subject matter for the weak of spirit and poor in information, for the creation of pseudo-religions, around supposed extraterrestrial ambassadors, bringing us the "universal panacea for good living," and formulae for never-ending peace. I know firsthand of several Colombian and Venezuelan towns where this emotional-psychic disarrangement has occurred, where many people dangerously propose these formulae for peace and harmony, of supposed extraterrestrial origin, and seek physical contacts in lonely places, after establishing telepathic contact with "them," in order to get further explanations on a personal basis.

The candid and naive may believe that as long as they are extraterrestrial, they must be good and loving, and that we must be the only disgraced ones who have not reached the fullness of cosmic consciousness. The UFO phenomenon is thus a pole of attraction for the religious misfits, the fanatics, and the ignorant, who get together in a group with the well-meaning objective of improving the world, where all tend to become seers and prophets of heavenly punishments for human sins. (One of those sins, I would say, is to be ignorant of the implications of the phenomenon.)

Not only in Colombia and Venezuela, but in other countries where I have visited and given talks, I have been witness to these dangerous games of direct contacts with aliens.

If time had permitted, I would have brought up horrifying cases of physical attacks on adult men and women, and a couple of children also, well documented, which have not been divulged for various reasons. It is a mistake to believe that all aliens are good and pacific, because they have been able to "know God" and his laws.

The features of the UFO occupants are very complex, and therefore their description and evaluation are also complex. Some eminent investigators have proposed at world congresses the advisability of giving out information at schools and universities about the different varieties of alien visitors, by means of talks, pamphlets, etc., just in case of a massive confrontation in the future. Others advise not to give out information about something we know is there, but whose intentions or purposes we don't know.

Salvador Freixedo speaks of a quasi-intelligent-residual energy, which has made itself felt since olden times and which now increases its activity on account of the difficult times and social decomposition we live in.

Dr. Vallée says that this psychic force tends to control and seek equilibrium for humanity, but does not explain who directs it.

According to Major (retired) Kolman von Kievizki, there is an extragalactic conspiracy to occupy our planet militarily and enslave us. He claims to have evidence and clues that this will happen sooner or later. Some of the UFO occupants are space "animal-monsters," with a metallic-like caparison. Once in a while they visit earth and are gifted with great intelligence and almost human abilities.

I would like to mention also my friend Erich von Daniken, whose theory has become very popular, about some space rovers who performed a mutation experiment on our planet, inoculating intelligence into the first hominids, who would become our ancestors. This involves a very swift jump in intelligence, which science has not yet been able to explain, but von Daniken's theory has some serious followers in the world.

UFO activity might seem to have dropped off, but this is not actually the case; veritable flaps have taken place, with virtual climaxes, such as happened in Puerto Rico, Chile, and some European countries, where the media shows little interest about this rather commonplace occurrence. These flaps have stressed the *psychic* component, a powerful element in their behavior pattern. Almost all of the witnesses in close encounters have experienced a radical change in their personal and religious viewpoints. Others, additionally, become the subject of paranormal experiences, which usually have a powerful and unsettling effect in their lives.

Statistics show that these psychological events produce marked mental-spiritual effects in some people. In others, more open-minded and cultured, the changes tend towards a search for higher values. In still others, the changes can be harmful, causing mental imbalance.

UFOs have caused, during the last thirty-eight years, from my viewpoint, an incredible impact on the field of beliefs, affecting in a positive way not only the great majority of the witnesses, but other people from differing social groups, as well.

There have been a high number of encounters with women of different ages and social status, who have been exposed to close encounters with these navigators, in several countries, wherein they are forced to have sexual intercourse, possibly for experimental purposes. These encounters do not usually cause physical damage, but an irreparable trauma, because the women involved usually acquire a strong revulsion for the sexual act. Some of the affected are under medical and psychical care, so far without success.

All of them today have psychological problems, plus some burns on their bodies, because of the radiation, not only from the vehicle, but from the instrumentation used on board to examine them. These are only a few examples of what can happen.

You may realize the diversity of visitors we can have. Definitely, there is a great multiplicity, surely with different degrees of evolution—scientific, technological, and spiritual. During my talks with several very important investigators, I have become acquainted with many instances of aggression, kidnapping, and sometimes death of the witnesses, by attacks of the ufonauts. And still there are some who believe that all of them are "angelic brothers from space."

As a case in point, I received a few days ago some information from Brazil, where on November 3, 1981, a UFO attacked several hunters, killing four of them with terrible radioactive burns. There are other cases of child kidnapping, and the mutilation of a whole group of explorers, who disappeared and were later found 500 kilometers away, where pieces of their bodies, as well as their clothing, were dropped from above on the roofs of a hamlet. I omit more details, to avoid further revulsion. In this way, some of our very dear space brothers visit us, and leave us their bloody calling card, in cases such as the one I have just mentioned tangentially. Cattle mutilations have been carried out, also, most probably by some type of aliens.

Not all is negative and somber, however; there are well-documented cases showing very clearly that another kind of visitor is also affecting the human consciousness, and here it is where I can state categorically that there is a plan, a directive, which is subtly affecting all humanity, for a great cosmic-mental change, and that some of the UFOs play a most important part in this plan.

It might seem that there is a contradiction in my words. But my warning was clear about what they send through subtle waves, the great change that will open the door to the New Man on earth in the following generations: the mutant. And when I say this, I am not taking a great risk, because I know with certainty that I am telling the truth. Within the next ninety years, we will find that the main effect of the UFO phenomenon will be to genetically engrave, in a silent way, throughout hundreds of years, the information required to improve the human race that will populate this lovely but vexed, fratricidal, and nuclearized planet.

The psychic component of the new humanity already shows some of the new paranormal capabilities, such as "dermoptics," the ability to see through the skin of one's hands, or telekinesis, the ability to move objects with mere will power, the controlling of mechanical and electrical devices at a distance, the bending of objects through induced plasticity, self-healing, telepathy, etc. These will be the future dwellers of this earth.

It is not a Utopia, my dear friends. Facing this new human reality will be fantasy for some, but for those with a futuristic outlook, it is a positive fact; it is our destiny. But this future requires a quota of sacrifice. The children who will come with these improvements incorporated shall not be the children or grandchildren of smokers, to give just one example. Do we want a new race? In what ways have we formally advanced in order to face the responsibility of this fantastic future world?

This Congress has met, upon great effort, to make known these facts, this new science, which, without frontiers, will marvel our descendants in the third millennium. By then, the psychic-man shall be born, dweller of this small planet of cosmic learning.

Are the ufonauts responsible for this awakening? Are they directed by some cosmic-planetary organization that oversees this great change without harming evolution? I believe so.

The idea of the UFO phenomenon, as a means of psychic control of a very complex type, is arriving to fruition and serves the needs of human beings in a changing world. Perhaps, the UFO and its phenomena during a close encounter serve to break the barrier of accepted concepts, and allow us to reach the true reality that surrounds us. Some investigators consider the possibility that UFOs are the product of physical, astral, and mental phenomena taken all together.

To see a UFO, to feel overwhelmed and paralyzed by its blinding lights, to sense one's vital psycho-biological processes being suspended, while an energy of indescribable nature shakes one's neurons and provokes short-circuits in the nervous system, is a unique experience, which always leaves an indelible imprint in the deepest layers of the psyche, and often—I am sure—has the capacity to overwrite the genetic code hidden in the chromosomes . . . !

Parallel to the fear of death, ridicule, pranks, or any other unexpected happening, is the touch of magic and the mysterious in the physical encounter with unknown intelligences. The insistent knocking in your mind that you are living a hallucinating and unique experience, gives you the bravery to let yourself be fascinated by the unknown, the marvelous.

I compare these encounters of today with those experienced directly by many of our prophets and forebears, who were unable to find a rational and valid explanation. During the several investigations that I undertook after my encounters, I realized that a goodly number of the "contactees" were phony, that they wanted to make themselves noticed, and that UFOs, of course, were one of the best ways to achieve it.

These individuals did not seek to appear in the press, or in TV interviews; they just have a deep longing for recognition, for receiving special treatment from those who struggle to meet them, or to belong to their group of chosen ones—to receive special treatment from people who would consider them special. These people otherwise lack real affection, and the ETs have become their excuse to obtain it.

The serious problem with this madness is the effect produced on the people who associate themselves with the fake contactee, a new type of mystic, personal terrestrial representative, or carrier of calamitous predictions, that are always to be kept secret until the ET orders that "chosen one" to speak up. As long as there is a chance of a break in the silence, the group members expect to be the first to know. With this "message-trap," the disciple eventually ends up getting sick and tired of his master, who wastes his time and money without any spectacular news, and he ends up leaving the "contactee," not without slandering the untrustworthy ET.

This singular drama has been experienced by many people associated with these false Messiahs or contactees, in almost all the Latin American cities where I have observed this situation at close range. I have encountered during my investigations instances where the leader of the group claimed to have received instructions to practice sexual exchange (swapping), in order to obtain a supposed "coupling of supermen." Married and separated women, as well as single girls, have fallen naively into this exploitative situation. Of course, the leader of the group, carrier of the superior genes, is the one to accomplish the distressing assignment of impregnating all the women of the group, even with the approval of their husbands and other group members. This dangerous experience has brought these people many terrible consequences, once they discover that their phony master is only one more "smart-aleck," who not only enjoys himself with the girls of the group but also takes away from them whatever money they have.

Sociologists and psychologists could study and explain this type of situation and give warning to other people, who are in search of higher values and honestly seek a new, better world, full of understanding and love. This type of situation has led many people to desperation in Colombia, Venezuela, Perú, and Ecuador. Without giving names, many have needed psychiatric attention for many months, without gaining a complete recovery. Some people have sold their property and belongings, on supposed orders from the ETs, with the idea of traveling to another planet, where worldly goods are a hindrance. Of course, the money goes to the earthly "master" (master of deceit), who uses it to buy a few necessary things for the trip to Utopia.

The "Colonies of Love" are another facet, where disciples go to live communally away from the cities, in a place selected "by the ET," and dedicate themselves to tilling the earth and learning to live without hate and envy. The typical outcome is: fights between families, indiscriminate sexual interchanges, eloping with the other fellows' wives and the younger girls of the group, separations, abandonments, and so on. Some of these phony "incarnated prophets" believe they have God's authorization to exploit their followers and subject them to exhausting labor, as "tests from the Lord."

Some of the members of these surprising communities return to their places of origin, once they realize their mistake, completely broken—and

Left to right: Dr. Enio Hernández F. (parapsychologist), Enrique Castillo R., and Dr. James Hurtak of the U.S.A. during the UFO International Congress in San Cristobal, State of Tachira, Venezuela.
Photo: Carlos Torres

Enrique Castillo, Dr. J. Allen Hynek, and Carlos Vilchez. Mexico, 1978
Photo: Ricardo Vilchez

broke—physically and morally, very ashamed. They are not willing to accuse anyone, for fear of being considered, and rightly so, credulous idiots of phony ET teachings.

Changing the subject, it is necessary to mention that there are several levels of existence: various dimensional levels, and also other terrestrial entities that are not duly registered in the mysterious records of our history. Some of them have great supernatural powers, and sometimes they like to experiment or play tricks on us. They share the planet in a quasi-physical plane of existence, from which they can manifest, emerging as if they were "extraterrestrial." So far, we lack information on what are the objectives of these bothersome neighbors. Regarding the "legitimate" ET, it is also very risky to give definitive answers. As far as we know, there are fourteen different "typologies" or "identi-kits" of occupants of alien ships, varying from robots, humanoids, humans, and certain creatures more animal than human.

Nevertheless, through this tangle of fraudulent and confusing facts, there emerge true, legitimate contacts.

Such is the case with the experiences I lived in November, 1973, featuring the good extraterrestrials, friendly and spiritual. The comparisons that I have been able to establish show that perhaps there is a well-designed plan, conceived by some of these benevolent entities, to awake our human consciousness and raise us to higher evolutionary levels, accelerating normal evolution. I am sure, also, that they carry out psychic tests intended to improve us at an individual or collective level, without tampering with our daily activities.

As in the movies, the so-called "Westerns," there are also the equivalents of the showdowns on Main Street. They watch and fear each other, and this is part of the information received from the ETs. These power-to-power confrontations are not known by us in their terrifying scope, because we lack the necessary background to comprehend the complexities of this cosmic struggle that takes place "right in front of us." I only know for sure that, thanks to men of great courage and bravery in adversity, these mysteries shall unravel little by little, with reason and logic throwing light on the great mysteries before man, which is the subject matter of this Congress, for the purpose of dissipating the fog that obscures all that was formerly considered taboo, miraculous, or impossible.

During the development of these Congresses, there is something else worth mentioning:

During 1975, in Wiesbaden, Germany, I received the first threat to my personal integrity, if I "talked" about something that I was cautioned not to mention. I was aware that I had to be judicious when delivering the information I had received. Who was afraid that I could uncover "something," which I supposedly knew? Were they the MIB (Men in Black)?

Of the four threats that I received during different years, the last one was in 1985, during the World Congress in Costa Rica. The letter arrived when Charles Berlitz spoke on the subject of the Bermuda Triangle and Atlantis. When the messenger handed me the envelope, I was sitting between Jacques Vallée at my left and Dr. Jacobo Grinberg at my right.

I opened the envelope, and with newspaper clippings and strange symbols, the senders threatened me about not talking about "something," of which they knew I was aware. Who are they? When I showed the note to Dr. Vallée, he said that it seemed to be rather voodoo-like. I still don't know who could be affected by what I knew at that time; I have always been very careful in handling information.

In San José, Costa Rica, during the two years I spent in the country where I was born (1987-1989), a Congress took place, the Third Esoteric Congress of Costa Rica. I was invited to participate, and for personal reasons I did not attend, but I sent a paper, to be read by a friend who attended the Congress. At that time, this was my position:

"THE UFO PHENOMENON AND ITS ESOTERIC ASPECT"
San José, Costa Rica
April 13, 1988

Dear public in general, organizers of the Third Esoteric Congress of Costa Rica, representatives of related organizations, ladies and gentlemen:

The human race has been moved by curiosity since the very first days of its appearance on Earth to unveil the great mysteries that surround its true origin or genesis. This curiosity, perpetuated by genetic memory, seeks to unravel "Memories from the Future." Generation after generation has engraved, first in stone and rock and then on animal skins and papyrus, an oral tradition which has passed down from parents to children, from race to race, throughout history, telling of the arrival of messengers from the stars, and the ways to interpret their teachings and spiritual legacy.

This knowledge, delivered to various races in different parts of the world and during different epochs, gave birth to the major religions of the world, as well as the esoteric and hermetic organizations dedicated to preserving intact the original, superior teachings. On the other hand, the knowledge delivered to man gave birth to an authentic scientific-spiritual body of knowledge: the "extraterrestrial science."

We should notice that this science has a special characteristic, being both the oldest knowledge and the newest. In order to preserve this knowledge, it was kept secret, away from the common people, and accessible only to the "worthy ones" in charge of its preservation for future use. A special generation would be able to make correct use of it. This was the origin of the esoteric organizations, preservers of the knowledge furnished by the very gods themselves, as a legitimate heritage for the human race.

The visitation to our planet of these superior beings contributed a wealth of knowledge and technology that man, by himself, could not have achieved easily. From August 5-8, 1971, during a scientific congress held in Byurakan, Soviet Armenia, where more than a thousand people met, including personalities of international science, and under the patronage of the Academies of Sciences of the Soviet Union and of the United States, it was decided to officially consider this subject as "EXTRATERRESTRIAL SCIENCE." It is

Left to right: Carlos Vílchez, the author, Juan José Benítez, and Ricardo Vílchez, during the visit of Mr. Benítez to the UFO Congress in 1997. (Photo taken at the author's home.)
Photo: Ana Castillo

Juan José Benítez and Enrique Castillo at the author's home, April 1997.
Photo: Ana Castillo

well to repeat, for the ignorant who deny facts of such importance, the statement of the illustrious Alexis Carrel: *"Summing up, scientists are only men. They are saturated with the prejudices of their milieu, and of their time. They believe quite honestly that facts which cannot be explained do not exist."*

Let's take into account that man is essentially "cosmic" by birth, by tradition, and by all of his actions. Let's think for a moment about Foster's theory, according to which man constantly receives certain cosmic particles, which gradually unlock an immense data file, and a constant inflow of radiation which will inexorably lead us to our true cosmic nature. If the intelligent universe is striving to communicate and establish contact with us—and due to our lack of attention the process is slow—let's understand, in all certainty, that man is pre-programmed for knowledge and enlightenment.

We should realize that the time is ripe for moving from the external to the internal, and that the greatest human finding is to grasp and understand with our five senses and our intuition that our greatest conquest is here, on earth: Man to the rescue of Man!

The presence and behavior of the visiting gods—whose history makes them part of our ancestry—was more direct in the past. Nowadays, they make themselves evident through UFOs—their unbelievable displacements, astonishing movements, and instant materialization and dematerialization, which seem both magical and mysterious, because they challenge our present physical concepts.

Esoteric Ufology denies that UFOs are manned spaceships from other, physical—or perhaps parallel or other-dimensional—worlds. It is undeniable that these sightings, unexplainable by present science, include great esoteric and symbolic components, as has been pointed out by several important researchers. But there is something undeniable: they are present on our earth here and now, as a challenge to all human scientific rules, to all our values and beliefs, shaking collectively the passive life of the distracted man, challenging the incredulous, provoking thought among intellectuals, and evolving human behavior patterns to acquire new mental possibilities that will give us the key to avoid a collective panic that could destabilize the planet.

Assuming that sometimes UFOs can originate paraphysically or extradimensionally, reaching vibratory levels that we cannot register, the opportunity arises to explore an esoteric approach in order to penetrate the inner nature of a separate, marvelous reality.

Writer Vicente Anglada in his book, *The Hierarchy, The Solar Angels, and Divinity,* says:

"Final liberation, or the entry of the human being into the Divine Kingdom, takes place precisely when the last embers of the solar body have melted in the mysterious crucible of the space dwellers, a particular kind of being who assists in the initiation process. This way, upon the dawn of the Aquarian Age, this esoteric teaching concretizes in respect to the great cosmic intermediaries."

Author "Brother Phillip," in his book, *The Secret of the Andes*, says:

"In the towers of the lost cities there is a resplendent crystal that shines eternally. This crystal is, without doubt, the Maxin light of antiquity and is related to the same power utilized today by the UFO visitors from space. . . .

Spacemen are three-dimensional beings like ourselves; they are not ghosts. There are beings from other dimensions who are working with the 'Space Confederation,' but they will not show up in our living rooms. They are mentors of the Space Brothers, who come in physical form."

Paul Brunton, in his book, *The Wisdom of the Overself*, page 33, states, *"Intelligence must accept, in this varied universe, that there is a place for a being superior to Man."*

I conclude with a teaching from the extraterrestrial master, Krunula:

"You are made with parts from infinity and from the stars,
but you do not know it, because you are asleep."

Peace, peace, peace . . . to all truth-seeking men.

Enrique Castillo Rincón
San José, April 23, 1988

Chapter Note

[1] Translator's note: Perhaps they can violate the physical laws, because they helped establish such laws and have control over them, or because they understand physical laws more comprehensively than we do at present.

Afterword

THESE FINAL LINES are added to the English translation of the book, which is to be published in the United States of America, where so recently the mass suicide in San Diego, California took place, an event linked one way or another with the UFO phenomenon.

Readers and the general public are urged to use caution and discrimination about venturing into the realms of the spiritual and the occult, especially when seeking an escape from the spiritual frustrations that are so frequent nowadays. For, many cult-like or "pseudo-religious" groups take advantage of people who are innocent and lacking experience and knowledge. My specific and strong recommendation is to abstain from joining any such groups.

To provide some background in the subject, it may be helpful to know that, according to international news releases of the last ten years, in the United Kingdom alone there are about 700 officially registered cult-type groups. Numerous examples also operate in Switzerland, Canada, the United States, South Korea, Japan, Philippines, France, and Guyana. Italy, Spain, Colombia, Venezuela, Peru, and other countries also have dangerous levels of fanaticism, of groups led by "super-endowed" individuals who claim to have links with UFO entities. These groups often have as their aim the interference with an individual's freedom of thought and discretion, while controlling their members' minds and rights to act as free human beings. The phenomenon is not restricted to the UFO realm and involves religions and pseudo-religions as well, apparently arising from people's inner need for certain values that are no longer found in the established religions.

As addressed previously in the text, such groups typically isolate their followers from families and friends, enroll them in a program of renunciation from their worldly goods, and eventually take possession of their income and properties. In exchange, they offer members "Eternal Freedom" in illusory worlds where money and suffering do not exist, and they organize fake meetings with supposedly superior beings, whose grandiose ships are supposed to take them on board.

I have witnessed such leaders offering people this type of "brave new world," then convening meetings in lonely places, such as mountains or forests, where the expected otherworldly ships never arrive. The waiting eventually becomes distressing and unbearable for the seekers, who then begin weeping and lamenting desperately, because they realize that their properties have already been sold or given away to others, usually the leaders of the group. These are examples of the "mild quotas" that believers are required to pay. Others "contributions," well-documented in the media, include voluntary death or mass suicide, examples of which have occurred year after year in different countries around the world.

When this continues to occur, again and again, I ask myself how best to stop these evil leaders, who are so capable of corrupting people's minds and of thoroughly brain-washing them into terribly wrong beliefs. Liberation from such fanatics can occur only when we use our free will, powers of inquiry and discrimination, and conscience to recognize, fight against, and defeat all falsity and deceit. Those who let themselves be led into this type of path-of-no-return, accepting unquestioning membership in these sects, will lose their most precious gift: their freedom. The words of Jesus Christ point the way to the only hope:

> ". . . and you shall know the Truth, and it will make you FREE."
> —John 8:32

The Bogota Specimen: A New Physical Investigation

Before ending this book, I consider it important to include the results of an investigation carried out by Dr. Jacques Vallée, on the analysis of a physical sample from a UFO sighting that was found in Bogotá, Colombia.

June 1987
by Dr. Jacques Vallee

SCIENTISTS INTERESTED IN THE UFO phenomenon have long hoped that some sort of physical evidence would be found in connection with a well-documented sighting. Such evidence could be analyzed in the laboratory, and it would provide, if not a proof of the reality of UFOs, at least a good basis for a fruitful dialogue among the supporters of various theories about them.

In real life, things are not so simple. The combination of a good sighting with a physical specimen is rare. And given such a specimen, it is often difficult to find competent laboratories to analyze it. Not only is the cost of such an analysis significant, but it is a complex task to determine what questions should be asked and what equipment should be used. A fascinating book could be written about the mistakes that have been made over the years in the handling of such samples, from careless labelling to outright destruction, as was the case in the first "analysis" of the Ubatuba magnesium sample by the U.S. Air Force!

Over the years a number of cases have been found in which a physical specimen was in fact recovered. A short summary includes:

A. The Maury Island (Washington) case of 21 June 1947.
B. The Ubatuba (Brazil) case of 1933 or 1934.
C. The Swedish case of 11 October 1959.
D. The Alaska (Kiana) case, date unknown.
E. The Council Bluffs (Iowa) case of 17 December 1977.
F. The Jopala (Mexico) case of 1978.
G. The Campinas (Brazil) case of 14 December 1954.

None of these cases has provided conclusive evidence for any particular theory of UFOs, although the Ubatuba material has successfully resisted "explanation" at the hands of the Condon committee—after surviving partial destruction at the hands of "Project Blue Book . . . That particular sample is now under active and very competent analysis at a large American university."

The new case I am introducing here is likely to fall into the same category: intriguing enough to deserve study, yet more frustrating in terms of investigation techniques and research methodology than in terms of the physics of the phenomenon. My hope is that we will eventually have enough cases of this type for a pattern to emerge.

Background

The Bogotá specimen was brought to my attention in October 1985 by two respected Latin American researchers, Messrs. Enrique Castillo (director of the Venezuela Institute for Research on Extraterrestrial Phenomena) and Ricardo Vilchez (of the Costa Rica Institute for Scientific and Exobiology Investigation). The occasion was an international congress on paranormal research held in San José, Costa Rica.

Mr. Castillo, who had conducted the initial investigation in Colombia, told me that he had secured a piece of some physical evidence that witnesses had found at the site of a UFO sighting. He had subsequently given it to Mr. Vilchez, who was kind enough to turn it over to me for further study. They mentioned that a preliminary analysis had already been performed in Central America.

The Sighting

Two students who were walking on the campus of the University of Bogotá at about 4:00 a.m. one night in 1975 or 1976 heard a metallic sound overhead. Looking up through the rain that was falling heavily at the time, they saw a disk swinging in the air as if it were having difficulty navigating. They estimated its diameter at four meters and its altitude at 1000 to 1200 meters.

While this object seemed about to go out of control, they observed four other disks that flew to the vicinity of the first one as if to assist it. They were of the same shape and size.

It is at this point that, according to the witnesses, they took refuge under a tree and secretly saw a bright liquid fall into the rainwater puddles in the street, producing a vapor. The five objects then rose and disappeared into the low rain clouds.

The witnesses recovered two metal chunks, about four inches by one-and-a-quarter inch in size, after letting the material cool for about ten minutes.

Preliminary Analysis

The first analysis of the metal chunks was performed at the request of Mr. Castillo by a mechanical engineer with a petroleum company. He concluded that the sample was an aluminum alloy with magnesium and tin. It was non-magnetic, seemed to contain no iron, no nickel, and no molybdenum, but included traces of materials that remained unidentified. He also stated that the metal was soft (easily cut) and presented a very fine granulation.

Analysis in the United States

When the sample was turned over to me by Mr. Vilchez, I initiated a "chain of evidence" by sealing it inside an envelope and having him place his signature next to mine on the flap of that envelope. I carried it back to the United States and placed the envelope in a secure location after summarizing the case for the record at the office of my attorney and signing an affidavit. The envelope was not opened until arrangements had been made with a high-technology company whose executives were interested in the case. They provided access to the required tools for a detailed investigation. After witnessing that the original signatures were present on the intact envelope, the group extracted the sample and made the following observations:

1. The sample is approximately 51mm long, tapering in width from 39mm to 33 mm with a 7mm thickness. It shows signs of melting, with a rough surface on one side. We observed a crude cut, apparently made by a shop saw during the first analysis.

2. The process of metal solidification on the "top" side shows violent activity with bubbling of the metal. Some embedded organic material, possibly from the road asphalt, was also noted. The sample is quite light, with low density and little corrosion. It flakes easily when attacked with a sharp scalpel.

3. The sample is an excellent electrical conductor. An ohmmeter test across the narrow dimension of 36mm shows only a fraction of an ohm in resistance. The sample must be purely metallic in composition, and aluminum is suspected.

4. A small corner of the sample was cut with a hand jewelry saw, except for a small portion, which was bent by hand. This remaining "bridge" broke after six bends, showing the metal to be very ductile, with very strong grain growth. We noted that the sample showed weld marks and clamp marks, probably from the earlier analysis.

5. We designated the small portion we had cut off as "Sample A." It is on that portion that all subsequent tests were conducted.

Scanning Electron Microscope Analysis

This is a technique that produces an X-ray fluorescence spectrum. It was applied to the small part of the sample that had been broken by hand and thus represented a typical, uncontaminated section of the inside matter of the specimen. Microphotographs showed a rather sizeable cavity, which was probed further during the analysis. The results of this test showed the sample to contain ninety percent aluminum, with small amounts of phosphorus and iron. There was no tin and no magnesium.

The metallurgical experts doing the analysis commented that the sample was "melted through and through" and that nothing could have survived of the initial structure. The appearance, in fact, is typical of an "overheat." Such heat would have ruined a casting and is consistent with the blow-up of a machine.

The test produced agreement about the following composition:

Aluminum	93.72%
Phosphorus	4.75%
Iron	0.91%
Trace elements	0.62%

Auger Analysis

In this technique, a scanning ion mass spectroscope is used to explore the material deeper and deeper, from its surface layer into its interior. Placed in a very high vacuum, the sample is hit by an electron beam. The measurements are repeated at several points for consistency. An average of five points was used. This analysis surprised us, in that it showed no aluminum at first. The surface layer was composed of carbon, oxygen (not combined with aluminum), and nitrogen.

Beyond this layer appeared the following elements: aluminum, magnesium, potassium, sulphur, sodium, and silicon. Phosphorus and iron also show up in this analysis, in small amounts.

Summary of the Analysis

The Bogotá specimen is a sample of aluminum with a high degree of purity, combined with phosphorus and iron, with trace elements including sulphur, magnesium, silicon, and an oxy-carbide layer.

The sample is unusual in what it ***does not contain***. In particular there is no fluoride, a common by-product of the aluminum refining process. Aluminum fluoride is very stable and would be expected in this material. The absence of heavy materials is also noteworthy. Another substance whose absence is intriguing is water.

The significance of the oxy-carbide layer that was found in the sample is unknown at this point. This layer goes deeper than a surface contaminant would.

Questions for Follow-up Tests

The analysis of this specimen is continuing. Although its composition has now been established, a number of questions remain.

1. We have not investigated the list of all possible aluminum alloys this material could match.
2. Tests of radioactivity need to be performed.
3. We have not had the opportunity to consult an aluminum production expert to find out if the absence of fluoride and of water were truly significant.
4. It would be interesting to determine just how hard an average laboratory would have to work in order to duplicate this sample.
5. A neutron activation analysis and an attempt at carbon-14 dating of the organic material have been suggested to us.
6. A microscopic examination of the surface, followed by chemical analysis of surface contaminants such as asphalt would be useful in completing our assessment of the case.
7. An attempt should be made to locate the witnesses in Colombia and to document their story in greater detail.

Conclusions

The most useful result of this work has been to refine our methodology and give us greater experience in the testing of alleged UFO material. We have also put into place a procedure for the preservation of a "chain of evidence" that would have validity in the legal sense, although it does not completely eliminate any possibility of trickery on the part of the scientists involved in the test. The probability of such manipulation of the data decreases, of course, as the tests are repeated by independent laboratories.

The range of explanations for the Bogotá sample has now been narrowed down to three hypotheses. It could have come from a UFO, as claimed by the witnesses. But before we can definitely "prove" this conclusion, we must eliminate the possibility that we are dealing with satellite re-entry material, or with a hoax. It is difficult to exclude the satellite hypothesis as long as the date remains imprecise, hence the high priority on finding the witnesses again. Unfortunately, the file containing the original interviews has been lost, and we do not know the exact year of the observation.

The hoax hypothesis can be eliminated only through the internal consistency of the test results and their match with the witnesses' story. So far we have noted several facts that seem to indicate that the case is genuine: the sample is very clean and does not seem to have been formed by pouring aluminum over the ground or over a factory floor. Aluminum picks up dirt very easily, and the sample would have been contaminated.

Also, the impurity level is quite different from what would be expected from slag. These observations encourage us to continue with our program of tests, but they do not constitute final proof that the case is genuine.

In coming months, we hope to be able to determine whether this sample is truly unusual. It will then be interesting to correlate its composition with that of other alleged UFO samples.

APPENDIX

Testimonials about Enrique Castillo Rincón[1]

OPINION 1

Some time had elapsed after I began investigating the UFO phenomenon, when the engineer Enrique Castillo arrived in Costa Rica, in late 1976. Enrique was offering talks and conferences in auditoriums, and on radio and TV, telling about his experiences and claiming to have had direct contact with extraterrestrial beings.

As a beginner in UFO investigations, I never missed a single one of the talks given by Enrique, because it was my conviction that in order to carry out any research, it is mandatory not to reject *a priori* anything that could contribute significant elements for the study at hand. Now, after several years of investigation, I do not have the slightest doubt that to carry out a good investigation, the first requirement is the disposition not to reject or to accept the available data, no matter how unlikely or appealing it might seem. The second is to learn to listen to people and to avoid judging or criticizing them hastily, because these actions can cause harm to us and to them. Later, my brother Ricardo and myself[2] realized that, besides giving his talks, Enrique had the intention of establishing in Costa Rica an institution to be dedicated to the investigation of UFOs and related phenomena, similar to others he had already created in Venezuela, Colombia, and Ecuador. By the end of 1976, a provisional Executive Board had been elected, and thus was created the ICICE, Instituto Costarricense de Investigaciones Científica y Exobiológicas (Costa Rican Institute for Scientific and Exobiological Investigations).

We became personal friends but never abandoned our spirit of investigation. In fact, since then, Enrique has been investigated by my brother and myself, in relation to his experiences as a "contactee," and also as an individual. This ongoing investigation has not ended, and Enrique knows it. During these four years, we have found in him only friendship, sincerity, loyalty, and a great humility.

Often, to be true, he has been like a guide for my investigations, because upon knowing him better, one realizes that he is a scholar regarding his own experiences, with a knowledge and an astonishing memory that—I am sure—few individuals can match. I must say that my own outlook on life has changed since I met Enrique, not only by listening to his extraterrestrial experiences, but mainly because of a statement I heard him make before one of his talks, which impressed me exceedingly: *"Before starting this talk, I would like to tell you not to believe what I am going to say, but rather, investigate it."* This helped me much in my own investigations and gave me the chance to make a better judgment about him. He was encouraging people not to believe blindly in what he said but advising them to investigate, to meditate on the subject matter. This was the customary way Enrique handled these matters.

He never dogmatizes; instead, he has thrown much light where there was only darkness, helping many to get rid of the skepticism common among us, which acts as an unconscious defensive armor against our ignorance of UFOs and related subjects.

Enrique has been subjected twice to hypnotic regressions, and nothing has ever been found to cast doubt on what he says regarding his experiences, outlandish as they may seem.

As far as I am concerned, I must say that I have not the slightest doubt that the events described by Enrique actually took place. This does not mean that I believe, or have to believe, that what the extraterrestrials told him is true, for a very simple reason. As an investigator, I have information from people in other countries who have been given similar information through contacts with supposed extraterrestrials. I have reason to believe that the information received should be doubted and questioned in most instances, be it messianic, apocalyptic, or scientific.

I hope many of the events announced through Enrique come true; others I wish would never materialize. Either way, it is my belief that every human being should discern, investigate, and study the subject matter exhaustively, and thus arrive at his or her own conclusions.

By experience and conviction, I know that true friendship, I mean fraternal friendship, is hard to find. Musing over this subject, I often think how few true friends I have. One thing is sure: among them, I can always count on my friend and brother, Enrique Castillo.

Carlos Vilchez N.,
Founding Member, ICICE
Writer and UFO investigator, author of the books, *UFOs: What You Never Suspected* and *Invest and Retire in an Authentic Democracy*
San José, Costa Rica, 1980

OPINION 2

If there were a single word that could describe a person with the characteristics belonging to Enrique Castillo, that word would be "integrity." I met Enrique, not by chance, but as a consequence of my keen interest in the UFO phenomenon. In October or November 1976, he arrived in Costa Rica, giving talks and conferences everywhere, telling about his experiences with the extraterrestrials. From then on, my eagerness to learn all about UFOs increased relentlessly—an indescribable force pushed me to know more and more about this subject.

This is how I met Enrique. From that moment on, my personal investigation of him began (and continued): what were his objectives and motivations, what did he do and why? He proposed the possibility of creating an institution for the investigation of the UFO subject, and with him, I was one of the founders of ICICE, an institute that in Costa Rica investigates everything related to the UFO phenomenon. Previously, Enrique had founded the ICIFE in Colombia and the IVIFE in Venezuela, parallel organizations. Eventually he organized similar institutions in Ecuador and Honduras.

From the very beginning we became conscious of his honesty and humility. I had many doubts about him and his word, and interrogated him rather roughly, but he was able to distinguish curiosity from malice.

From the human side, he is one of the kindest persons that I know, although sometimes I do not quite understand the way he acts, which often breaks with established patterns; of course, I am not in a position to judge other people's way of handling things. But he impresses me with the uncommon certainty he has about what he does and with what purpose he does it. He knows himself better than most, and he is a better human being than most.

He has a clear mind and an impressive memory. Being a "contactee," he is the only one who has become a tireless investigator, widely recognized in Europe and America as one of the most dependable and knowledgeable. He has attended many congresses. We have attended such meetings together in Mexico, Venezuela, and Costa Rica.

I know his family and friends: his personal life is just as normal as that of anybody else, although his outlook changed after he saw the two great ships above a volcano in Costa Rica. He looks at life a little differently than ordinary people. His ends are not the same; now they are more universal, more human, and less selfish.

Regarding his fantastic story about the extraterrestrials, as far as Enrique himself is concerned, I am sure that the events actually occurred. Of course, I am not sure if what he was told by the entities is true or not, because I don't know them and cannot speak on their behalf. Enrique does know them, so it is then necessary to talk to him. Much slander has been scattered about him: he has been variously described as insane, paranoid, illuminated, or prophetic. I believe that such judgments can come only from ignorant or misinformed individuals, because once you know Enrique, you can truly appreciate what kind of a person he really is.

For me, it is an honor and a pleasure to have met him, and not only that, I am very proud to be called his friend. To my brother, because that is the way I feel, I thank him for his friendship, which only he knows how much I treasure.

Ricardo Vilchez N.,
Founding Member, ICICE
Writer and UFO investigator, author of the books, *All Costa Rica, All Caracas,* and *Conscious Democracy*
San José, Costa Rica, 1980

OPINION 3

I met Enrique Castillo during the International UFO Congress in Acapulco, Mexico, in 1977. I had heard about him, but it is one thing to hear about him and a different thing to meet him in person.

I had the opportunity to interview him twice, together with my wife, Mercedes Castellanos, thus starting my first investigation of Enrique as a "contactee" of the extraterrestrials.

During the interviews, he answered my questions, at times inquisitively, and always accurately and quite sure of what he was talking about.

As he narrates, he was "contacted" by extraterrestrial beings from Pleiades, starting November 3, 1973, near a lake, some 80 kilometers north of Bogotá, the capital of Colombia, in South America. He was invited to the above-mentioned Congress as a "contactee," in order to present his experience to the public and to the investigators. Enrique was allowed to narrate his experience only at a private and personal level, such as he did with my wife and myself.

Those interviews were meant to be the beginning of a full investigation that I expected to pursue, which for various reasons was impossible to complete. However, Enrique showed great certainty and self-assurance when

Enrique Castillo R. and Andreas Faber Kaiser at the Pyramid of the Sun, Mexico, 1977. Photo: Samuel Medina

faced by my sometimes nearly foolish questions. As a contactee, he can generate quite a stir, because he is really sure of what he says and has a prodigious memory, backed up by an uncommon charisma. Besides, his wording and the way he presents his story about the encounters is very convincing, free of false mysticism or beliefs about him being a "chosen one" to save humanity, as is frequent among other so-called "contactees."

He confessed to having no specific agreement with the Pleiadeans, but that what he does is to create awareness among people, so that through enlightenment, human beings can improve themselves. I never noticed in him the slightest trace of self-aggrandizement.

"I want to be accepted for what I am, not for my experiences with the ETs," he used to tell me. I have always seen him as a simple and self-assured man, who gives the impression of being truthful. His many explanations are all coherent and easy to understand. I am positive that Enrique is not a crackpot or a cheap mystic. Something happened to him, and we the investigators should find an explanation for it. He himself confesses that he doesn't know the real motivations for his experiences.

I am not in a position to guarantee his experiences, but I shall continue investigating him as long as I can and the opportunity permits, because we live thousands of kilometers away from each other.

Enrique tells me that he has finished his book containing all the details. That will be a great opportunity to carry on the research, not only for me, but for anyone interested, given the wealth of details that he says are available. Besides, a great friendship has grown between Enrique and myself, which I am sure will not suffer, regardless of the outcome of the investigations.

Since our meeting in 1977 in Acapulco, we have corresponded several times. One of his interesting letters contains a prophecy, which according to Enrique was given to him by the Pleiadeans, under the striking title of "The Nine Times That Will Change the World."

The most significant prophetic accuracy is the appearance of AIDS, announced with an anticipation of eight years. I must stress that Enrique sent me the prophecy in 1980 (it was given to him in 1974-1975). A short war between Arab countries is also mentioned, with several countries involved. Today, I write this opinion about Enrique, while the World Congress Regarding Great Human Mysteries is underway in Costa Rica, in 1985.

I must add that Enrique has surprised scientists and investigators. I myself find him more solid, humble, and sure of himself than when I met him, together with his pretty wife, Ana. He gave me two more interviews about his interesting experiences. One was in the lobby of the hotel where the Congress was meeting (Hotel Irazú), and the second in a private room where he was more precise and forceful.

Today, even more than before, I believe that what Enrique says about the "sky people" has more validation than ever, because now more attention is paid to the contactees, due to the more frequent occurrence of abductions and cattle mutilations, etc., that have been taking place lately. It is no longer possible to ignore these events, odd as they are, especially when the very survival of the planet may be involved.

Andreas Faber Kaiser[3]
Spanish investigator and writer, founder and director for many years of the international magazine, *Mundo Desconocido*, with an international reputation.
Author of *¿Sacerdotes o Cosmonautas? (Priests or Cosmonauts?); Jesus Lived and Died in Kashmir; The Cave of the Treasures; Clouds of Deceit; Out of Control.*

OPINION 4

The case of Enrique Castillo Rincón began physically on November 3, 1973, and, taken as one of several other contacts, I personally classify it as a concrete reality, with certainty, by UFO behavior standards, which I have followed and investigated for twenty-five years.

Since 1975, when I met the protagonist, to whom I am united by a very deep friendship and affection, I have never stopped investigating him under varying circumstances,[4] and today, in 1985, twelve years later, I find more than ever, the apparent "lack of reason" behind this contact. Fundamentally, the personal investigations that I have completed regarding contactee individuals, show more and more the true existence of these "absurd but real" abductions—outside our time frame, outside our science, outside our culture—but still present, giving hints about life on other planes of existence.

Thanks for being, Enrique.

Fabio Zerpa
Director of ONIFE, Organización Nacional para la Investigación del Fenómeno OVNI, Argentina (National Organization for Investigation of UFO Phenomena, Argentina).
Founder and director of the international magazine, *Cuarta Dimensión*.

OPINION 5

Anything I can say about Dr. Enrique Castillo Rincón[5] may be not totally impartial, because, before all and above all, I am his personal friend. Friends look at each other with benevolent eyes and tend to ignore defects and weaknesses. Even so, on this occasion I will pretend to come from another planet in order to gauge him. Offhand, he is a well-balanced individual, both physically and mentally. Thus, we must discard the presumption that he could have been the subject of some hallucination, through confusion taking as real the experiences that he reports as a contactee. Not so. Besides, the subject matter in his book has enough qualities to present on its own in the wondrous world of Ufology.

Castillo stands halfway between the sickly mysticism of some ignorant UFO buffs and the stubborn objectivity of the traditional scientists.

When contactee Eugenio Siragusa stated in Colombia that Enrique Castillo was the reincarnation of Luke the Apostle, Enrique laughed willingly. When an astronomer, during a radio forum in Caracas, propounded once more the old arguments of traditional science about the impossibility of the existence of life on other worlds, Castillo smiled philosophically, saying, "Such is man!"

When I speak out like this regarding mysticism, it is not my intention to proscribe spiritual values. On the contrary, this huge universe where we have our being is directed, or rather, *self-directed*. Until now, I think I am the first to proclaim publicly that the most basic driving force in the universe is a universal psychic force, to which all other aspects or types of force are subordinated. I have called it psychic, for lack of a more adequate term.

But let us return to Castillo's experiences.

Ufology is a new science; it is observational and not experimental. Thus, and to date, the contactees are our largest and best source of information. We find that we have had contacts with extraterrestrials of the most varied and diverse kinds and categories, something to be expected, given the multitude of worlds that surround us.

And we find ourselves with a multitude of disconcerting "contacts," that we must evaluate, classify, and coordinate as quickly as possible in a harmonically structured scheme.

But that is not all: the problem becomes very acute when our cognitive capacity is exceeded by the complexity of the phenomena. And then comes the problem of our mental deficiencies that manifest themselves as false, secular ideas that we take as unfinished truths, which obscure our perception of the investigated phenomena. I have discovered that there are twelve hindrances that intermittently curb the advancement of human knowledge, slowing it down. So impressed have I been by this, that I have written a book about the subject, *Los Doce Traumas del Pensamiento Humano (The Twelve Hindrances of Human Thought,* unpublished).

But there is another aspect in Castillo's Ufological task, which I consider of extreme importance. I refer to his continuous effort for the dissemination of the available knowledge on this subject, in a good number of countries of the American continent. He has lived a constant and relentless struggle in this respect. Something like this is not viable unless one is dedicated completely to a cause, an idea, or a purpose, regardless of the consequences, even if these be repudiation, jail, or even death. This he has been carrying out tenaciously and without rest, becoming in this way a veritable Cosmic Messenger.

Dr. Francisco Aniceto Lugo
Venezuelan scientist, writer, and investigator.
Author of more than twenty books on numerous subjects.
Member of several international scientific associations.
Caracas, Venezuela, 1981[6]

OPINION 6

Although I believe that the UFO phenomenon is more psychic than physical, cases such as that of contactee Enrique Castillo Rincón make me consider seriously the involvement of "nuts-and-bolts" alien ships, "manned" by flesh-and-bone individuals.

Whether or not the origin of the phenomenon is from other planets, the thesis that there are initiatory processes of the Ufological type applies to

Enrique Castillo. I believe that all of the experiences that he underwent during the years after his physical contacts can be classified as potentiating, with the effect of shaping a new vision of existence and a mental opening in Enrique, as well as a solid personality, balanced, human, and noble.

Lic. Carlos Ortiz del la Huerta
Mexican writer and investigator, co-organizer of the World Congress in Acapulco, 1977, and "The World Congress on the Great Mysteries of Man," Costa Rica, 1985.
Caracas, Venezuela, 1978

Chapter Notes

[1] In Spanish-speaking countries, it is customary to use the mother's maiden last name (Rincón), after the father's (Castillo).

[2] Carlos and Ricardo Vilchez are brothers, twins to be exact. Both are outstanding writers and investigators, very well known in the intellectual circles of Costa Rica.

[3] Translator's note: Unfortunately, Andreas Faber Kaiser, courageous investigator and journalist, died in his country, Spain, in 1995 under mysterious circumstances, a victim of AIDS. Honor to his memory.

[4] Because this is my *raison d'être*, my reason for life, and perhaps to give justice to the nickname given to me by my good friend Pedro Ferriz: "The Investigating Machine."

[5] In Colombia and Venezuela it is customary to refer to any professional as "doctor," whether in medicine, engineering, law, etc.

[6] Dr. Lugo passed away in Caracas, in 1982.